Comparative Ethics Series /
Collection d'Éthique Comparée

Comparative Ethics Series / Collection d'Éthique Comparée

As Religious Studies in its various branches has spread out in recent years, it has met with a newly emergent discipline: Comparative Ethics as the study of moralities as cultural systems, rather than as the philosophical investigation of particular moral issues. To study a morality as a dynamic whole in its social nature and functioning requires a context in which other instances of a comparable kind are considered. Moral action-guides and religious action-guides have historically been brought together in mixed, moral-religious or religious-moral systems. The different paths followed by moralities as cultural systems in the varying contexts demand comparative study.

The series embraces three kinds of studies: (1) methodological studies, which will endeavour to elaborate and discuss principles, concepts and models for the new discipline; (2) studies that aim at deepening our knowledge of the nature and functioning, the scope and content, of particular moral systems, such as the Islamic, the Hindu and the Christian; (3) studies of a directly comparative kind, which bring differing moral systems or elements of systems into relationship.

GENERAL EDITOR: *Paul Bowlby* Saint Mary's University (Halifax)

Comparative Ethics Series /
Collection d'Éthique Comparée

Doing Ethics in a Pluralistic World

Essays in Honour of Roger C. Hutchinson

Phyllis D. Airhart, Marilyn J. Legge and Gary L. Redcliffe, editors

Published for the Canadian Corporation for Studies in Religion /
Corporation Canadienne des Sciences Religieuses
by Wilfrid Laurier University Press

2002

We acknowledge the financial support of the Government of Canada through the Book Publishing Industry Development Program for our publishing activities.

National Library of Canada Cataloguing in Publication Data

Doing ethics in a pluralistic world : essays in honour of Roger C. Hutchinson / edited by Phyllis D. Airhart, Marilyn J. Legge and Gary L. Redcliffe.

(Comparative ethics series ; v. 6)
Includes bibliographical references.
ISBN 0-88920-410-1

1. Social ethics. 2. Christian ethics. 3. Hutchinson, Roger, 1935- . I. Airhart, Phyllis D. (Phyllis Diane), 1953- . II. Legge, Marilyn J. III. Redcliffe, Gary Lorne. IV. Canadian Corporation for Studies in Religion. V. Series.

BJ401.D65 2002 170 C2002-900018-1

Cover design by Leslie Macredie. Cover image: untitled monoprint by Stu Oxley, courtesy of the artist.

(∞)
Printed in Canada

Order from:
WILFRID LAURIER UNIVERSITY PRESS
Waterloo, Ontario, Canada N2L 3C5
http://www.wlupress.wlu.ca

Table of Contents

Acknowledgments

We want to thank a host of contributors in this collaborative venture. We are grateful to Roseann Runte, then president of Victoria University, who provided funds to make publication possible and arranged a lovely celebration to surprise Roger with this festschrift. Paul Bowlby, editor of the Comparative Ethics Series, vetted the manuscript with alacrity and the peer reviewers offered helpful comments to strengthen the collection. Moira Hutchinson, in addition to doing the bibliography, colluded in providing special information and smoke-screens to keep this project a secret. Heather Gamester undertook the arduous task of editing the entire manuscript in its many stages, assisted by Jeralyn Towne and Gail Allan. At Wilfrid Laurier University Press, Brian Henderson, director, readily welcomed this project; Jenny Wilson did the copy editing; and Leslie Macredie prepared the publicity. A grant from the Emmanuel College Academic Initiatives Fund, with the support of principal Peter Wyatt, has ensured that this volume see the light of day.

INTRODUCTION

PHYLLIS D. AIRHART

MARILYN J. LEGGE

GARY L. REDCLIFFE

Doing Ethics in a Pluralistic World is an apt title for this collection of essays in honour of Roger Hutchinson. His academic life has been devoted to serious inquiry into the role and function of ethics at points of interplay between religious conviction and social transformation. His abiding interest in social ethics and religious engagement with public issues has animated his many decades of involvement in ecumenical and scholarly ventures. He began his studies at the University of Alberta in chemical engineering and worked as a professional engineer for five years in the Alberta oil industry. He undertook his initial theological degree at Queen's University in Kingston, Ontario, and his master's degree at the University of Chicago Divinity School in ethics and society. He completed his doctorate in Christian ethics at the Toronto School of Theology. For nearly three decades Hutchinson has been based at Victoria University in the University of Toronto, first in religious studies and then at Emmanuel College (its faculty of theology) as professor of church and society and as principal from 1996 to 2001.

Roger Hutchinson has consistently claimed throughout his career that in a pluralistic world there is no one set of religious convictions that alone should define a democratic society. From his Chicago experience as a graduate student he has carried into all his academic endeav-

Notes to introduction are on p. 12.

ours a conviction that, in their methodologies, social ethicists must take account of the fact that democratic societies are not built by a direct application of the insights and inspirations of religious beliefs and practices. The process, he argues, is both more complex and more interactive than that, as can be seen in his ethical method outlined below. His doctoral research led him to develop an approach to social ethics that has proved to be an invaluable tool for allowing people of diverse moral convictions and conflicting opinions to engage constructively in open dialogue.

In a society that is diverse and divided in its values and vision, social ethicists need methods by which reasonable contentions for truth-in-action can be discerned. One of Hutchinson's many notable accomplishments is his method for ethical clarification. Students, peers, policy-makers, academics and religious inquirers have engaged in debate with him about his method. He prods all who have sincere perplexities, issues or contending visions to enter into a method of ethical clarification that will bring them into conversation with others of different views. His method is grounded in the presupposition that everyone has a right to speak and be heard, no matter how profoundly people may differ in their positions.

Hutchinson's method consists of four levels. It begins with storytelling and definition of the problem by all parties involved in an issue. Next comes the level of factual clarification in which questions are raised: What counts as a fact and how is it verified? What claims does each party make about the truth that could be measured in some way? How could one prove whether these claims are true? The third level is ethical clarification: To what moral standards or norms does each party appeal? What obligations are claimed? What positive or negative consequences would arise? What good or value is being served or undermined by these arguments? Last but not least (once the dialogue is seasoned) is the level of post-ethical clarification in which issues of faith and world views are explored: What symbols, metaphors, images, sacred texts and traditions ground each approach/story (personal and/or communal)?[1]

Hutchinson's ethical method also challenges social-policy planners, politicians and academics not to ignore the contributions of religious thinkers and theologians in their discourse. Equally, his method protects policy planners, politicians and academics from a naive application of religious conviction in the public domain, and ensures that their dialogues about important social issues are not dominated by any power groups in society, whether religious or secular. His ethical method stimulates and demands intellectual rigour and personal engagement, but it also encourages and enhances open political processes that include society's most vulnerable members in discussions of issues of greatest importance to them. This observation holds whether the subject is the Mackenzie Valley Pipeline debate in the 1970s or health-care delivery in Canada at the turn of the millennium.

In a conflictual situation, Hutchinson's principled methodology has served as a helpful tool for staying power despite discomfort. Indeed, it seems to summon further resources of energy because of an inherent concern to help sort out the degree to which the conflict is based on fundamental differences or on difficulties the parties may be having in understanding each other as a result of their varying perspectives, world views and methods of communication. His approach encourages people of diverse views to move beyond a destructive cycle of constant social and political contention. Difference is expected, and social values and policies are constructed because of shared discernment rather than through the triumph of one particular set of convictions over another. Given his assumption that difference and diversity are essential to a democratic society, all voices need to be invited to speak and to participate in the construction of a just society.

At the heart of Hutchinson's vocation is his desire to encourage and to participate in shaping social ethics within a Canadian context. For this project, his operative conviction is that the dynamic intersection of church, community and university provides the proper arena in which to discern appropriate ethical principles and action. He has always focused on the role of the churches' public witness in a pluralistic world. As David Hallman points out in his essay, Hutchinson's role as a Christian ethicist in major public issues also comes with a significant degree of complexity in terms of both how he perceives his function and how others experience his involvement:

> As an ethicist, I have a role to play in the conversation through which church activists, other church leaders and members and church-related academics together assess the

> faithfulness and effectiveness of particular activities. Looking back upon these activities to see how the issues were perceived, how judgements were made and defended, and how different groups within the churches related to one another is an integral part of the action-reflection process of the churches themselves. Just as the surgeon adopts a specialized focus and disciplined detachment to diagnose and remove a tumour, the ethicist applies her or his specialized training to diagnose and cure distorted communication. In neither case does specialization and detachment reflect a lack of commitment to the remedy being sought.[2]

Hutchinson's approach is framed by ongoing conversion to a multiple-world outlook and a deepened double vision (Northrop Frye). In a pluralistic world, when is one to use the language of a particular faith and when is one to use shared public language? Hutchinson responds to this conundrum: it is a matter of both timing and sensitivity based on attention to the particularity of the context. To do ethics contextually, Hutchinson calls for a "trifocal vision"—the ability to see the world clearly at the level of empirical reality and hard facts; to see it at the level of symbols and stories; and, within the realm of symbols and stories, to see the difference between confessional and public languages. For example, his long commitment to a habitable planet led him to participate in the 1991 World Council of Churches' consultation in Bossey, Switzerland, where the term "one earth community" was formulated as being most appropriate for speaking theologically of creation in interfaith dialogues. Based on this work, the 1994 United Church of Canada's Division of Mission's Record of Proceedings appropriated this language for its own use. Contextuality, therefore, requires ongoing interpretation and action for transformation. In this process, Hutchinson has encouraged the intellectual development of countless students, peers and colleagues in Canada and beyond, to which this collection of essays is a profound testament.

The foregoing may help to explain Hutchinson's hallmark hospitality—why his office door is always open, and why he entertains the questions and comments of all who enter. Perhaps his upbringing on a farm in Alberta helps to explain why he respects every individual's point of view and listens with an open mind. His formative life experiences gave him his first taste of the claims of cooperation. Was it early on that he also first learned the importance of ingenuity and of new ideas? Did he learn from that small community the importance of being able to live with diverse agendas and their consequences for people's lives? Hutchinson has never lost his engineer's curiosity about the way things work, perhaps another testament to his Western roots. So, too, the expansiveness of Western Canadian geography is reflected in Hutchinson's active and open mind. The connections between topics and ideas that he injects into conversations are often as intriguing as they are challenging. His serendipitous mind continues to be dedicated to the same intellectual inquiries that first drew him into the field of social ethics.

Equally abiding has been his investment over the years in nurturing his students and colleagues in a wide range of intellectual and organizational pursuits, from encouraging congregational participation in major social issues, to shaping ecumenical tasks with the World Council of Churches, to teaching an ethics course in the faculty of forestry, to collaborating with the faculty of law located across the road from his office. This collection of essays provides a sampling of such collegial work. Each contribution from former students and colleagues manages to deal with some matters of method and substance that build on and connect with Hutchinson's own work. Some refer directly to his method, others address issues that have been important to him and still others reflect on their involvement in particular struggles for justice.

The volume opens with an essay by C. Douglas Jay, "Roger Hutchinson as Ethicist and Educator in an Age of Religious Pluralism." A colleague since he supervised Hutchinson's doctoral thesis on the Canadian tradition of social ethics in the 1930s, Jay traces, often in relation to his own intellectual journey, key influences on the development of Hutchinson's work. This braiding depicts how the ethical norm of love, when translated into mutuality, became the key procedural norm and foundational symbol for Hutchinson. Jay elaborates on Hutchinson's development, in keeping with this commitment, of a method for the clarification of ethical issues. As Jay attests, "The main feature of his approach is the identification of different levels of clarification which can help bring into sharper focus different dimensions of a debate over controversial social issues....Thus, essential to his method is genuine dialogue as key to the problem of communication." This approach is not without its critics, however, and some objections to what has been called his "reformist" strategy are discussed. Nonetheless, Hutchinson has persevered in his commitment to principles of dialogue in a pluralistic age, and Jay explores his contributions as an educator, research advocate and promoter of a wider rationality based in action. In sum, Hutchinson's work is characterized by a "non-imperialistic way of pursuing truth, justice and reconciliation through respectful dialogue and disciplined research."

Hutchinson's early work in religious studies had a major focus on religion, ethnicity, multiculturalism and public policy. The contribution by Gregory Baum, "The Church and Pluralism in Quebec: An Account of a Participant," contextualizes pluralistic ethics through an examination of how the Catholic Church, particularly in its official statements, has responded to the new cultural pluralism in Quebec. Tackling the complex history of French Quebec, with its minority status in North America, Baum explores how the concept of "multiculturalism" has functioned. Quebec's official version of multiculturalism distinguishes between the welcoming culitre (*la culture d'accueil*) and the arriving cultures (*les communautés culturelles*). He finds that the church shares the "double orientation" of Quebec society: of a growing openness to ethnocultural pluralism that would enable new cultural communities to feel more at home in Quebec, and of efforts to enhance, under the new conditions of the globalization of the economy and the massive transmigration of peoples, the historical identity of Quebec as a French-language minority. Citizenship, pluralism and solidarity are promoted as interconnected values, which Baum discovers include "an appreciation of the cultural communities, support for an evolving Quebec culture in continuity with its history, and concern for social cohesion and joint responsibility." Through his participation in the Centre justice et foi, Baum assesses the church's commitment to the flourishing of Quebec society.

David Novak's contribution, "Karl Barth on Divine Command: A Jewish Response," addresses the relationship of revealed religious truth and a religious person's participation in public/secular space for the common good. From a Jewish perspective he discusses the practical problem raised by Karl Barth's theology of divine command for a pluralistic world. He engages Barth philosophically on two issues: how Barth deals with the relationship of commandment and law; and how he deals with the problem of keeping God's ethical commandments in public, that is, in space that is essentially secular. Novak explores the relationship of law and commandment in terms of natural law theory. Some modes of Christian theological ethics such as Barth's have been characterized as divine command ethics, attempting to move directly and deductively from language about God to questions about human agency. While Barth contends that the command of God directly addresses the totality of life and brings all cultural forms, including religion, to judgment, Novak argues that the indirect commands of God prepare for the direct commands of God, which are therefore understood as mediated in communal, and only abstractly individual, moral agents. Thus, the necessarily human gestalt of the commandments of God is upheld as appropriate. Religious persons can participate with integrity in the public shaping of common good.

Following up on the theme of the participation of churches in a pluralistic world, Harold Wells, in "Not Moral Heroes: The Grace of God and the Church's Public Voice," asks if it is still possible in post-Christendom Canada for the church to have an effective public voice for social justice. The key concern that Wells raises is what doctrine best enables the church to have an effective public voice. The core Christian teaching is that God's gospel is free, beyond all ecclesial bounds. Reconciliation is based in the grace of the Incarnation. Exploring the theological message of the Incarnation, he asserts, will enable the sort of preaching that offers a credible empowering message of grace in today's context. In turn, this witness, in the tradition of political theology, will inspire a public ethics of compassion and generosity.

In keeping with this aim, Ian Manson, in "'O Day of God, Draw Nigh': R.B.Y. Scott, the Church and the Call for Social Reconstruction," explores as ethical resource the terrain of social gospel history in Canada to discuss certain contextual commitments and precedents of the public witness of the churches. R.B.Y. Scott was one of the leaders of the Fellowship for a Christian Social Order, the group of Christian socialists featured in Hutchinson's dissertation and early publications. Co-editor of and contributor to *Towards the Christian Revolution*, Scott modelled the commitment to church, academy and public life that has marked Hutchinson's own professional choices. Manson notes that a recurring theme in Scott's work is the spiritual dimension of our political and economic dilemmas and, hence, the indispensability of spiritual rebirth for social transformation. His scholarly studies of the Old Testament prophetic tradition and his involvement with a number of

United Church committees on public issues made that point, as did his hymns invoking God to bring justice to the land.

"Ethical Values and Canadian Foreign Policy" by Cranford Pratt addresses the effects of the erosion of social welfare values in terms of the international context of a Canadian public ethics. Pratt builds on Hutchinson's long-term involvement with the efforts of Canadian churches to make public policy more ethically responsible and to clarify the relationship of the activities of Canadian churches to their Christian faith. Pratt asks what success the churches and other concerned civil society organizations have had in their efforts to promote a more ethically responsive Canadian foreign policy. He responds by examining the continuous efforts of inter-church and non-governmental organizations over several decades to influence Canadian policies in regard to two major foreign policy issues—foreign aid and apartheid South Africa. Given a meaner, less compassionate Canada, he concludes that civil society structures can no longer press internationally for the ethical values that are dominant in Canadian society. "Rather, they are engaged in the more substantial and daunting task of generating, within Canada itself, a greater moral concern for the welfare of those beyond its borders."

David G. Hallman's essay, "Ecological Ethics: Roger Hutchinson's Methodology and Engagement in Canadian Initiatives," provides a comprehensive guide to ecumenical ecological ethics and Canadian initiatives through the lens of Hutchinson's methodology. He begins by reflecting on Hutchinson's book, *Prophets, Pastors and Public Choices: Canadian Churches and the Mackenzie Valley Pipeline Debate* (1992), and examines his engagement with the Canadian ecumenical Taskforce on the Churches and Corporate Responsibility and its work on forestry issues. Hallman then focuses on Hutchinson's involvement in ecumenical and secular debates regarding attempts to prepare an "Earth Charter" before and after the 1992 Rio Earth Summit. The third area of Hutchinson's work he explores is with the World Council of Churches on the issue of climate change. In conclusion, he looks at Hutchinson's participation in some denominational and ecumenical reflections on the increasing role of biotechnology in Canadian society. Hallman's basic argument is that "Hutchinson has consistently pressed the United Church of Canada and the broader ecumenical community to avoid romanticizing or demonizing participants in contentious ecological struggles, to create opportunities and atmospheres in which people holding varying perspectives on an issue can listen to each other with respect, and to analyze issues and engage in advocacy based on the best possible information and the clearest possible appreciation of realizable goals and objectives."

In "Genetically Modified Food: Beauty or the Beast?," Karen Krug demonstrates her appreciation of Hutchinson's method. She discusses how it "fosters integrity by supporting action based on reasoned reflection and engagement with the views of those with whom one disagrees." Her case study uses Hutchinson's method to compare two authors' differing positions on food-related biotechnology. While "no analysis in and of itself can dictate right action," Krug argues that clarity about the visions we consciously or unconsciously embrace is a necessary and constructive element.

Drawing on extensive field research, Cameron R. Harder, in "Beyond 'Survival of the Fittest': Pastoral Resources for Rebuilding Rural Community," assesses the Prairie farm crisis in theo-ethical terms. He develops a four-stage method, indebted to Hutchinson's, which can attend to what is happening, identify underlying values and beliefs, assess their "truthfulness" and their capacity to carry rural hopes and dreams, and nurture a rebellious imagination. This fourth task is designed to help a community deal with the operative belief system that supports its economic structures. "Once the stories of suffering have been told, and the 'truth-telling' strengths of the belief structure have been tested, the final task is to develop a 'habitable' world view for this community." To this end, Harder engages biblical sources (for example, about the land) to re-frame what is happening and to offer alternatives. His final pastoral strategy is not to develop a biblical ethics of farm economics, but rather to rediscover and turn toward a broad vision of human life under God that challenges us to find new ways to organize our common life.

Hutchinson has long been involved in biomedical ethics. His method for ethical clarification as applied in hospital settings is the central reference point for the next essay. In "Fetal Assessment: A Feminist Approach to a Bioethical Case Study Using Hutchinson's Method of Ethicial Clarification," Tracy J. Trothen examines a single case in which a fetus is at risk of having a serious heart defect. Through the eyes of each participant/moral agent in the case, she describes the complexities of decision-making and asks: What are the possible courses of action available should the fetus have this condition? One of the features of Hutchinson's method is to broaden the field of the ethical conversation. For Trothen, the insights of feminist biomedical ethicists provide an appropriate breadth for the process of ethical clarification. Employing a feminist perspective in tandem with Hutchinson's method, she moves from the particular case of fetal assessment to broader socio-economic considerations.

Christopher Lind's essay follows, with an examination of how pastoral ethics are actually practised. In "Are Clergy Ethics a Matter of Common Sense?" Lind draws on the database of a study of ethics in ministry that he has undertaken with his research colleague, Maureen Muldoon. In this essay, he establishes that "common sense is relied on by both clergy and laity, and especially so by laity." Following cultural anthropologist Clifford Geertz, Lind affirms that "common sense has a common form but not necessarily a common content, for it does not spontaneously apprehend a fixed reality but affirms suppositions arrived at on earlier occasions. Where disagreement is fuelled by competing claims to common sense (as in the United Church debate on ministry and sexual orientation), there is no alternative but to unearth the presuppositions and expose them to a critical analysis. By this, one may hope to arrive at some truly common understanding." To do so, we will have to expose deliberately the extent to which our common sensibilities are not held in common. Lind asserts that it will be painful, but it will also be essential to institutional and community survival: "The survival of communities is directly related to the survival of the institutions they inhabit."

Joe Mihevc concludes this volume by outlining key principles for "Spirituality and Justice-Making in a City Context." Mihevc describes the efforts of social activists in Toronto, where he serves as a city councillor, as a spiritual quest for community wholeness. Housing, homelessness, hunger and ecology are issues that unite the "soul of the city" in a common cause for justice. Does justice-seeking action bring people of diverse backgrounds together more fruitfully than belief-based efforts to do the same? How is spiritual sustenance generated and sustained in a pluralistic ethos? "An ecumenism of works rather than an ecumenism of faith is at the root of the spirituality of social justice in Toronto." Mihevc's careful reporting of statistics, his relating of the narratives of social activists, and the courageous gathering together of people for action and reflection in support of those on the underside of a particular urban context, provides a practical example of Hutchinson's method at the grassroots, local level.

Hutchinson's commitment to public engagement, transformative ethics and theological education stands out in the bibliography of his published works, cited in the closing contribution to this volume. It has been compiled by Moira Hutchinson, his partner in life and marriage, church and community, political work and shared projects. She has organized the bibliography chronologically and alphabetically. Unlike a curriculum vitae, the bibliography does not list the numerous conferences Hutchinson organized or speeches, sermons, guest seminars and lectures he delivered; nor does it name many of his preoccupations over the last several years—for example, his animation of community discussions about the shape of the Canadian health-care system. It also, by definition, omits book reviews and any "technical" reports he has written, which did not seem to fit the category of publications—for example, his authorship of a 1993 "Submission of the Ecumenical Study Commission to the Royal Commission on Learning." Finally, not reflected in his publications or in the authors' contributions is Hutchinson's major preoccupation from 1978 to 1994 with ecumenical deliberations on Canada's population policy, as illustrated by his active participation in the Inter-Church Project on Population, the Ad Hoc Committee on Church Preparations for the 1984 World Population Conference in Mexico and the Ecumenical Monitoring Group at the International Conference on Population and Development.

Nonetheless, in the bibliography and in these contributions we witness his commitment to the study of contemporary ethics in its many contexts. His vocation has helped to close the gap between the worlds of classroom (always a favourite space of his), congregation, community and various other publics in a pluralistic world. He has also endeavoured to appreciate the diversity within each setting and to make connections among them. Above all, we celebrate with Roger Hutchinson his life and his desire to facilitate "the kinds of consensus and self-knowledge required for co-operation in the search for a just, participatory, and sustainable society."[3]

Notes

1 For example, see Roger Hutchinson, "Study and Action in Politically Diverse Churches," in Roger Hutchinson and Cranford Pratt, eds., *Christian Faith and Economic Justice: Toward a Canadian Perspective* (Burlington, ON: Trinity Press, 1988), 178-92.

2 Roger Hutchinson, *Prophets, Pastors and Public Choices: Canadian Churches and the Mackenzie Valley Pipeline Debate* (Waterloo, ON: Wilfrid Laurier University Press, 1992), 9.

3 Roger Hutchinson, "Towards a 'Pedagogy for Allies of the Oppressed,'" *Studies in Religion/Sciences religieuses* 13/2 (1984): 150.

1

ROGER HUTCHINSON AS ETHICIST AND EDUCATOR IN AN AGE OF RELIGIOUS PLURALISM

C. DOUGLAS JAY

In this attempt to locate Roger Hutchinson's work and significance as ethicist and educator, I have found it necessary to combine some of his intellectual history with my own, for reasons that should become clear later. When I was assigned to direct his graduate studies, I was intrigued at the outset by his expressed interest in continuing his research in the field of Christian ethics in the Toronto School of Theology (TST) context, which he perceived to have a different theological focus from the University of Chicago Divinity School, where he had studied for a master's degree. I had made the same choice for a similar reason over two decades earlier.

Becoming a Religious Social Ethicist

Hutchinson's own account of the evolution of his theological education identifies three stages, moving from an "applying the tradition" model, through approaches that represented varying degrees of responsiveness, to the challenges of secularization and pluralism.[1] After spending five years as a petroleum engineer in Alberta, Hutchinson entered Queen's Theological College to qualify for a second career as a United Church minister. There, he found no reason to challenge the "empty

Notes to chapter 1 are on p. 35-37.

bucket/full bucket" model of education, which assumed that the object was to gain enough knowledge about the tradition to be equipped to apply it effectively in some form of ministry. In retrospect, he saw this as corresponding to a phase in the development of social ethics as a discipline characterized by applying the received tradition to the routine functions of congregational life and to the problems of secular life, personal and social.

By the end of his B.D. program at Queen's, he realized that, before engaging in ministry, he wanted more knowledge about the tradition, and he began the second phase of his theological education by enrolling in the M.A. program in ethics and society at the University of Chicago Divinity School. In the summer interval between Queen's and Chicago, Hutchinson accompanied his spouse Moira (who was representing the Political Commission of the World Student Christian Federation) to the landmark Church and Society Conference held in Geneva in 1966—his introduction to the World Council of Churches. The opportunity to meet delegates from Asia, Africa and Latin America provided him with a foretaste of the challenges to come to his Western male assumptions about understanding and applying the Christian tradition.

At Chicago, Hutchinson was profoundly influenced by Gibson Winter's changed direction from neo-orthodox assumptions in his earlier works to the search for a new foundation for social ethics through the development of a closer working relationship between theology and the empirical sciences. This approach, reflected in Winter's *Elements for a Social Ethic* (1966) and his *Being Free: Reflections on America's Cultural Revolution* (1970),[2] seemed more relevant to contemporary societies that were more and more secular, while religion was a private or confessional matter.

However, after completing his M.A. in ethics and society, Hutchinson decided to switch from the Chicago Ph.D. to the Toronto Th.D. program. In his application, he gave the following reasons, which I quote at length, for they are germane to our inquiry:

> At this point in my career as a "might-be" minister and a "would-be" theologian or Christian ethicist my interests and commitments are somewhat different from those which dominate the Ethics and Society field here. My immediate aim is to prepare myself, on behalf of believing, hoping Christians, to think through the implications of the indus-

> trial, scientific and technological revolutions for the ways in which the faith, hopes and institutions of Christians, and the larger society, must relate to, or rebel against, different aspects of contemporary society. In contrast to this "churchy," theologically oriented concern, the main interest of the Ethics and Society field is to work out a methodology that will allow us to grow out of our concern for a special tradition or a special community of faith. The challenge of working with staff and students who are convinced, not only that the church is disappearing, but that it should, has been stimulating and has caused me to think carefully about a lot of things I previously took for granted. However, if one is not attracted to the new answers the stimulation of the challenge fails to make up for the lack of serious attention to the task of relating what Christians have, do and should believe, to the ways of looking at and understanding our world provided by the various sciences.
>
> In addition to being more "churchy" and theologically oriented than is convenient here, I am becoming increasingly convinced of [the] value of being involved in the Canadian situation, and the life of the Canadian church in particular, both as the subject matter and the context of my studies. One further consideration is that as I reflect on my reaction to those who in some way or another claim to be speaking for the Christian community, but who have rejected the biblical confessional traditions, I realize that my interests are shifting back to the problems of the church, its social teachings, and its theological education, and that it is becoming less important to me whether I have a Ph.D. or a Th.D. In other words, although it is very much out of tune with the times, I find my interest shifting away from departments of religion to theological colleges and other types of ministry tied up more closely with the life of the church.
>
> I feel that studying at Toronto would be a good way to combine my present background in the methodological problems of social ethics with a better knowledge of the history and sociology of Canadian institutions, churches and social movements, and a deeper appreciation and knowledge of the theological tradition that has, can and should inform the life of the church.

However, as we shall see, Winter's approach continued to influence Hutchinson after he entered the doctoral program at Emmanuel

College in 1968. A short time after being appointed his thesis director, I was also appointed founding director of the TST, so that a major portion of my time and energy was diverted to administration. But Hutchinson was a quick study and came with a clear sense of direction, as indicated in the quotation above. By his own account, at Emmanuel he found "an alternative tradition in the United Church that had resisted the neo-orthodox rejection of 'natural' theology."[3] This enabled him to continue his questioning of the "applying the tradition" model of social ethics, which Gibson Winter's new direction had encouraged, while finding credible roots for this position in the United Church and World Council of Churches traditions.

He found grist for his mill in a number of Canadian scholars whom he discovered for the first time, and others who had influenced them. These included John Line and Eric Havelock of Victoria University; Gregory Vlastos and Martyn Estall, two philosophers from his old alma mater Queen's University (although he was unfamiliar with their work); and R.B.Y. Scott of McGill University, an Old Testament scholar. As well, he was influenced by the philosophical theology of John Baillie and the philosophy of John Macmurray of Edinburgh. (Although our backgrounds were different in key respects, it soon became apparent in directing Hutchinson's thesis that we had common interests and perspectives, as exemplified by our shared interest in these scholars, not least Macmurray and Baillie who were influential in my own studies.) What united the Canadian scholars mentioned above was their common membership in the Fellowship for a Christian Social Order (FCSO), and their authorship of chapters in the seminal *Towards the Christian Revolution*,[4] published in 1936. John Macmurray had profoundly influenced this Canadian group, many of whom had met him at an SCM of Canada conference; and, while John Baillie did not have as direct an influence, he had left his mark at Emmanuel as its first professor of systematic theology (1927-30). His work complemented the writings of Donald Baillie which were featured in Hutchinson's B.D. work at Queen's under Donald Mathers.

Hutchinson found Macmurray's work especially to be of great significance for his doctoral thesis, entitled "The Fellowship for a Christian Social Order: A Social Ethical Analysis of a Christian Socialist Movement." At this time, Hutchinson began the third stage of his theological education. He became particularly interested in interfaith dialogue and pluralism. It was the mid-1960s, and the United Church's General Council acknowledged the significance for missiology of religious pluralism. I had been involved in developing a portfolio with the Division of World Outreach to promote dialogue based on mutual respect with persons of other faith traditions, a development that led to an involvement in the World Council of Churches as a founding member of the subunit on dialogue with people of living faiths and ideologies. Hutchinson acknowledged that this work "reinforced my growing conviction that the real challenge (and opportunity) facing religious social ethics was not secularization but pluralism."[5] Hutchinson later affirmed that the concrete measures taken to address religious pluralism (including the R.P. MacKay Memorial Lectures in 1967, in which the challenge of secularization as well as pluralism had been emphasized) marked "the third—and current—phase of my theological education…characterized by the awareness that an adequate understanding of the functions and foundation of social ethics must deal explicitly with both secularization and pluralism."[6]

This is in no way to suggest that Hutchinson is not an independent thinker, but only to acknowledge that it has been gratifying that our perspectives and interests have coincided in many important respects, and that we have learned from each other. Coming from a science background, he was concerned to promote creative dialogue between science and theology[7]; in my case, I shared the same concern with respect to philosophy and theology. A significant measure of Hutchinson's independence of thought is manifested in the creative way in which he has been able to relate insights from the group of Canadian social critics/reformers identified above to those from the later thought of Chicago's Gibson Winter, and to develop a distinctive methodology for both social ethical analysis and theological education. Key to both are the concept of mutuality as an ethical norm (which he found "remarkably similar to Winter's use of the 'we-relation'")[8] and dialogue as a method of developing consensus regarding social analysis and policy formation in a pluralistic society, as well as an indispensable method of seeking truth. These themes are foundational in his development of a distinctive methodology for social ethics, whether designated as Christian, religious or comparative.

Mutuality as Ethical Norm

Mutuality was a dominant theme for most of the authors of *Towards the Christian Revolution*, but especially those most influenced by John Macmurray. Vlastos dealt with this theme repeatedly as a foundational symbol not only in the FCSO volume, but also in other articles dealing with the relationship between love and justice and the religious foundations of democracy, connecting the biblical and Western philosophical traditions. Estall, who thought it expedient while teaching at McMaster to deal with "the Marxist challenge"[9] under the pen name "Propheticus," used the concept of friendship in place of mutuality, but the underlying argument was similar. Both agreed that love as an ethical norm needs to be translated into a pattern of equal social relationships, "one that replaces the dominance of master to submissive slave by the co-operative solidarity of a circle of friends."[10]

This translation of love into mutuality as a procedural norm was severely criticized by Reinhold Niebuhr, who accused the authors of reverting to the immanental theology of earlier liberal interpretations of the social gospel.[11] Niebuhr distinguished sharply between perfectionist love and pragmatic justice, whereas Vlastos maintained that love and justice were both grounded in the fact of human community. For Niebuhr, sacrificial love is the ultimate expression of love. For Vlastos, love is the recognition of community, which justice serves by protecting each member through principles of common action and mutual obligation. The content of love and the rights protected by justice will be different in different communities. When a community is broken up into castes or classes, the prevalent sense of justice will enforce these divisions. Thus, the Christian demand for love is simultaneously a demand for justice, condemning all institutions, whether economic, political or religious, that cause divisions within communities. When justice and love are separated, justice becomes legalistic and love sentimental. Thus, for Vlastos, the source of both is mutuality. Mutuality is the aspect of reality in which what ultimately *is* the case and what absolutely *ought to be* promoted converge.

Vlastos identified the major obstacle to mutuality in an article entitled "Love and the Class Struggle."[12] As he interprets the term, "class struggle" does not refer to hostility between capitalists and workers, but to the capitalist social structure that breaks our common life into two groups, mutually dependent yet mutually antagonistic. The class struggle is thus both an economic and a moral fact. Fidelity to God, who commands us to love, requires solidarity in the struggle to overcome class divisions; by the same token, the struggle for justice is conducted in God's name.

Niebuhr commended the members of the FCSO group for their radical activities in a review of *Towards the Christian Revolution*, but feared that the Kingdom of God of Christian hopes had been reduced to the socialist commonwealth for which the authors were striving. "The crucial problem of every religious radicalism is how to relate the proximate goals of politics and relative values of history to the unconditioned demands of the gospel. If these unconditioned demands are merely reduced to a demand for increased mutuality (after the fashion of John Macmurray, to whom most of the authors express their indebtedness), the result is not only a corruption of the historical meaning of the gospel but also an evasion of the actual human situation."[13]

Niebuhr insisted that forms of utopianism, including Marxism, tend to ignore the deeper alienation of human beings from their Maker and thus falsify the ultimate problem of human spirituality, however correctly they may analyze the mechanics of justice. But, as Hutchinson correctly observed, Vlastos agreed with Niebuhr that mutuality would never be fully achieved in any imaginable social order and sin would not be abolished through social engineering. Thus, he insisted that Niebuhr's perfectionist love-ethic was a mistaken reading of the gospels and a failure to distinguish between love as an emotion and love as an ethical attitude. The dialogue between them continued in Vlastos' review of Niebuhr's *The Nature and Destiny of Man*,[14] in which their differing views of mutuality were in turn related to different concepts of God. For Niebuhr, God is wholly transcendent, whereas the image of God in us is based on the capacity for self-transcendence, including transcendence of nature and social relations, which drives people to sins of pride and self-glorification. Vlastos, on the other hand, stresses God's immanence and the rootedness of human life in natural and social relationships. God is referred to as "the structure of reality which men must discover and express in their ideas in order to conform to it in their action."[15] Hutchinson thus saw Vlastos as balancing Niebuhr's emphasis on freedom as self-transcendence with the complementary truth that personal life is possible only in community.[16]

But Hutchinson also saw Niebuhr's view of the human condition as severely limiting the role of reason, an issue that would recur in his approach to theological education as a whole, as discussed below. Niebuhr claimed that reason mechanizes human relations, and his interpretation of the Christian faith was avowedly supernaturalistic. Vlastos and his FCSO colleagues found in Macmurray a position that was more helpful in relating faith to the human condition than the dualistic supernaturalism of Niebuhr. For Macmurray, the Other is found in the experience of mutuality, of rational human life. In reviewing Macmurray's *The Structure of Religious Experience*, Vlastos agreed that the spiritual world to which we belong by our transcendence of the natural order "is not another world but the natural world known and intended."[17] Whereas, for Niebuhr, the central problem was the finiteness of the human spirit and the fact that persons achieve not only good but evil in attempting to overcome that finiteness, for Vlastos the central problem was the tension between a lingering divisive society of economic classes and the new possibilities of cooperative community. As humans are social beings, the structure of the social order is the key for discerning the forces of life and death, and thus the nature and will of God. Mutuality and a rational empirical faith were key to Vlastos' understanding of the religion of Jesus, the prophets and the biblical idea of covenant. Hutchinson recognized that some criticized Vlastos' theology as too immanental, but argued that "those who share Vlastos' conviction that the 'unconditioned demands of the gospel' can be expressed as 'a demand for increased mutuality' will perhaps discover that their preoccupation with conditions in this world has not made them thoroughly secular after all."[18]

I have dwelt at some length on the role of the concept of mutuality in the thought of Macmurray, Vlastos and other FCSO colleagues, and on those who challenged it, Reinhold Niebuhr in particular, for, as Hutchinson has acknowledged, it was this concept that became for him a foundational symbol as he returned to continue his graduate studies in Canada. In his own words, "the path toward that awareness involved being *uprooted* from one set of assumptions and *rerooted* in a different strand of my own tradition which had been *challenged* when it emerged in the 1930s but *reaffirmed* by recent feminist scholars."[19]

For Hutchinson, mutuality included an awareness that the context within which social ethical judgments were to be addressed had become dramatically more pluralistic than had been apparent in the 1930s, which in turn had important implications for understanding the role of mutuality as foundational symbol and procedural norm. However, this did not render the concept obsolete. On the contrary, Hutchinson found its relevance reaffirmed in the late twentieth century by missiologists dealing with interfaith dialogue and a host of other disciplines, including philosophers of law and, importantly, feminist scholars. For example, he used Carol Robb's analysis of the relationship between Beverly Harrison's feminist social ethic and the wider discipline of religious social ethics to show how respect for diversity can be combined with acceptance of a shared framework to sustain disciplined moral discourse.[20]

But it should be emphasized that Hutchinson's self-described rerooting in a strand of his own tradition was integrally connected with the strand of the Chicago tradition represented by aspects of Winter's *Elements for a Social Ethic*. The evolution of his thought included a measure of reappraisal of the earlier rejection of Niebuhr, as he developed a methodology of ethical analysis and clarification in which dialogue with those holding differing views was an essential instrument.

In his early analysis of the Niebuhr-Vlastos debate, in the course of developing his thesis on the work of the FCSO group, Hutchinson was primarily concerned with refuting Niebuhr's dualistic supernaturalism and defending the Macmurray-Vlastos approach from the charge that it was a naturalistic philosophy without a theological foundation. As his thought evolved, he became more pluralistic with regard to foundational symbols, including Niebuhr's, though he remained critical of Niebuhr's contextual judgments.

Hutchinson's Methodology

The methodology that Hutchinson developed, drawing on insights identified above and reached in collaboration with colleagues specializing in the social sciences, such as Gibson Winter of Chicago and political scientist Cranford Pratt of the University of Toronto, is designed to be relevant to changing social contexts. The decades following the 1930s and 1940s, when the FCSO was flourishing, were characterized not only by profound economic changes, but also by a degree of cultural and religious pluralism that could not have been anticipated in the earlier period. The initial goal of Christianizing the social order has a triumphalist ring in our contemporary post-Christendom, pluralistic society. With the benefit of hindsight, it is now apparent that the authors of the 1930s documents were relatively insensitive to issues of gender equality, racial and ethnic diversity, and the environment. But Hutchinson has shown how the central concepts, such as mutuality, the organic sense of the relation of the individual to society and the realization of the self-in-community, which informed the work of Macmurray, Vlastos, John Line and others, are of continuing relevance as Christians seek to work for individual, social and cultural transformation with those of other traditions who share our core values.[21]

Although, in identifying his reasons for continuing his graduate studies in Toronto, Hutchinson mentioned his desire to work in a more explicitly theological context as opposed to that of religious studies, he accepted an appointment to teach religious studies while completing his doctoral dissertation. The fact of religious and ideological diversity in the non-confessional context of religious studies provided the initial motivation for him to develop a method for the clarification of ethical issues that takes nothing for granted regarding religious commitment. As well, his experience with church groups convinced him that it is as difficult to deal with controversial issues within a particular religious group as it is in more mixed settings. This coincided in time with the efforts of the United Church and the World Council of Churches to develop methods and protocols for ecumenical and interfaith dialogue. Hutchinson perceptively observed that these were in many ways more advanced than our practices for dealing with other members of our own group.[22] The truth of this perception from the 1970s has been more than confirmed in the last decade and a half in the ways in which the United Church has struggled over issues ranging from the ordination of homosexuals to biblical interpretation and Christology. Thus, the method Hutchinson developed is as pertinent to ethical analysis in the context of theological education as it is to that of religious studies, for in any contemporary context, whether identified as religious, theological or secular, it is necessary to deal with the fact of diversity and the need for disciplined inquiry.

As his method evolved, Hutchinson came to identify it under the heading of "comparative ethics." This was not to suggest that it pertains only to a comparison of different religious traditions, or even to different Christian traditions, for it is intended to apply equally to debate within a particular denomination. The main feature of his approach is the identification of different levels of clarification which can help to bring into sharper focus different dimensions of debate over controversial social issues; a major aim is to help persons who are often silenced in such debates to see that their concerns are heard in an undistorted fashion. Thus, essential to his method is genuine dialogue as key to the problem of communication.

The first level of clarification consists of storytelling, in which all participants are invited to report their feelings about the issues or alternatives being discussed. The object is to reach a tentative agreement regarding the problem being discussed. In the course of the discussion, the group may discover that the problem as initially defined is not the real issue, so that the problem needs to be redefined.

The second level involves testing initial claims against the evidence. Important in this process is the recognition that lying behind conflicting factual claims are often different interpretative frameworks, assumptions and world views in relation to which facts are selected and interpreted. While it is important to assess factual claims in their own right in the light of empirical evidence, Hutchinson insists that it is no less important to consider the bearing of these interpretative frameworks on factual claims. While it is useful, up to a point, to distinguish between fact and value, Hutchinson challenges the common tendency to separate fact and value altogether, rightly insisting that value judgments are often embedded in claims of fact, and underlying assumptions need to be examined in their own right in the course of clarifying options.

The third level is that of ethical clarification. Whereas the factual level of clarification involves the relationship between ethics and the empirical sciences, Hutchinson draws on moral philosophy as a means of clarifying value judgments and ethical arguments. This serves the purpose of identifying different types of moral reasoning to help overcome the tendency to equate ethics with a single ethical theory, whether utilitarian, deontological or idealist. Different circumstances may call for different methods to do justice to a particular issue, but Hutchinson believes that there needs to be clarity about the kinds of claims being made and challenged at any particular moment, and has illustrated this in relation to a variety of issues, including the Mackenzie Valley Pipeline debate.[23]

The fourth level is called "post-ethical clarification," to indicate a shift from documenting factual claims (and identifying the value judgments embedded in them) and giving reasons for one's ethical judgments, to "confessing" one's faith. As foundational convictions are discovered and confessed, a basis is laid for mutual acceptance and understanding, creating the conditions that facilitate a return to the arguments carried on at the factual and ethical levels. At this level, attention is given to the religious beliefs, symbols, metaphors and myths that shape the stories and convey the most basic convictions of the participants. The main objective at this level is the mutual clarification of identities.

Hutchinson's overall objective in developing this educational approach is to help to produce the kind of consensus required for cooperation in the search for what the World Council of Churches has variously called a "responsible society" or a "just, participatory and sustainable society." Cooperation in the struggle for justice requires an educational approach designed to clarify perplexities and disagreements and an organizational strategy that can capitalize on agreement but accommodate disagreement. This educational approach has served well as a methodology for teaching, not only in academic courses in religious studies and theological contexts, but also in other academic contexts such as the University of Toronto's Department of Forestry and its Joint Centre for Bioethics, in symposia, in the supervision of research under the auspices of Emmanuel College's Centre for the Study of Religion in Canada (later renamed the Centre for Research in Religion), in publications on a remarkably broad range of issues and in ecumenical coalitions. The centrality of the principle of dialogue has been manifested in the collaboration and debate with a broad spectrum of theologians, philosophers and social scientists, both religiously oriented and secular.

Hutchinson's Critics

But the methodology is not without its critics. One example is the response to *Christian Faith and Economic Justice: Toward a Canadian Perspective,*[24] which Hutchinson edited and contributed to in collaboration with Cranford Pratt. This book grew out of a series of lectures given at Bloor Street United Church in Toronto, designed to expose church members to the findings and perspectives of socially concerned, but not necessarily radical, scholars whose views were being neglected by church-sponsored groups dealing with development issues. In the authors' words,

> We were concerned that an intruding ideological exclusivism and a too easy transfer to judgments on social policies of the authority granted to our faith have taken their toll on the quality of some Christian contributions to discussions on social issues in Canada. Our second concern is that tendencies towards ideological narrowness and an uncritical fusion of faith claims and policy conclusions have undermined an older tradition of ecumenical social ethics. The Oldham-Abrecht approach sought rigour and relevance through an open, public engagement with a wide range of expert and non-expert opinion. In recent years, however, Abrecht found that in World Council of Churches programs it has become increasingly difficult to combine solidarity with victims of injustice with the subjection of policy proposals to the scrutiny of experts.[25]

Abrecht's experience led him to conclude that "ecumenical work on social issues is almost at a standstill."[26] I quote this at some length because Hutchinson felt a sense of indebtedness to Oldham's and Abrecht's methodology. He shared personal conversations with Paul Abrecht on the subject of the impoverishment of the aspect of the ecumenical movement noted in the quotation. This reference is pertinent to Pratt's and Hutchinson's response to criticism by a TST colleague, Lee Cormie of the University of St. Michael's College. Cormie affirmed the value of collaboration across academic disciplines in relating ethics to economics, as well as their emphasis on comparative ethics and the importance of pluralism in ethics.[27] But he argued that Pratt and Hutchinson were primarily concerned to improve communications rather than to arrive at an authoritative declaration of what is true or right.[28] He was particularly critical of their characterization of an "option for the poor" ethic, in the course of criticizing the Roman Catholic bishops' *Ethical Reflections on the Economic Crisis* and some GATT-Fly writings.[29] They criticized these documents for their lack of clarity regarding the relationship between particular policy proposals and basic ethical precepts, and for failing to take detailed account of the consequences of proposed policies. Cormie concluded that they equated an "option for the poor" ethic with that lack of clarity or failure to account for consequences, substituting a reformist, developmentalist ethic. More seriously, he charged that their proposal for a framework for comparing different ethical approaches was intimately linked to their "reformist" way of thinking, and questioned whether they had a vision of an alternative social order and an adequate strategy for social change.

Pratt and Hutchinson responded that there was evidence of their views on both these issues throughout the book, but that the main aim of this book was not to articulate a vision or develop a strategy for social change. They contended that this misperception of their aim had led to inaccurate claims about their approach. In arguing that the views of sensitive, concerned, well-intentioned people working in major corporate headquarters should be enlisted in the effort to reform these institutions, Pratt and Hutchinson did not mean that these institutions did not need to be reformed. The key issue was not tactics for reforming reactionary institutions, but which voices were to be included or excluded from conversations within the church regarding which economic policies would in fact help the poorest of the poor, and whether we can learn from analyses that are not rooted in our own ideology.

Thus, they disagreed with Cormie (as well as with Travis Kroeker and Janet Silman, whose critiques are found in the same issue of the *Toronto Journal of Theology*)[30] that their openness to the contributions of scholars and practitioners to public debates represented either the marginalization of theology or a lack of attention to the voices of the poor. I would add that the personal commitment of both Hutchinson and Pratt to social democracy and strategies to promote it is a matter of record throughout their publications and activities. But the issue here is rather the propriety of advocating openness to a variety of stances to determine which is the most likely to be achieved in a given context. To be open to the possibility that a "reformist" strategy is more likely to help the poor than a "prophetic" one in a given context is not necessarily a compromise to be judged as a less Christian contribution; rather, it may complement the prophetic stance, an important position in creating an awareness of how great are the social transformations that are still needed.

Cormie's final criticism involved "the option for the poor and oppressed itself, in its hermeneutical dimension."[31] He charged them with making a simple distinction between facts and values, and separating the spheres of the social sciences from theology and ethics. This was a rather curious charge in light of the consistent emphasis throughout so many of Hutchinson's writings on the interrelationship between fact and value, the importance of relating social sciences to ethics, and his frequent collaboration with social scientists, of which this book is an example.

In their defence, Pratt and Hutchinson cited Pratt's comments about the need to go beyond Gregory Baum's claim that a guide for Christian social action is provided by the demand to be in solidarity with popular movements.[32] Pratt pointed out that such a goal in itself is an insufficient guide for action. In order to judge which movements are struggling with the issues of justice and truth and which are not, we must have canons of judgment other than whether the movement is or is not a popular movement of protest. This was consistent with Hutchinson's support of Abrecht's critique of the World Council of Churches regarding the role of "experts," noted above.

Finally, in their response Pratt and Hutchinson identified a distinct characteristic of their conception of the task of Christian social ethics, distinguishing between defending a particular social ethic (whether prophetic or reformist, for example) and the discipline of social ethics. As professors in a publicly funded university and in the ecumenical theological context of the TST it is imperative to respect ideological and theological diversity. Speaking from their own experience, Hutchinson sees his mandate as a social ethicist "to help his students think clearly and critically within an ecumenical and cultural commitment to peace, justice and the integrity of creation and in relation to their own traditions;" Pratt, as a political scientist, "insists that the professional requirement of his academic discipline to weigh all evidence, to avoid claims that go beyond persuasive evidence, and to be open to contrary arguments must not be abandoned when he seeks to give social expression to the central values of his religious tradition."[33]

Hutchinson and Pratt recognized that as social democrats they would inevitably appear "lacklustre" to those more assertive, but they insisted that the validity of their attempts to clarify options should be judged by criteria other than their credentials as socialists, radicals or prophets, and remained convinced of the importance of frameworks for public moral and political discourse that attempt to transcend particular ideological stances and political judgments. As a case in point, they saw a danger that the public witness of the churches, based on the type of research and advocacy carried out by groups such as the Taskforce on the Churches and Corporate Responsibility and Project Ploughshares, could be undermined by distracting debates about the correct analysis and proper language for professing the preferential option for the poor. In support of their caveat, I recall hearing the Indian theologian, Archbishop Paulos Mar Gregorius, arguing in a World Council of Churches debate that, if poverty is deemed to be the central problem, the solution is wealth, and therefore that analysis of the problem is far too simplistic. As archbishop of the Mar Thoma Church of South India, and as an articulate theologian and social critic of international repute, Gregorius was surely qualified to speak with some authority on behalf of the marginalized. At any rate, this concern about the churches' practice was what prompted Hutchinson and Pratt to stress the importance of discerning when to accept diversity and when to seek consensus. Cormie's criticism that they seemed to have "no commitment beyond contributing to the debate itself"[34] was surely belied by their contention that "study and advocacy, the detailed study of consequences and the ability to make decisions and to take action, should not be separated from one another," and that, "although not all Canadian activists would agree, we remain convinced that it is more useful to focus on issues rather than to attempt to reach consensus about the churches' stance in relation to capitalism or about the scriptural foundations for Christian social action."[35]

In spite of the disagreements noted between Cormie and Hutchinson (and his colleague Pratt), I can think of few who have more effectively exemplified Cormie's affirmation that "a fundamental key must be the education and mobilization of the rest of us to promote radical changes in ways of naming the problems, articulating alternatives which will require basic changes in the institutions and structures shaping our lives, and choosing among them."[36]

Locating Hutchinson's Contributions as an Educator

While we have focused thus far primarily on Hutchinson as social ethicist, it must be apparent that education is at the heart of his approach to social analysis. It is intimately connected to the need for mobilization, consistent with the ground rules inherent in his methodology for respecting diversity in a pluralistic society. In reflecting on his contribution as an educator, therefore, it is necessary to take account of the whole corpus of his work, rather than be limited to his role in the classroom, whether under the aegis of religious studies, theology or forestry, or to his administrative roles in educational institutions, including his principalship of Emmanuel College. As with his approach to social analysis, dialogue is key to his role as an educator—dialogue across lines of discipline, faith, culture and any other pertinent forms of division. A course offered in his last year before retirement illustrates his method in the classroom. Entitled "Ethical Clarification in Multifaith Contexts," the course was team-taught with Andreas d'Souza, director of the Henry Martyn Institute in Hyderabad and currently a visiting Islamic scholar in residence at Emmanuel. Always, however, dialogue is informed by disciplined research, and Hutchinson's teaching has been enriched throughout his career by primary research related to a wide range of current social issues.

Consistent with his commitment to principles of dialogue in a pluralistic age, Hutchinson has also been notably committed to promoting the research of colleagues—faculty and students within or outside the college. Thus, in addition to his own substantial body of research, in 1986 he played a key role in the establishment of the Centre for the Study of Religion in Canada at Emmanuel College, an initiative resulting from a Lilly Endowment faculty development grant. As principal at the time, I can testify that Hutchinson not only was the primary source of the rationale for the Centre, but has chaired the administrative committee from its founding. The Centre has provided support facilities for a wide variety of both short- and long-term research projects. Hutchinson has provided administrative support to and participated in literally dozens of events sponsored by the Centre or co-sponsored with other agencies. Theologians, social scientists, philosophers and other academicians, clergy, health professionals, lawyers, and informed and inquiring lay people have engaged each other on a wide range of current social issues. Subjects have included different aspects of the current crisis in public health care, multifaith literacy, law and religion, population, consumption and sustainable development, a wide range of peace and environmental issues, and issues around ethics, science and religion. While the range of issues has been wide, the methodology has consistently followed the principles of clarification and respect for diversity enunciated above.

An unpublished outline of an address given on 19 April 2000, entitled "Training for Ministry in Modern Times," offers significant clues to Hutchinson's philosophy of theological education. He begins with the text from 1 Peter 3:15b-16, "Always be ready to make your defence to anyone who demands from you an accounting for the hope that is in you; yet do it with gentleness and reverence." The task is identified as "education for church and community leadership to equip the saints for the mission of God who is love" by demystifying and recovering Christianity's initial intelligibility. This he proceeds to do, beginning with an appeal again to Gregory Vlastos who, in *Christian Faith and Democracy* (1939), wrote: "the essential thing in this religion is not a mysterious act performed by [a small group] on behalf of the whole community; it is intelligible, reasonable service performed by [all] members of the community on [their] own behalf and on behalf of the whole community. It is an affirmation of a covenant, an understanding that the whole community makes with God…there is nothing essentially mysterious about it: the best human insight must be brought to bear upon it, re-interpret, and transform it with advanced understanding."[37]

Hutchinson notes that, in an earlier period, one could assume that United Church theological students began their formal studies with a background in family and church that provided a broad spiritual formation, so that the task of the theological school was to deconstruct some of the students' theological perceptions in order to reconstruct a more intellectually viable way of helping them to understand life and ministry in a particular denominational context. This older conventional wisdom no longer applies, since a large percentage of students now lack the kind of formation the church provided in an earlier time. Thus, since the theological school may be the student's point of entry into the faith tradition, the school has a larger responsibility for spiritual formation than in an earlier time. This includes not only attention to personal development and interpersonal skills, skills in social analysis and practical moral reasoning, but also socialization into the United Church as a religious institution and tradition. It is important to be self-consciously contextual in the way all disciplines are taught. The present context calls for heightened awareness of the diversity of religious backgrounds of students, both within and outside the United Church. The religious diversity of contemporary society must be seriously addressed in the curriculum, not only in the traditional ecumenical sense but also in multifaith and interfaith senses.

Hutchinson concludes by returning directly to the text from 1 Peter, stressing the importance of developing an intellectually mature as well as an emotionally satisfying sense of being Christian, as the necessary foundation for "giving an account of the hope that is in you," and for doing it with gentleness and reverence. This is consistent with his understanding of the concepts of mutuality, dialogue and persons in community that we have seen to be so central to all his work, as well as with his articulation of the role of reason. For example, dealing with the current debate around biotechnology and genetic engineering, Hutchinson again makes the point that facts and values are never completely separable, for in a sense the way in which facts are selected and weighed will always reflect a person's values and interests. Theology helps to define both values and our interpretation of the facts.[38]

Another case in point, which is instructive with regard to the epistemology underlying his philosophy of education, is the conference Hutchinson hosted in June 2000, entitled "A Wider Rationality: Science, Religion and Ethical Directions." As we noted above, Hutchinson was severely critical in his doctoral thesis of Niebuhr's limited view of reason. He therefore sought support for the concept of "a wider rationality," which was the central theme of the conference and was demonstrated by contemporary scholars from a variety of disciplines. For example, Jean Porter, a professor of moral theology at the University of Notre Dame, argued that natural law theory, rather than being seen as ineluctably foreign to Christian theological ethics, can credibly be embedded within and shaped by contemporary Christian theology. Jennifer Nedelsky, professor of the philosophy of law at the University of Toronto, argued that we need a language that turns our attention to the full dimensions of our humanness, rather than to a stripped-down image of the rational agent—attention therefore to embodiment, to difference, to emotion and to our essentially relational nature, as well as to our creative capacity.

These and other examples from authors in a range of disciplines with whom Hutchinson is in dialogue offer striking contemporary parallels to Macmurray's concept of reason, especially as reflected in *Reason and Emotion* and in his Gifford Lectures.[39] It is not surprising, therefore, to find throughout Hutchinson's writings, including these most recent examples of his views on education, a continuing consistency with Macmurray's concept of reason. For Macmurray, action, not abstract thinking in isolation, is the defining feature of human identity and expression. Action is conceptually prior to thinking, and is the mode of unity constituting personality. The impersonal cannot explain the personal, but the personal can explain the impersonal, for it contains it. He distinguished faith from knowledge, but contended that a deep integration in knowledge is possible between religion and science. Faith is not a form of knowledge, but a practical attitude of the will that is needed to do science as much as to embrace religion. As his thought evolved, the personal became central to his philosophy and theology, for he argued that personality is realized in the unity of persons in communion; if personality is the fullest bearer of value, then Absolute Reality is personal and God is a Personal Absolute. The most complete expression of reality is communion with God. But this is not achieved solely through thought, for thinking is derivative from action. The self is to be understood primarily as agent: "I do" precedes "I think." Moreover, a purely individual self is a fiction. The philosophical implication of this is that the unity of the personal can be understood only through the mutuality of a personal relationship.

The underlying assumption of Macmurray's philosophy of knowledge is that reason is not a private but a mutual possession. His Gifford Lectures, published in two volumes as *The Self as Agent* and *Persons in Relation*, represent his fullest articulation of the "form of the personal." The thesis of the first volume is that all meaningful knowledge is for the sake of action, and all meaningful action is for the sake of friendship. In the second volume, as well as in *Reason and Emotion,* he argues that transferring the centre of reference of the self to action enables us to understand all human activity as a functional unity, so that even our emotions, instead of being disturbances to the placidity of thought, take their place as necessary motives which sustain our activities, including the activity of thinking. But, above all, it ends the solitariness of the thinking self, and restores us to our proper existence as a community of "persons in relation," for whom the norm of ethical behaviour is mutuality.

Macmurray succeeded such eminent philosophers and theologians as Samuel Alexander, A.N. Whitehead, J. Dewey, G. Marcel, Reinhold Niebuhr and Michael Polanyi, but his Gifford Lectures were judged to be the most systematic of the natural theologies. At the outset of the first volume Macmurray affirms that he is treating these themes as a *philosopher* "for that is my only competence." He is embarrassed by the widespread doubt as to whether a natural theology is at all possible, however, and argues that if

> human reason, unaided by revelation, can contribute anything to theology, it is through a philosophical analysis of the personal....If there is no point at which faith and reason can meet, then it is unreasonable to accept the deliverance of faith, and atheism is the reasonable conclusion....But the view that there is no path from common experience to a belief in God; that religion rests upon some special and extraordinary type of experience apart from which it could not arise—this seems to me hardly credible....[But] religion is the...one universal expression of our human capacity to reflect....These considerations do nothing...to prove the validity of religious belief; but they do make it unlikely that our common, primary experience provides no evidence tending to support it.

So, while affirming that he is speaking as a philosopher rather than as a theologian, he goes on to say that, "if this leads, as I believe it does, to modifications of outlook which require a theistic conclusion, I shall have fulfilled the intentions of the founder of the Gifford lectureship."[40] I quote this at some length on the ground that it is an important source of what Hutchinson described as "an alternative tradition in the United Church that had resisted the neo-orthodox rejection of 'natural' theology,"[41] and which he found so compelling on his return to Canada.

Thus, to sum up my attempt to "locate" Hutchinson philosophically and theologically: in the whole corpus of his work, I find him consistently, though critically, interpreting and reinterpreting in the contemporary context the tradition of Canadian social ethicists of the 1930s, including both philosophers and theologians who in turn were deeply indebted to Macmurray, as were World Council of Churches pioneers in the field of church and society. Both J.H. Oldham and George MacLeod, founder of the Iona Community, were widely influential; but Hutchinson uniquely integrated this tradition with that of the United States represented by Gibson Winter's work from the 1960s (he, in turn, being influenced by Wieman, Tillich and H.R. Niebuhr, among others), to promote the methodology of ethical analysis and clarification that we have examined above. And, as noted, these approaches to ethical analysis, based on an epistemology and philosophy of education presuming a wider rationality, locate him with other contemporary scholars in different fields, such as Jean Porter (Roman Catholic moral theology), Jennifer Nedelsky (philosophy of law), and Protestant feminist theological ethicists such as Beverly Harrison. The theologians among these, including Hutchinson, have been criticized for basing their social thought on theologies judged to be too immanental and insufficiently transcendental. However, the logic of Hutchinson's methodology of clarification requires respectful dialogue between proponents of differing options, together with disciplined research. This debate is not new; I well recall from my student days at Edinburgh fifty years ago how Thomas Torrance, the then rather rigid Barthian, dismissed George MacLeod's social analysis as being too focused on the Incarnation to do justice to the Crucifixion. MacLeod was guilty of being too influenced by Macmurray. On the other hand, while sensitive to the Vlastos-Hutchinson critique of Niebuhr, I have to take seriously Ricouer's claim that "the cross is the privileged symbol of Christianity," and submit that the logic of Hutchinson's methodology requires continuing dialogue between these positions. As Hutchinson himself acknowledges, while in his early analyses of the Vlastos-Niebuhr debate he was insistent on defending Vlastos-Macmurray from the charge that theirs was a non-theological, naturalistic philosophy, in his later work he adopted a more pluralistic attitude toward foundational symbols.[42]

Concluding Remarks

Hutchinson's methodology is particularly relevant within the contemporary pluralistic context, and not least within the United Church which, as we noted above, has been characterized by unprecedented polarization in recent decades regarding issues ranging from homosexuality to biblical interpretation to Christology and atonement. In an article entitled "Atonement Theories and the Scope of Salvation,"[43] Michael Bourgeois offers a salutary reminder that the image of Jesus Christ as sacrifice, satisfaction or substitute for the sins of humanity is but one of the ways in which Christians have expressed his saving significance. Throughout history, his Incarnation, healing and teaching have been among the other dimensions of his saving work that have been recognized, just as the evil from which we are saved also has multiple dimensions—all the evils that enslave us, including sin, suffering and death, and unjust relations, are based on hierarchies of wealth, race, gender and sexual orientation. The educational approach that underlies Hutchinson's unique methodology is designed to clarify perplexities and disagreements and to develop an organizational strategy that can capitalize on agreement but accommodate disagreement. It is singularly appropriate for a pluralistic, post-Christian era. While preserving the integrity of Christian commitment by recognizing the multiple dimensions of God's saving work in Christ and wherever else God has spoken and been recognized, it offers a non-imperialistic way of pursuing truth, justice and reconciliation through respectful dialogue and disciplined research. Above all, the validity of Hutchinson's theory has been remarkably exemplified in his practice as ethicist and educator.

Notes

1 Roger Hutchinson, "Social Ethics and Social Transformation," in *Action Training in Canada: Reflections on Church-Based Education for Social Transformation,* ed. Ted Reeve and Roger Hutchinson (Toronto: Centre for Research in Religion, Emmanuel College, 1997), 115ff.

2 Gibson Winter, *Elements for a Social Ethic: Scientific and Ethical Perspectives on Social Process* (New York: Macmillan, 1966); and *Being Free: Reflections on America's Cultural Revolution* (New York: Macmillan, 1970).

3 Hutchinson, "Social Ethics and Social Transformation," 118.

4 R.B.Y. Scott and Gregory Vlastos, eds., *Towards the Christian Revolution* (Chicago and New York: Willett, Clark & Company, 1936; reprint Kingston, ON: Ronald P. Frye and Company, 1989).

5 Hutchinson, "Social Ethics and Social Transformation," 119.

6 Ibid.

7 It was Hutchinson's interest in science-religion issues that first drew his attention, quite by accident, to the FCSO group of scholars. After a lecture on the Darwinist-Creationist controversy, he purchased a book in a second-hand bookstore for ten cents. It had a damaged dust jacket, which he thought referred to *evolution*. However, he did not examine the book until coming to Toronto, when he discovered that it referred to *revolution.*

8 Roger Hutchinson, "Mutuality: Procedural Norm and Foundational Symbol," in *Liberation Ethics: Essays in Religious Social Ethics in Honor of Gibson Winter,* ed. Charles Amjad-Ali and W. Alvin Pitcher (Chicago: Center for the Scientific Study of Religion, 1985), 98.

9 Roger Hutchinson, "Introduction," in *Towards the Christian Revolution*, reprint edition, xxx.
10 Hutchinson, "Mutuality," 98-99.
11 Ibid., 100, citing Reinhold Niebuhr, "*Towards the Christian Revolution*: Review," *Radical Religion* 2 (Spring 1937): 43.
12 Gregory Vlastos, "Love and the Class Struggle," *Radical Religion* 3 (Spring 1938): 26.
13 Niebuhr, "*Towards the Christian Revolution*: Review," 43.
14 Gregory Vlastos, "Sin and Destiny in Niebuhr's Religion," *The Christian Century*, 1 October 1941, 1202-04.
15 Gregory Vlastos, "The Ethical Foundations," in *Towards the Christian Revolution*, 70.
16 Roger Hutchinson, "Love, Justice and the Class Struggle," *Religious Studies/Sciences religieuses* 10/4 (1981): 475-76.
17 Gregory Vlastos, "*The Structure of Religious Experience*: Review," *Christendom* 2/2 (1937): 293.
18 Hutchinson, "Love, Justice and the Class Struggle," 479.
19 Hutchinson, "Mutuality," 97 and 107; he is particularly interested in Carol Gilligan's ethic of responsibility, which employs mutuality as an operative norm, as well as the work of such scholars as Judith Plaskow, Beverly Harrison and Elisabeth Schüssler Fiorenza.
20 Roger Hutchinson, "Social Ethics and Mission in a Post-Liberal Age," in *Theological Education in Canada*, ed. Graham Brown (Toronto: United Church Publishing House, 1998), 30-31.
21 On John Line, see Robert H. Craig, "Ungodly Capitalism: The Canadian Protestant Left in the 1930s," in *A Long and Faithful March: "Towards the Christian Revolution" 1930s/1980s*, ed. Harold Wells and Roger Hutchinson (Toronto: United Church Publishing House, 1989), 52; see also Roger Hutchinson, "Social Action and Mission in the Eighties," in *Justice as Mission: An Agenda for the Church*, ed. Terry Brown and Christopher Lind (Burlington, ON: Trinity Press, 1985), 89-90.
22 Roger Hutchinson, "Towards a 'Pedagogy for Allies of the Oppressed,'" *Studies in Religion/Sciences religieuses* 13/2 (1984): 145.
23 Roger Hutchinson, "Comparative Ethics and the Mackenzie Valley Pipeline Debate," *Toronto Journal of Theology* 1/2 (1985): 242-60.
24 Cranford Pratt and Roger Hutchinson, eds., *Christian Faith and Economic Justice: Toward a Canadian Perspective* (Burlington, ON: Trinity Press, 1988).
25 Roger Hutchinson and Cranford Pratt, "A Response," *Toronto Journal of Theology* 7/1 (1991): 51-52.
26 Ibid., 52.
27 Lee Cormie, "Option for the Poor and Oppressed," *Toronto Journal of Theology* 7/1 (1991): 19ff.
28 Ibid., 24.

29 Ibid., 23-25, citing Cranford Pratt, "Faith and Social Action," in *Christian Faith and Economic Justice*, ed. Cranford Pratt and Roger Hutchinson (Burlington, ON: Trinity Press, 1988), 167ff. See Cranford Pratt and Roger Hutchinson, "Religious Commitments and Public Choices," in *Christian Faith and Economic Justice*, 5-7 and Cranford Pratt, "International Development and Christian Responsibility," in *Christian Faith and Economic Justice*, 148-54. GATT-Fly is a pun on the word "gadfly" and the General Agreement on Tariffs and Trade (GATT). The coalition was organized in 1973.

30 P. Travis Kroeker, "Pluralism and Policy Monism: The Political Irrelevance of Theology," *Toronto Journal of Theology* 7/1 (1991): 35-43; Janet Silman, "An Open Letter to Cranford Pratt and Roger Hutchinson," *Toronto Journal of Theology* 7/1 (Spring 1991): 44-50.

31 Hutchinson and Pratt, "A Response," 54.

32 Ibid., citing Pratt, "Faith and Social Action," 168-69.

33 Hutchinson and Pratt, "A Response," 54-55.

34 Cormie, "Option for the Poor and Oppressed," 31.

35 Roger Hutchinson, "Study and Action in Politically Diverse Churches," in *Christian Faith and Economic Justice*, 190-191.

36 Cormie, "Option for the Poor and Oppressed," 29.

37 Hutchinson, "Training for Ministry in Modern Times," citing Gregory Vlastos, *Christian Faith and Democracy* (New York: Association Press, 1939), 20.

38 Taskforce on the Churches and Corporate Responsibility, *Biotechnology and Genetic Engineering: Current Issues, Ethics, and Theological Reflections* (Toronto: United Church of Canada, 2000), 90.

39 John Macmurray, *Reason and Emotion* (London: Faber and Faber, 1935); "The Form of the Personal," Gifford Lectures, 1953-54, published as *The Self as Agent* (London: Faber and Faber, 1957); and *Persons in Relation* (London: Faber and Faber, 1961).

40 See Macmurray, *The Self as Agent* (Faber and Faber: London, 1957), 17-21.

41 Hutchinson, "Social Ethics and Social Transformation," 19.

42 Hutchinson, "Mutuality," 107.

43 Michael Bourgeois, "Atonement Theories and the Scope of Salvation," *Emmanuel College Newsletter* (Fall 2000): 6-7.

2

THE CHURCH AND PLURALISM IN QUEBEC

An Account of a Participant

GREGORY BAUM

Today's church is challenged by pluralism in several contexts. Let me mention three of them. There is, first, the difficult theological problem of religious pluralism in a church that believes in a single saviour. There is, second, the political challenge of the new ethnic or cultural pluralism in the developed countries of the West, in which the church must play a reconciling role. And there is, third, the pastoral problem of cultural and spiritual pluralism within the church itself.

In this essay, I wish to examine the Catholic Church's reaction to the new cultural pluralism in Quebec. I am, of course, also interested in the theology of religious pluralism and hence duly unhappy with Cardinal Ratzinger's recent declaration.[1] I have also been involved in the pastoral effort of Montreal's Centre justice et foi to promote solidarity and tolerance in Montreal's pluralistic church. In this essay, however, I shall deal only with issues related to Quebec's cultural pluralism and the Catholic Church's response to it.

Because of the unjust distribution of wealth, resources and power globally and the grave suffering inflicted upon people in many parts of the world as a result, a stream of immigrants has arrived and continues to arrive in the developed countries of the West. Who can blame these people for wanting to better their lives? If we had lived in their part of

Notes to chapter 2 are on pp. 55-56.

the world, we would probably be immigrants with them. Yet, there is something new in this shift of population. Thanks to the highly developed technology of communications and transportation, the new immigrants are able to retain their ties to their places of origin, remain in conversation with their cultural centres and obtain resources for preserving their own cultural inheritance. Because immigrants of the past were largely cut off from their homeland, they rarely exhibited the same cultural self-confidence. The new immigrants believe that becoming citizens of their new country does not interfere with the preservation of their own collective identity.

Today, this effort to preserve cultural identity is respected in most developed countries. As a result of several social movements, including the women's movement, contemporary culture honours the values and the commitment involved in the pursuit of the politics of identity. The urgent question that emerges from this is how the developed countries should modify their self-understanding and reform their institutions to make room for these new cultural identities. All Western developed countries are currently wrestling with this issue.

Pluralism in Quebec

Pluralism in Quebec has a different history from that in the rest of Canada. The descendants of the French settlers in North America thought of themselves as *les canadiens*, the French-Canadian nation, the core and centre of which was Lower Canada, later the province of Quebec. A vigorous sense of national identity, supported by the Catholic Church, enabled them in the past to define themselves in a manner at odds with the dominant North American culture created by Protestant values and secular modernization. At that time, French-Canadian nationalism was to a large extent ethnically based. The great majority of immigrants who settled in Montreal desired integration into the English-speaking world of Canada and the United States. French Canadians preferred to remain among themselves. Conscious of their minority status in North America, they thought this seemed the best way to protect their cultural identity. The Catholic Church reinforced this by stating that the French language protected the faith (*la langue, protectrice de la foi),* without warning that resistance to outsiders easily generates xenophobia.

After World War II, the desire to catch up with the modern North American world became strong in certain sectors of Quebec society, including the Catholic Action Movement. This trend came to a climax on 22 June 1960, when the Liberal Party under Jean Lesage was elected to form the provincial government, replacing the conservative Union Nationale. What took place was a major cultural upheaval, the so-called Quiet Revolution. Quebecers wanted to catch up with the democratic, technological and commercial orientation of North American society; they wanted to replace the Anglo economic elite and become controllers of their own province; they wanted to preserve and promote a strong sense of social solidarity, inherited from the past; and they wanted the state to foster economic development in the hands of the French-Canadian bourgeoisie and to redistribute society's wealth in favour of workers and the poor. The Quiet Revolution was accompanied by a cultural creativity, an artistic renaissance and, as we shall see, the secularization of society.

Quebecers now began to observe themselves as "a nation." They started to think of themselves as a people settled on a territory with defined boundaries, enjoying a common cultural heritage, a democratic political organization, a reasonably sound economy and the capacity to welcome people of other origins. They no longer referred to themselves as *les canadiens*, but as *les québécois*. The sense of nationhood was affirmed by their newly elected Liberal premier, Jean Lesage, who made becoming "*maîtres chez nous*" and "*égalité ou indépendance*" the slogans of his government. As French Canadians in the province of Quebec expressed their collective will no longer to be second-class citizens, they came to think of themselves as "a nation" within the Canadian federal framework. They called the provincial parliament "*l'assemblée nationale*," the provincial highways "*les routes nationales*" and Quebec City "*la capitale nationale*."

This new thinking had important political consequences. First, French Canadians outside Quebec now no longer belonged to the same national family. In other words, the old ethnic notion of the French-Canadian nation collapsed. Quebecers believed, possibly quite unjustly, that French Canadians outside Quebec were becoming increasingly assimilated into the English-speaking world and that their French language was acquiring a folkloric character. For many such French Canadians, this exclusion was a painful experience.

The second political consequence of the new sense of Quebec's nationhood was that all people living in the province, whatever their ethnic origin, were now regarded as equal citizens of Quebec. Quebec's national identity came to be defined in territorial terms, no longer by ethnic categories. This political evolution was a gradual process, as documented by the official statements of successive governments, political parties and social institutions.[2] What interests us for the purposes of this essay is this evolution as reflected in the statements of the Catholic Church.

A pastoral letter written by all the Canadian Catholic bishops, anglophone and francophone, in the centennial year of 1967 still refers to the "French Canadian nation" from sea to sea, with its core and centre located in the province of Quebec,[3] while a decade later two pastoral letters, written by the Quebec bishops (in 1977[4] and 1979,[5] respectively), define the "Quebec nation" in pluri-ethnic terms. The Quebec bishops insist that *les québécois* are the people living in Quebec: the French-speaking majority, the English-speaking minority of long standing and the ethnocultural communities that have arrived more recently.

> It is together with these that the francophone people of Quebec ponder their future and search for an answer....The future of Quebec shall not be decided by the francophone majority alone, but by all citizens, that is by all who live within its boundaries, develop its economy, form a significant community, enrich its common culture, share the same legal and political institutions, inherited from a common history. It is in this sense then, providing for all the necessary nuances, that one may refer to "the people of Quebec."[6]

In these two letters, the Quebec bishops refer to the Native peoples living in Quebec as part of the Quebec people. It was only later, in 1984, that the bishops recognized the nationhood of the Aboriginal peoples and honoured their right to self-determination.[7]

Responding to Quebec's pluralistic self-understanding, the Quebec government adopted a Charter of Human Rights and Freedoms in 1975, seven years prior to the corresponding Canadian charter. Following the United Nations' Universal Declaration of Human Rights of 1948, the Quebec charter included both personal and social human rights, while the Canadian charter preferred to limit itself to personal rights. To protect human rights in Quebec, the government created a special commission, the Commission des droits de la personne, to which individuals and groups experiencing discrimination could apply for support. A group of Quebecers who felt that government agencies were not aggressive enough in the fight against racism founded a civil liberty organization, the Ligue des droits et libertés, which involved itself in the struggle against all forms of discrimination. Since I had been a member of the Canadian Civil Liberties Association when I lived in Toronto, I decided to join this organization when I moved to Montreal in 1986. Since the Quebec charter also included social rights, such as the rights to work, education and a decent standard of living (articles 39-48), the Ligue inevitably had a left-leaning agenda, quite different from the liberal orientation of the Canadian Civil Liberties Association.

Protecting Francophone Space

Because of the minority status of a French-speaking society in North America, Quebec's acceptance of ethnocultural pluralism is a complex process. As a result of Quebec's self-affirmation in the Quiet Revolution, Quebec came to see itself as a francophone space on the North American continent. French was made the public language of Quebec in 1974 by the Liberal government's Bill 22. This was strengthened in 1977 by the Parti Québécois government's Bill 101 and later, in 1988, somewhat weakened by the Liberal government's Bill 178. For Franco-Quebecers, constituting over 80 percent of the population, these laws are in keeping with a people's collective right to cultural and political self-determination, acknowledged by the United Nations; for some Anglo-Quebecers, these laws put undue limitations on their personal freedom.

Quebec's francophone majority is keenly aware that it is a minority on the North American continent. As English is at present becoming the lingua franca of the world, mediated by technology and scientific research, the globalization of the economy and the spread of the U.S.-based entertainment industry, Quebecers continue to fear that their language might deteriorate. I appreciate their anxiety. In my opinion, legislation is not enough to protect the French language in Quebec; what is equally necessary is the personal discipline of its francophone citizens to cherish and cultivate their own language. (As an immigrant of long standing, I am keenly aware of the vulnerability of language. Unless immigrants make an enormous effort, unless they have access to means of education, their mother tongue soon becomes corrupted—they insert words from the common language and make use of ungrammatical constructions. I have been fortunate. Since I have lived in privileged conditions, I have been able to keep my German mother tongue intact.)

The Catholic Church has approved Quebec's language legislation in principle.[8] When a group of anglophone Catholics appealed to the bishops to intervene in the public debate and oppose the language legislation as restricting the rights of a minority, the bishops declined their request. They argued that the majority had the right to rectify the past exclusion of French from many areas of public life and to make it the public language of society, as long as the inherited English-speaking institutions—schools, universities, hospitals and social services—continued to be supported to enable the anglophone communities to thrive.[9]

One consequence of Quebec's language legislation is the arrival of francophone immigrant communities from former French colonies around the world. Montreal boasts large French-speaking, Jewish and Muslim communities from North Africa, francophone groups from several African communities, and a substantial French Creole-speaking Haitian community. Another consequence of the language legislation is that immigrants from non-francophone parts of the world—immigrants who speak English fluently—are obliged, like all other immigrants, to send their children to francophone schools. Immigrants who come to Quebec in the hope of being integrated into the language of North America are disappointed. They often find it difficult to think of themselves as citizens of Quebec; many prefer to see themselves as Canadians or simply as North Americans, and they leave Quebec when they have an opportunity. The minority status of French Quebec in North America makes the entry into ethnocultural pluralism a complex process.

A Convergence of Cultures

The Quebec government under the Liberals and the Parti Québécois has rejected the concept of "multiculturalism" as defined by the federal government.[10] According to this concept, Canada is a country with two official languages and many cultures. This definition makes no distinction between the receiving cultures of British and French origin and the incoming cultures of other backgrounds. To many critics, not only in Quebec, the federal concept is self-contradictory. For, if English and French are the two official languages, the public schools will teach these languages, teach their literature and teach the history of how these languages came to Canada—which in fact privileges two cultures, one of British and the other of French origin.

Quebec's official approach to cultural pluralism distinguishes between the welcoming culture (*la culture d'accueil*) and the arriving cultures (*les communautés culturelles*), encourages interaction between them and envisages a certain convergence of these cultures, each changing under the influence of the others, yet each retaining its identity. This approach anticipates an enrichment of the welcoming culture in continuity with the Quebec heritage and a certain adaptation of the cultural communities to the conditions of Quebec society. To foster cultural pluralism in Quebec, the government has taken several initiatives. Sometimes, the accent has been on the convergence of cultures. At other times, the emphasis has been on the development of a common set of public values (*la culture publique commune*) that would protect the diversity of cultures and at the same time enable all citizens, whatever their cultural inheritance, to cooperate in the building of a common society. Quebec's version of multiculturalism includes an appreciation of the cultural communities, support for an evolving Quebec culture which recognizes its distinctive history, and the concern for social cohesion and joint responsibility.

At present, the government is stressing the common citizenship of all Quebecers, whatever their origin. The idea behind this effort is to awaken all Quebecers to their responsibility as citizens and to stimulate them to become actively involved in the building of civil society. While the omnipresence of the market makes people see themselves increasingly as customers and clients, the government wants to persuade all Quebecers, those of old stock (*les québécois de souche*) and those of other origins, to see themselves primarily as citizens responsible for their society's well-being.

To promote the interconnected ideas of citizenship, pluralism and solidarity, the Quebec government organized a consultation in Quebec City, on 21-22 September 2000, to which over 400 people were invited, many of them representatives of the various cultural communities. The purpose was to evaluate a document written by the Ministère de la citoyenneté et de l'immigration. The meeting opened with a panel of four invited speakers, two of whom (including myself) were attached to the Centre justice et foi. Christian activists were also well represented among the participants. The assembly was critical of the document proposed by the Ministry. While the document lauded the responsibilities of citizens, affirmed ethnocultural pluralism, fostered increasing social solidarity and called for a joint effort to combat racism, xenophobia, prejudice and discrimination, it failed to analyze the structural exclusion of people of all backgrounds through unemployment, low wages, substandard living conditions, poverty and the absence of linguistic competence. The document did not analyze the social conditions necessary for the exercise of citizenship, nor did it acknowledge the government's responsibility to help create these conditions where they were absent. While the official discourse on pluralism and solidarity is excellent, many of the participants felt that behind this discourse stands the neo-liberal philosophy, today's political orthodoxy (*la pensée unique*), that has begun to influence the Parti Quebecois government and the Liberal opposition. We are witnessing a waning of the social-democratic ethos that characterized Quebec society during and after the Quiet Revolution, and that found expression in Quebec's Charter of Human Rights and Freedoms and important policy statements of previous governments. As the government withdraws financial support from the wide network of groups, centres and movements that enable people at the base and in the margins of society to assume responsibility for their lives and become active citizens, the politically correct discourse in praise of openness, pluralism and a common set of public values remains powerless.

Quebec Pluralism and Nationalism

Involved in the debates about pluralism, citizenship, immigration and refugees are a good number of Christian groups in Montreal that pursue a theological perspective and become actively involved in helping minorities of various kinds.[11] Several of these groups are sponsored by religious orders and congregations of women and men. These Catholic activists join boards of cooperation (*les tables de concertation*) where, as members, they work with secular groups and representatives of the Protestant and Jewish communities to deal with multicultural issues.

A very active Catholic organization is the Jesuit social justice centre, the Centre justice et foi, whose work includes educational projects of various kinds, the publication of the monthly review *Relations*, and a special task force, called *Vivre ensemble*, that deals with cultural pluralism in the church. I am associated with the Centre as a member of the editorial committee of *Relations*. We are committed to social justice, the option for the poor, cultural pluralism and a society free from discrimination.

I am keenly aware that our perspective differs from that of corresponding social justice centres in Toronto and other parts of Canada since, in addition to these common values, we promote the flourishing of Quebec society, in continuity with its past and enriched by the presence of its cultural communities. This nationalist dimension is absent from similar justice centres in Toronto and other parts of Canada, where English as the public language is not threatened. My participation in the Centre has forced me to engage in ethical reflection on nationalism. The majority of Quebecers, whether federalist or sovereigntist, think of Quebec as a nation and assume its right to self-determination. Quebec federalists are convinced that the nationhood of Quebec, that is, its distinct character as a society, can find a place within Canadian confederation.

Is nationalism an ethical option? Since this issue troubled me, I decided to write a book on the ethical implications of nationalism, called *Nationalism, Religion and Ethics.*[12] I was helped greatly in my reflections by the pastoral letters of the Quebec bishops. The bishops insisted that it was not their duty to tell Quebecers how to vote in a referendum on sovereignty, but that it was their job to propose ethical norms that must be observed in any struggle for political self-determination. According to them, such a struggle is ethical only (i) if it aims to make society more just and more open; (ii) if it respects the rights of minority communities; (iii) if it anticipates cooperative relations with neighbouring societies; and (iv) if it refuses to look upon the nation as the highest value—for that would be idolatry.[13]

At the Centre justice et foi, we find inadequate the distinction commonly made between "ethnic nationalism" based on a common ethnic origin and "civic nationalism" based simply on common citizenship. While ethnic nationalism leads to xenophobia and discrimination, civic nationalism creates unity and equality among the citizens yet brackets the nation's historical continuity. Both of these seem problematic. If nations are creative human communities, they will be able to retain the memory of the historical drama that has formed them and, at the same time, be capable of welcoming groups that want to join them, embracing them as citizens on an equal footing and desiring their help in building their society and shaping their future. Fr. Julien Harvey, SJ, was a passionate defender of the rights of immigrants and refugees and, at the same time, an ardent nationalist who believed in Quebec's social-democratic vocation. A respected progressive social thinker in Quebec, Fr. Harvey was an active member of the Centre justice et foi until his untimely death in 1997. He shared the concern of many Quebecers that openness to pluralism might threaten Quebec's vulnerable national identity. Yet, reflecting on the various aspects of Quebec's history, he concluded that this history has made Quebecers a creative people with the capacity to adapt to new social conditions, embrace the arriving communities in a fraternal manner while respecting their difference, and integrate them into an ever-to-be-renewed Quebec society.

Is this an impossible dream? As I mentioned at the beginning of this essay, recent immigrant communities have such a strong sense of their cultural identity that all the developed countries of the West are currently wrestling with the question of how they can, under these new conditions, modify their self-understanding and reform their inherited institutions. Britain, France and Germany have not yet found a clear direction. Will Quebec succeed? Or will the globalization of the economy and the massive transmigration of peoples transform the very notion of the state? This has become a debated issue.

The Growth of Secularism in Quebec

What I have so far mentioned only in passing, even though it is related to the topic of this essay, is that the Quiet Revolution initiated the modernization of Quebec culture, leading to the rapid secularization of society. The Quiet Revolution was enthusiastically supported by many committed Catholics encouraged by Vatican Council II, which was at this very time redefining the church's relationship to society.[14] These Catholics opposed the control that the Catholic bishops had exercised over Quebec's public institutions and advocated greater independence for the Catholic lay organizations. Recognizing the crisis in the church, the bishops created a commission, chaired by Fernand Dumont, a well-known sociologist, to examine the conflicts in the church and come up with new pastoral proposals. But, by the time the Dumont Report was published in 1970, practising Catholics had become a minority in Quebec. Quebec had become an essentially secular society.

Yet the Dumont Report, entitled *L'Église du Québec: un héritage, un projet*, had a strong influence on the self-understanding of Quebec's Catholic Church.[15] It urged the bishops not to become nostalgic for the church of the past, nor to lament the loss of their power. To be faithful to its heritage, the report proposed that the church continue to accompany the Quebec people on their journey and offer support for Quebec's historical project. The bishops accepted this advice. Conscious that they now speak only for a minority in society, they continue to address public issues in Quebec society—not in a tone of authority, but rather as contributors to the public debate that defines a democratic society. When the church represented the whole of French Quebec, it felt bound to sanction the existing social order and exercise a conservative function. Now that it represents only a minority, the church is free to react to society in theological terms, to become critical of social injustices, and to express its solidarity with working people, the unemployed, the poor and the marginalized. In this context, the bishops have affirmed the cultural pluralism in society and denounced racism, prejudice and discrimination.

Every year on 1 May, the bishops publish a labour day statement in Quebec offering critical reflections on various aspects of society, seen from the perspective of the people at the base and in the margins of society.[16] While these and other episcopal statements on social justice are gladly received by the social justice movement in the church, they have on the whole been ignored by the wider, secular society. The major newspapers hardly ever mention the bishops' pastoral statements.

By presenting the church as "a project," *un chantier*, (a building site) or even a provisional institution ever ready to respond to new challenges, the Dumont Report has influenced Catholic life in Quebec. Since these images corresponded to the experience of the Quebec church, the bishops accepted this bold discourse. They have developed a sense of the provisional, they acknowledge theological and spiritual pluralism in the church, and they are ready to listen to Catholics critical of the church's official teachings.

Because of this development, there now exists a considerable difference between the Catholicism of Quebec and the more traditional Catholicism of many of the ethnocultural communities.[17] Most of Quebec's practising Catholics prefer a simple liturgy with active lay participation; they shy away from the traditional devotions; they are unhappy with expressions of clericalism; they take with a grain of salt what the parish priest and the local bishop tell them; and they have a generous interpretation of sexual morality and are tolerant of divorce. These Catholics participate in parish life or, if they prefer, associate themselves with one of the spiritual or social movements in the church. For Franco-Quebecers, be they liberal, conservative or radical, the church has become *un chantier*—a building site.

Since the long-established, English-speaking parishes and the more recent ethnocultural communities have not experienced a cultural upheaval, they tend to retain a more traditional form of Catholicism. For them, the Catholic Church is neither a building site nor a social project in which they participate, but a completed house into which they try to fit themselves. Many of these people are suspicious of Quebec's Catholicism and its (francophone) literature of religious education.

Quebec is one of the few Canadian provinces in which Catholics are involved in a public debate over the continuing usefulness of Catholic schools.[18] Catholics in other provinces are united in the defence of Catholic schools. Yet, in response to the new pluralism, and as a result of rapid secularization, many Quebec Catholics have questioned the confessional or denominational form of the public school system. Because this topic is related to Quebec's pluralism, I will discuss it briefly, even though the topic deserves a full report.

Until recently, the Quebec school system was divided into two commissions: Catholic and Protestant. Soon after the Quiet Revolution, the control of the Catholic commission was removed from the bishops and entrusted to a body called the Comité catholique, in which the bishops, as well as Catholic lay leaders, were represented. Yet, in view of the new pluralism, many Quebecers, including members of the government, have come to look upon the confessional division of the school system as dysfunctional. The Catholic schools are filled with students whose backgrounds are indeed Catholic, but who often come from families that have become secular and wish to remain so; the Protestant schools, most of which are anglophone, are populated by Protestants,

Jews and pupils of other religious backgrounds. Many Quebecers think that it would be more reasonable to have two non-confessional school commissions, one francophone and the other anglophone. Several times in the last thirty years the issue has triggered a heated debate. The most recent was sparked by the publication of the government-sponsored Proulx Report in the spring of 1999, which recommended the de-confessionalization of the schools and the introduction of cultural studies of religion.

It is interesting to consider the diverse Catholic responses.[19] The bishops defended the confessional schools in a modest way, proposing adjustments that respected the religious pluralism among the students. Some conservative Catholic groups asked for the restoration of strict Catholic schools. Of special interest are two briefs: one, submitted by the Comité catholique, calling for "une confessionalité ouverte," and the other, by the Centre justice et foi, proposing "une laïcité ouverte."

Recognizing that the Catholic schools had in fact become open to pluralism and taught religion with attention to Quebec's religious plurality, the Comité catholique advocated the retention of the confessional schools as long as their openness to pluralism was guaranteed. In fact, the bishops were rather close to this position.

By contrast, the Centre justice et foi had, for pastoral reasons, advocated for several years the de-confessionalization of Quebec's school system.[20] While, in the past, the common opinion was that children brought up in a Catholic school would remain Catholics later in life, social-scientific research has shown that this is no longer true in today's Quebec.[21] The existing schools are Catholic only in name: they are already largely secular and pluralistic. The Centre argued that the church can no longer rely on the schools for the transmission of the faith to the next generation. What has to take place, the Centre proposed, is faith education in the parish communities, which requires specialized teachers and the cooperation of parents. At the same time, the Centre opposed a non-confessional school system that would exclude religion from the curriculum altogether. It advocated "une laïcité ouverte," a secular school system in which religion is taught following a phenomenological approach, with special emphasis on the religions practised in Quebec. The Centre offered its support for the Proulx Report in two briefs, one submitted to the bishops and the other to the government's Commission on Education.[22]

Religion in the schools remains a hotly debated topic. Reacting to the Proulx Report and the public debate, the government has opted for a compromise: it has de-confessionalized the school system, creating two linguistic school commissions, French and English, but has preserved in the curriculum, at least for the time being, the teaching of Catholic and Protestant religions, albeit for fewer hours.

Racism in Quebec

So far I have said little about racism. In my estimation, racism in Quebec has had a different character from racism in English-speaking North America. It would be of interest, for instance, to compare French-Canadian and English-Canadian anti-Semitism in Montreal in the 1930s. In English-speaking communities, racism has been inherited from empire, where its function was to justify the conquest and subjugation of other peoples and possibly even the institution of slavery. This kind of racism was derived from a position of strength. It was based on presumed superiority and, in many cases, on the memory of former power. This racism has, in fact, been visited upon French Canadians.

By contrast, racism in Quebec is derived from a position of weakness. Small nations, whose place in history is not assured, easily develop an animosity toward strangers living in their midst, because they fear that these strangers will not join their struggle for cultural survival and political recognition. Racism in Eastern European countries, which have been repeatedly held captive within large empires, has been of this kind. In such societies, racism was based on the dread of inferiority and the memory of former humiliations. Such has been the racism in Quebec.

The culture of democracy is the most efficient remedy for racism. Recognizing the dignity of persons and their equality before the law drives out the devil of racist contempt, or at least generates feelings of guilt among people still caught in this vise. The national self-confidence of Quebecers produced by the Quiet Revolution and their will to become a modern democracy have given their society a new openness to people of other origins, an openness sustained by the mass media. This is noticeable in the historical accounts, documentaries and serialized stories (*les téléromans*) presented on Quebec television, which play an important role in Quebec society: they acknowledge what is sometimes called *le Québec au pluriel*, make room for faces of colour and reveal the meanness in the heart of prejudiced people. Contemporary Quebec literature shows that some authors enjoy the new pluralism and integrate immigrants into their stories, while others are still attached to the homogeneous community of the past. Public celebrations—for instance, the parades on 24 June, *la fête nationale*, formerly St. Jean Baptiste Day—offer visibility to African, Asian and Amerindian faces. Catholic parishes are pleased when altar boys and altar girls include young people of colour.

At the same time, racism reveals itself in the high unemployment among people of colour, their disproportionate presence in low-paying jobs, the difficulties many experience in renting apartments, the low percentage of immigrants among government employees, and many other situations that are part and parcel of people's daily lives. Attitudes toward Native people are often colonial. As in the rest of Canada, in Quebec racism is still a cultural undercurrent that is no longer articulated, yet continues to result in social exclusion. How has the church addressed this issue?

As I look over the pastoral statements and letters published by the Canadian bishops, I find many statements that condemn prejudice and discrimination, echoing in this stance the teachings of Vatican Council II. But I find only two documents dealing exclusively with overcoming racism and welcoming people, whatever their origin. The first, "Les travailleurs immigrants chez nous," is a message of the Social Affairs Committee of the Quebec bishops, published on 1 May 1980,[23] and the second, "A Prophetic Mission for the Church: On the Acceptance and Integration of Immigrants and Refugees," a pastoral message of the Canadian bishops, including those of Quebec, published on 16 March 1993. These documents describe the hateful character of prejudice and explore what love and justice mean in today's pluralistic society. They offer reflections on biblical texts that reveal faith-inspired love as the centre of the Christian life and show that the outreach of this love is universal, beginning with people in need. These documents also offer concrete proposals for what individuals, groups and entire parishes can do to wrestle with prejudice and discrimination and foster the fraternal integration of immigrants and refugees.

The bishops of Quebec asked themselves again more recently how the church could be of service in today's pluralistic society. They established a small commission, of which I was invited to be a member, to examine this issue and possibly recommend concrete actions. At the meeting of the Quebec bishops in March 2000, our study group offered a day-long seminar on pluralism, to which were invited witnesses from various ethnocultural communities as well as special speakers; among the latter was Pierre Anctil, who analyzed society's covert racism.[24] The seminar made an attempt to focus the discussion on the idea of citizenship to avoid separating the issues of pluralism, prejudice and discrimination from economic inequality and its consequences.

Conclusions

What I conclude from this examination of the church's response to cultural pluralism in Quebec is that the church shares the "double orientation" of Quebec society. The growing openness to ethnocultural pluralism is accompanied by an effort to enhance, under the new conditions, the historical identity of Quebec in French—a minority language in North America. The church supports this in the hope that open dialogue with other cultural communities will enable these communities to feel more at home in Quebec and simultaneously lead to an evolution of the inherited culture modified by its interaction with other cultural streams. While the social teaching of the bishops is critical of growing unemployment, the widening gap between rich and poor, and the decline of the welfare state, the bishops do stand behind the government's effort to promote a certain convergence of cultures and to develop a set of common norms that will allow all citizens to communicate with one another in French and cooperate in the ongoing construction of society.

What I have called the "double orientation" of the Quebec church reminds me of a contemporary movement in the Church of Scotland, which promotes Scottish national identity and, at the same time, stands against prejudice and discrimination, denounces social injustices, and engages in dialogue with other Christians and secular groups in the hope of enhancing national solidarity. The theological literature produced at the University of Edinburgh's Centre for Theology and Public Issues has an affinity with the thought and attitudes of the church in Quebec—envisaging openness to pluralism and the enhancement of national identity.[25]

Notes

1 See Gregory Baum, "The Theology of Cardinal Ratzinger," *The Ecumenist* 37/4 (2000): 1-3.

2 Denise Helly, "Le Québec face à la pluralité culturelle—1975-1994," Institut québécois de recherche sur la culture, Université Laval, Paper 36 (1995).

3 "On the Occasion of the Hundredth Year of Confederation," in *Do Justice: The Social Teaching of the Canadian Catholic Bishops*, ed. E.F. Sheridan (Sherbrooke, QC: Éditions Paulines, 1987), 122-34, esp. 126.

4 "La charte de la langage française," in *La justice sociale comme bonne nouvelle* (Montreal: Éditions Bellarmin, 1984), 110-18, esp. 114.

5 "Le peuple québécois et son avenir politique" (1979), in *La justice sociale comme bonne nouvelle,* 137-44.

6 Ibid., 139.

7 "Premières Nations au Québec: Lettre pastorale sur la situation autochtone" (Spring 1984). Also, "La lettre pastorale sur la situation autochtone," published Fall 1992 by Le Comité de pastorale auprès des autochtones.

8 "La charte de la langage française" (1977).

9 *L'Église de Montréal* (16 February 1989), 151.

10 Julien Bauer, *Les minorités au Québec* (Montreal: Boréalec, 1994), 74-96; Gregory Baum, "Ethnic Pluralism in Quebec," *Canadian Forum* (April 1996): 19-22.

11 The literature dealing with the Catholic Left and its activities is ample. See, for example, Jean Richard and Louis O'Neil, eds., *La question sociale hier et aujourd'hui* (Sainte-Foy, QC: Les presses de l'Université Laval, 1993); a series of books, published by Fides of Montreal under the rubric of *Défis de Société,* including the proceedings of *Les journées sociales*, the meetings of Catholic activists held every two years; Kevin Arsenault, ed., *Stone Soup: Reflections on Economic Injustice* (Montreal: Paulines, 1997), containing several articles written by Quebecers; and Gregory Baum, "The Catholic Left in Quebec," in *Culture and Social Change: Social Movements in Quebec and Ontario*, ed. Colin Leys and Marguerite Mendell (Montreal: Black Rose, 1992), 140-54.

12 Gregory Baum, *Nationalism, Religion and Ethics* (Montreal: McGill-Queen's University Press, 2001).

13 See Gregory Baum, *The Church in Quebec* (Montreal: Novalis, 1991), 159-70.

14 David Seljak, "The Catholic Church's Reaction to the Quiet Revolution" (Ph.D. diss., McGill University, 1995).

15 On the Dumont Report, see Baum, *The Church in Quebec*, 49-65.

16 Yvonne Bergeron, "Les Messages du 1er mai," in *Intervenir à contre-courant*, ed. Michel Beaudin et al. (Montréal: Fides, 1998), 63-88.

17 Raymond Lemieux, "Le catholicisme québécois: une question de culture," *Sociologie et société* 20 (1990): 160-76.
18 Micheline Milot and Fernand Ouellet, eds., *Religion, éducation et démocratie* (Montreal: Harmattan, 1997).
19 For an analysis of these responses, see Jacques Palard, "La confessionalité scolaire en débat," in *Religion et identité dans l'école québécoise*, ed. Solange Lefebvre (Montréal: Fides, 2000), 91-136.
20 Julien Harvey, "Une laïcité scolaire pour le Québec," *Relations* (September 1992): 213-17.
21 Micheline Milot, *Une religion à transmettre?:Le choix des parents* (Sainte-Foy, QC: Les presses de l'Université Laval, 1991).
22 "Pour une laïcité ouverte au phénomène religieux: Mémoire du Centre justice et foi à la Commission de l'éducation," *Relations* (November 1999): 276-79.
23 See the Social Affairs Committee of the Quebec Bishops, *La justice sociale comme bonne nouvelle* (Montreal: Bellarmin, 1984), 157-61.
24 Pierre Anctil's talk was published as "L'Église québécoise face au défi de la pluriethnicité," *L'Église canadienne* 33 (October 2000): 285-89.
25 Gregory Baum, "The Church and Scottish Nationalism," *The Ecumenist* 36 (August-September 1999): 4-7.

3

KARL BARTH ON DIVINE COMMAND

A Jewish Response

DAVID NOVAK

The Philosophical Engagement of Barth

Usually one does not include Karl Barth in contemporary Jewish-Christian dialogue. Unlike his Protestant theological contemporaries, Paul Tillich and Reinhold Niebuhr, there is no evidence that, during his long theological career, Barth had any real contact with Jewish thinkers.[1] The only contemporary Jewish thinker whom he engages, to my knowledge, is Martin Buber, but in Barth's magnum opus, *Church Dogmatics*, Buber is discussed almost en passant and with a rather hurried dismissal.[2] Barth's relations with Judaism are seriously complicated, but one gets the impression from reading what he says about Judaism that he is doing typology—engaging a type already created in his mind largely by Paul and those who followed in his path. He does not seem to be dealing with Judaism as a living tradition, indeed as a current rival religious option to Christianity. After all, how can one engage Judaism as a living tradition, let alone as a current rival religious option, if one has no serious contact with living Jews during the most productive years of one's thought?[3] For that reason, it would seem that an engagement of Barth's thought by a contemporary Jewish theologian could be, at most, only an arcane academic exercise with no real Jewish significance.

Notes to chapter 3 are on pp. 73-76.

Nevertheless, there are some very good reasons for a contemporary Jewish engagement of Karl Barth that does have theological significance here and now. Of these, perhaps the most important is Barth's concern with where Judaism's prime theological emphasis lies: the commandments of God (*mitsvot*). Moreover, since both Judaism and Christianity find the prime source of those commandments in the Hebrew Bible (for Christians, the "Old Testament"; for Jews, *kitvei ha-qodesh*—"the Sacred Scriptures"), and since many of the commandments that each community finds there are virtually identical, it would be strange if Jews could not learn some significant insights from Barth, a Christian thinker who spent much of his time, energy and overwhelming intellect thinking of the commandments of the biblical God. Hence, following this approach to Barth, contemporary Jewish thinkers might have something significant to say on this very subject to Barth's disciples who are still their conversation partners and, indeed, to any Christian whose Christian faith has been illuminated by Barth.[4] That is especially the case in the area of the commandments we would call "ethics," namely, what the rabbis called commandments pertaining to what is "between humans themselves" [*bein adam le-havero*].[5]

In addition, the ethical interests of Barth and modern Jewish thinkers have in common their very location in modernity, a major strand of which, since Kant, has seen ethics (in one form or another) as the most important type of thought in which humans can possibly engage.[6] For Barth, this has further significance, since the one Jewish thinker who did greatly influence him in his youth was the German-Jewish philosopher Hermann Cohen (1842-1918), with whom he studied at the University of Marburg. Cohen was the greatest Kantian of his time, and a thinker whose serious Judaism, which was so obviously integrated with his philosophy, especially his ethics, could not have escaped someone as perceptive as Karl Barth.[7]

For these reasons, then, it might be best not to engage Barth on what he actually said about Judaism, but to engage him on what he said about Judaism's prime concern. Nevertheless, it might be questionable whether that engagement can or should be properly theological, at least in the way Barth saw theology. Barth says, "the Law is the form of the Gospel."[8] But how can that theological statement, which epitomizes his approach to ethics, be directly engaged theologically by any Jewish thinker for whom the gospel is not the source of his or her religious/ ethical life? At this point we would be left with the Christian "yes" and the Jewish "no," and there would be nothing to mediate any further discussion between Jews and Christians that could possibly overcome this fundamental antinomy. (Lest one simply think of Judaism as the rejection of Christianity, however, the inverse response of "yes" and "no" would be the Jewish assertion, "the law is the form of the exclusive covenant of God with the Jewish people." Here, a Jew would have to say "yes" and a Christian "no.") Conversion by a Jew to Christianity or by a Christian to Judaism would be the only way to get beyond this impasse at this directly theological level. But, if this were to happen, there could be no more dialogue between distinctly Jewish Jews and distinctly Christian Christians. One side would have totally capitulated to the other.[9]

In order to keep the dialogue on track and to include Barth in it, perhaps one could engage that statement, and all it involves and implies philosophically, by employing philosophical reasoning as a mediation through which to translate that which is ultimately theological into that which is more immediately accessible to those outside Barth's theological circle. That possibility becomes more evident when one notices that, in the German original of the quotation above, Barth says *das Gesetz die Gestalt des Evangeliums ist.*[10] That could be translated as "the Law is the way the Gospel shows itself"—namely, how the gospel manifests itself in the world. The German word *Gestalt* is much richer in meaning than the English word "form." As such, the phenomenality of the gospel (which, for Christians, is the New Covenant) is not an object to be observed but a commandment to be obeyed. In that way, a Jew can appreciate, indeed learn from, Barth's phenomenology of some of the same commandments of God that Jews also accept (indeed, accepted before Christians). That perspective would not require Jewish acceptance of the primary ground of the law for Barth, which is Jesus Christ, for any such acceptance by Jews would make their continued Jewish identity impossible. Barth says about the word of God that "It is first Gospel and then Law....His grace is also Law."[11] For a Jew, Barth's "and/also" is where he or she can properly enter into dialogue.

Whether Barth himself would have approved such a methodological move is doubtful, since he usually insisted on all his statements being read within the circle of distinctly Christian theology.[12] Nevertheless, whenever a person writes something that will inevitably be read by others beyond his or her own communal circle, it is also inevitable that some of those others will deconstruct the author's words, bracketing the author's intentions for purposes that the author would probably not endorse. This is so because the object of the author's intention is not a project of his or her will but, rather, a datum given to him or her and to others as well—a datum that the author, by writing of it, must share rather than control. Only the word of God in revelation can claim to be interpreted according to the author's original intention, inasmuch as the very datum of which the word speaks is the creation of the divine author. No human author, however, can make such an absolute claim on his or her readers. Theologians can only dispute among themselves as to what the original intention of revelation was, but they may not propose meanings that in any way bracket the assumption of original intent. That is why a Jew can constructively dispute with Barth philosophically but not strictly theologically. A purely theological dispute between a Jew and a Christian could result only in an impasse. The infamous medieval Jewish-Christian disputations are clear evidence of that impasse.

This essay will address itself critically to two main philosophical questions: first, how does Barth deal with the relationship of commandment (*Gebot*) and law (*Gesetz*); and second, how does Barth deal with the problem of keeping God's ethical commandments in essentially secular space? Both of these questions have been dealt with by Jewish thinkers and contemporaries of Barth, and, like all the great questions Barth addressed or that can be addressed to Barth, these questions are by no means antiquarian. They concern living Jews and living Christians here and now. But the second question is about those who, at least functionally, act in public neither as Jews, nor as Christians, nor as members of any faith based on revelation (like Islam, for example). Indeed, one could very well see this question as the most important one for normative Jewish or Christian ethics in today's politically secular world. Politics is the necessary context of ethical action, that is, action that takes place in an inter-human realm.[13]

Commandment and Law

Barth is intent on showing the superiority of ethics over law, and then the superiority of theological ethics over philosophical ethics. Concerning the superiority of ethics over law, Barth engages his Jewish philosophical teacher, Hermann Cohen, when he writes, "morality may be understood, as in the teaching of H. Cohen, as the immanent power of all legality….But it has never yet occurred to anyone seriously to assert a simple equation of ethics and politics, of ethics and jurisprudence."[14]

But what is the essential difference between law and ethics? The answer is that law (*Gesetz*) is that application of ethics that can be adequately taught, administered and judged by human political authorities. Thus, Barth does not differ from Cohen in the assertion of law being based on ethics. Indeed, if law were not based on ethics, then what is right, which is the concern of law, would not have to be based on what is good, which is the concern of ethics. That being the case, the validity of law could be based only on the power of the human authority that makes the law. Might would then be the only other source of right possible. Surely that would have been unacceptable to Karl Barth, himself expelled from Germany in 1935 by the immoral Nazi regime, and writing the above words in 1941-42 when Hitler and his minions were trampling the rights of everybody within the range of their political and military power. Thus, what Barth seems to be saying is that ethics is the transcendent power of all legality; that is, ethics grounds law but is not subsumed by law. Indeed, in order for ethics to ground law sufficiently, it must have a range of operation outside of law and prior to it. Law should not exhaust ethics.

Barth's qualification of the range of law can be better understood, I think, when one compares his distinctions with the distinction in Jewish theology between "commandment" (*mitsvah*) and "law" (*halakhah*). In many ways, one could say in this context that the content of Jewish religious life (which is all of life) is the *mitsvot* (commandments), and the structure or form or gestalt of that life is the *halakhah*. Thus, if one were to look, for example, at the laws of the Sabbath, one would see there an intricate structure, but one would never experience the true content that is so structured by the *halakhah* unless one experienced through one's own action the sanctity that doing God's Sabbath commandment truly gives.[15] It is the same with ethical commandments, commandments that pertain to inter-human relationships. Here, the foundational norm is "you shall love your neighbour as yourself" (Lev. 19:18). That overarching commandment is structured by the *halakhah* in a variety of ways.[16] But the experience of the presence of another human person, whom we are commanded to love, can be experienced only by one's own personal deed in the commandment. How one actually sanctifies the Sabbath in one's own particular circumstances is largely a matter of to how one actually experiences the commandment in one's own moment. So, also, how one loves one's neighbour is largely left to how one experiences the commandment and responds to it in one's own moment. This fact of Judaism is illuminated by Barth's statement that "this command of God is an event [*Ereignis*]."[17] Only an antinomian, which Barth certainly is not, could object to a law that gave structure to the commandments, more by teaching what may not be done to fulfill them than by teaching what must be done to fulfill them as commandments and not as humanly imposed rules. Law has overstepped its covenantal function only when it has seen itself as identical with, indeed a substitution for, the directly given commandments of God to his people. "And its worship of Me has been a commandment of men [*mitsvat anashim*] learned by rote" (Isa. 29:13).

Barth's understanding of the relationship of commandment and law can be fruitfully compared to a Jewish debate in the 1920s between two of Barth's contemporaries, Martin Buber (1878-1965) and Franz Rosenzweig (1886-1929). Both Buber and Rosenzweig attempted to develop a new Jewish theology, which they hoped would go beyond the antinomy between Orthodox and Liberal Judaism in Germany at that time on the question of law and commandment. The Orthodox seemed to believe that the sanctity of the commandments is identical with the authority of the law, thus making the presence of the commanding God fully mediated by normative Jewish tradition. Thus, it would seem that, for them, the difference between divine authority and human authority was one of degree rather than one of kind. The rabbinical authorities were seemingly held to operate *in loco Dei*. The Liberals, on the other hand, seemed to believe that the commandments, even the commandments pertaining to the divine-human relationship, can be reduced to some universally evident ethical principles and norms. The commandments, for them, seemed to be *in loco homini*. In both cases, though, the distinction between law and commandment seems to have been elided. For the Orthodox, all law becomes commandment; for the Liberals, all commandment becomes law.

With a striking resemblance to the position of some of the most radical Christian reformers, Buber emphasizes the antinomy between commandment and law:

> What is it that is eternal: the primal phenomenon, present in the here and now, of what we call revelation [*Offenbarung*]?...Man receives and what he receives is not a "content" [*Inhalt*] but a presence [*eine Gegenwart*]...I know not of nor believe in any revelation that is not its primal phenomenon...that which reveals is that which reveals. That which has being is there [*das Seiende ist da*], nothing more.[18]

Buber is not denying the legitimacy of law in the secular (what he calls the "I-it") realm. He is not a complete antinomian. But, in the truly religious/ethical (what he calls the "I-thou") realm, he finds no law other than commandments, which are only directed to particular individuals at a particular time and place, whether their object be God or other humans. The commandments themselves have no continued duration or extension. In this realm, the very notion of law is at best irrelevant and at worst a negative hindrance, a blocking out of pure presence. As such, Buber has totally severed commandment from law, from any legal structure whatsoever. That is why many Jews have taken him to be a religious antinomian.[19] This comes out when Buber says to his friend and colleague, Rosenzweig, "I told you that for me, though man is a law-receiver, God is not a law-giver, and therefore the Law has no universal validity for me, but only a personal one. I accept, therefore, only what I think is being spoken to me."[20]

Rosenzweig answers Buber's religious/ethical antinomianism as follows:

> Whatever can and must be done is not yet deed, whatever can and must be commanded is not yet commandment. Law [*Gesetz*] must again become commandment [*Gebot*] which seeks to be transformed into deed at the very moment it is heard. It must regain that living reality [*Heutigkeit*] in which all great Jewish periods have sensed the guarantee for its eternity.[21]

How does Rosenzweig differ from Buber in his constitution of the relationship of commandment and law? And how does Barth enhance Rosenzweig's theological position for Jews? The key to understanding the difference between Buber and Rosenzweig, it seems to me, lies in the difference in their use of singular and plural reference, respectively, in terms of who the object of the commandments of God truly is. Buber speaks of the validity of the commandments being "personal" rather than "universal." Rosenzweig, conversely, speaks of "all great Jewish periods." Thus, Rosenzweig speaks of the Jewish *people* as the object or addressee of the commandments (understanding *Gebot* generically), whereas Buber speaks of *himself* (or any other individual self) as that object or addressee (understanding *Gebot* particularly). There is a fundamental difference between one seeing the commandments as being addressed to a communal self and seeing them as being addressed to an individual self. That difference, in this case, lies in the continuity and extension of the commandments in time and space.

Commandments addressed to a communal self must have continuity in time and an extension in space in order to have communal intelligibility. A community is continuous in time: it has a history and a destiny. A community is extended in space: it is a universe, a plurality of persons who participate in its present life. Each aspect of basically communal human existence necessarily entails thinking in universals. But a commandment addressed solely to an individual is exclusively an event (*Ereignis*), necessarily unconnected to any other event; it is what is unique (*eigentlich*).

Despite Barth's insistence that the commandment of God is an event, it is an event experienced by a communal self and, as such, it has communal significance. On this key point Barth would, it seems, agree with Rosenzweig (a Jewish thinker of whom, to my knowledge, Barth was unaware).[22] Thus, Barth writes:

> The question must actually be: What ought *we* to do? [*was sollen wir tun*?] and not what *I* ought to do? The former does not exclude the latter. Indeed, it can seriously be put only if it really includes the latter....The one absolute thing which is the object of God's command...is declared to us, [it] is not something that I am and have alone, but only in the community and solidarity, perhaps of all men....Even the claim which is addressed to me is not as a so-called personality or individual or special case, but as a responsible partner [*verantwortliche Genosse*] in the divine covenant.[23]

The question, though, is whether Barth (or Rosenzweig) adequately dealt with the communal character of the commandments of

God. That leads us to the question of the manifestation of the commandments as law, which admittedly is not an assertion that the commandments of God are derived from some prior universal manifestation of the being of God.

The Lawful Community

Barth is rightly concerned that the commandments of God not be taken as specific conclusions of more general premises. It is a point he emphasizes many times. For example:

> The Law of God [*das Gebot Gottes*] cannot be compared with any human law. For it is not merely a general rule but also a specific prescription [*Vorschrift*] and norm for each individual case. At one and the same time it is both the law and the Judge who applies it.[24]

In order not to fall into the trap of seeing the divine commandment subsumed under some prior universal, it would seem that Barth has to see the community of faith—that is, the community whose task it is to be responsive to and responsible for (both implied in Barth's preferred German term *verantwortlich*) the commandments of God—as being constituted by those who have heard the commandment of God addressed to themselves. For Christians, that suggests the image of the disciples becoming a community *after* they have heard Jesus' call to them to obey God's commandment to follow him. However, is that how the covenanted community comes into existence? Is the community the subsequent association of like-minded believers? Is the community constituted a posteriori, that is, after the fact of the plural hearing of the commandment of God? Does the community have any a priori status and function? These philosophical questions have profound implications for the way Jewish ethics and Christian ethics can be practised, especially in a context that has become increasingly secular. Furthermore, they raise the further question of whether secularity (which need not be confused with modern attempts to make it atheistic per se) lies in the background of the revelation-receiving community as well.

We must now ask: Does the commandment of God itself create the community *of* those who hear it, or does the commandment of God come directly *to* a community that is already lawfully constituted by transcendent criteria of justice not of its own making? If it is the former—that is, the community is made *de novo by* the direct commandment of God—then there is no human precondition necessary for the commandment of God to be intelligible, let alone desirable, to its human hearers. If it is the latter, though, then one must discover what this human precondition is and why it is necessary *for* the human acceptance of the commandment itself. Moreover, in order to comply with Barth's rightful concern that the commandment of God not be derived *from* something prior to it, one must show how this human precondition operates *for* the commandment of God. That operation has logical and chronological priority in human experience, but it does not have ontological priority. The commandment per se cannot be derived from anything other than God's revealed will. The precondition is not an existential ground. The commandment of God is *in* the world, not *of* it. It is a ground-clearing, not the grounding, factor.[25]

If Barth is right in his preclusion of any precondition for (let alone grounds of) God's commandment, then one might ask: How could one know what a commandment is if one had never had any experience of a commandment *before* the event of revelation? The rabbinic principle, "the Torah speaks through human language [*ke-lashon benei adam*]," is helpful here.[26] Full revelation of God's word occurs within a human history already in progress, a history that language not only describes but actually comprises. Revelation is not synonymous with the creation of humankind and its communities. As such, full revelation comes to a people already organized by its concerns for the persons in its care, however rudimentary that order is. Without that connection to creation and its order, specifically the creation of humans as political beings, one runs the risk of the Gnostic (for Christians, the Marcionite) rupture between revelation and creation. Revelation comes *to* and *for* us *in* the world; it is not meant to remove us *from* the world. Finally, revelation promises redemption (*ge'ulah*), which will come *into* the world but not take us *out of* the world.

At this level, there is no antinomy between commandment (*Gebot*) and law (*Gesetz*). Instead, we can understand law as the gestalt of commandment. The difference between the two, then, is not between commandment and law but, rather, between direct and indirect commandments of God. Each one of these commandments, both direct (what has been called "special revelation") and indirect (what has been called "general revelation"), comes with its own gestalt, its own law.[27] And we experience indirect revelation before we experience direct revelation.[28]

We first experience God's commandment in the claims our fellow human presences make on us. The reason we are bound to respond to these claims is that we gradually see the uniqueness of human existence as reflecting an innate relationship with what is, at this level, *the divine*.[29] The human "other" mediates the presence of the divine "Other," anticipating that "Other," as it were—but never able to force it. That is why we ourselves relate to that human "other" differently from how we relate to any of our other co-creatures, which (not who) are the products of the divine making *of* them, not divine speech *to and with* them, as is the case with humans only. Law is the way in which a human community coordinates and adjudicates the claims made by one human upon another, claims made by many humans upon one human, and claims made by one human upon many humans.[30] Natural law, or the "orders of creation" or cosmic justice (*mishpat*), comprises those standards deemed necessary for any human community to claim the moral allegiance of humans who are the image of God. Natural law governs with whom we need to be. It prepares us for God's covenantal entrance into our community which transforms it without destroying it.

Our desire for human others in all their variety, which is the basis of all ethical motivation, reveals to us our ultimate desire to hear the word of God. Our desire for that direct presence of God must first be mediated by our desire for the always indirect presence of humans. That is because, when the presence of God comes to us, it comes to us as communal creatures *already* aware of our communal nature and, thus, *ready* for the covenant that we hope will come *to* us, but which can never be conjured up *by* us. God's presence, then, speaks to us in a language we have been speaking among ourselves, even though its content is a *novum*. God's word comes to the community, which is always becoming his people, to do good for its members. Some of that good they already comprehend; more of it they are ready to apprehend thereafter. It is through our desire for human presence that we can best appreciate how revelation shows us that God too desires that human presence—indeed, that God, both before us and after us, desires that same community. "For the Lord's portion is his people…he found them in a desert land…keeping them as the pupil [*k'ishon*] of his eye" (Deut. 32:9-10).

Of course, it is true that the demands of others, whether human or divine, rightly make their claims on us, even when we are not ready for them, even when we dislike them. Nevertheless, for those claims to be properly fulfilled by us, we have to learn to love them. Learning to love them means discovering our primal desire for God—the desire that is more often repressed into unconsciousness than any other. Indeed, without the recovery of that desire, we could only come to hate the commandments and thus, inevitably, to defy them. And all love is desire; all love is erotic in one way or another.[31] In this way, we are commanded to love God and our neighbour—commandments whose immediate source and immediate object could be seen to be identical. This is unlike the other commandments, where the source of the commandment (God) addresses himself to the subject of the commandment (humans) to act upon the object of the commandment (for example, unleavened bread to be eaten on Passover).[32]

To be sure, the covenanted community takes on its unique identity *because of* the direct commandments of God. The content of these commandments is unique because, in one way or another, it celebrates what God has done for, with and through his people in their singular history together. In this sense, Passover is the paradigm for all other such commandments. Nevertheless, the gestalt or law of these commandments is often very similar to the gestalt or law of what has transpired between humans themselves before revelation. That is why commandments in which God is the direct object of our action (prayer being the best example), whose preferred (although not exclusive) locus is during communal worship, always have an immediate relation to ethical/communal concerns. Thus, God rejects the prayers of unrepentant murderers, thieves and adulterers: "Even when you pray in excess, I do not listen; your hands are full of blood" (Isa. 1:15). And, just as the ethical commandments of God have historical/legal precedents in human attempts to honour the transcendent intention of human personal existence, so the cultic commandments of God have historical/legal precedents in human groping toward a direct relationship with God, one that can come only from God himself.

Without the assertion of this human precondition, it is hard to explain why the gestalt of God's commandments frequently looks so much like the gestalt of human institutions, which are open to the coming of the ultimate end of their desire, and why this similarity is not accidental. Thus, the gestalt of the direct commandments of God has already been prepared by the gestalt of the indirect commandments of God. These indirect, mediated commandments are experienced in the human claims that always come first in our personal history, which is concretely communal and only abstractly individual. That is why Jewish or Christian theology need not and should not reject true historical scholarship of its respective histories, whether cultic or ethical. Such inquiry helps us better appreciate the necessarily human gestalt of the commandments of God. Jews and Christians need only reject the type of historicist reductionism that assumes revelation is impossible. Here is where critical philosophy, especially analytic philosophy, can serve a useful theological purpose.

Divine Commandments and Ethical Discourse

The practical problem raised by Barth's theory of divine commandment is that it does not seem to be able to address adequately the changed political context of most of our ethical action brought about by modernity—a political context that seems irreversible and that many, including many Jews and Christians, think ought to be irreversible. The fact is that today, indeed by now yesterday and probably tomorrow, most of our ethical action is necessarily conducted in secular space. Thus, even if I as a believing Jew am convinced that protecting human life from wanton destruction is directly commanded to me by God, I cannot argue for that commandment, which I believe is addressed to all humans along with me and my fellow Jews; I cannot argue for public policies to implement that commandment qua commandment (*mitsvah* or *Gebot*). Why? Because not everyone in the society in which I responsibly participate is a Jewish believer, or a Christian or a Muslim believer with whom I can share an acceptance of some basic divine commandments which function ethically—that is, which are addressed to inter-human situations. In other words, in the secular, democratic society in which most of my interpersonal relationships (except those that are most intimate, like those within my family and synagogue) are conducted and where I frequently want to be a public advocate, I cannot speak of the claims of *my* commanding God except as my *private* motivation. Publicly, I can only speak of divine wisdom manifest in human nature.[33] That is because membership in that society cannot, indeed should not, be based on acceptance of historical revelation, which is the only possible source of the direct commandments of God.

There are some Jews, and some Christians, who attempt to retreat into sectarian enclaves where they can live more consistently and continually according to the direct commandments of God to their respective traditional communities. Such retreats should be respected, but one can still doubt their wisdom. Because of growing national and international economic interdependence, economic survival requires more and more participation in the secular realm, whether it be desirable or even only necessary—a fact that cannot help but have an increasing effect on even the most sectarian enclaves. And because of that reality, which is beyond the control of any community to reverse, religious believers—Jews, Christians or Muslims—need to be able to argue for ethical positions that are consistent with the divine commandments they have accepted, but that cannot be deduced from them. Maximally, that means that religious believers can make some positive contributions to the democratic societies that have, in many cases, provided them with a haven from religious persecution. Minimally, that means that religious believers need to be participants in the moral discourse of their democratic societies, so that they can effectively oppose public policies that would make observance of the commandments of God more difficult and, in some cases, impossible, and so that they can support public policies that make the observance of the commandments easier by providing more public space for their observance.

Barth, and Jewish advocates of ethics limited to only what can be deduced from divine commandments, would seem to have no answer to the secular need of the religious believers described above. Nevertheless, since most of these Jews and Christians are not sectarians—not Hasidim or Amish—they cannot in good faith avoid at least an attempt to deal with the problem. And, even if Barth does not have an answer for us, can we find any hints in his work for those of us who do not want to avoid this secular, this philosophical, need?

Almost en passant, Barth recognizes some value in a non-theological ethics, which he calls "an ethics whose self-reflection, self-understanding and self-responsibility were from the outset overshadowed, determined and guided by a prior, even if more or less inexplicit, knowledge of the word of God."[34] Despite some hyperbole here, it would seem that such an ethics is "determined" by the word of God, not as a premise determines its conclusion but, perhaps, as a desire is determined if and when its object appears to it; this can be a desire which is, more often than not, yet to be self-conscious. Barth continues his speculation on this matter:

> An ethics of this kind would renounce all claim to try to speak a final word in solution of the problem of right conduct...without being guilty of that apotheosis in the background, without asserting that there is an ultimate reality either from or within the human self as such....It would be an ethics that knew the limits of humanity, and would not therefore treat humanity as an absolute but would for that reason do justice to it....Indirectly, it too would call man away from himself.[35]

In reading a passage such as this, I wonder why Barth had such antipathy to the idea of natural law. Could not one see natural law minimally as a few basic negative principles that delimit the pretensions of human will—collective, then individual—in claiming absolute authority for itself? And could not one see natural law minimally as a few basic positive principles that advocate the justice of certain essential human claims? Could not one call this type of law or justice (*dike* or *Recht*) "natural" insofar as nature (*physis*) functions as both limit (*peras*) and goal (*telos*)?[36] Could not natural law be seen as the necessary delimitation of the human subject for the sake of the human object? And could not one see this very enhancement of the human object qua person as the necessary precondition for the acceptance of revelation as that grace which recognizes and validates the ultimate dignity of the human person in community, which is to be capable of being addressed by God in revelation?

I think Barth has a blind spot regarding natural law. This is evident in how he seems to see only two natural law alternatives: the "neo-Protestantism" of Wilhelm Herrmann, and the Aristotelianism of Thomas Aquinas and his disciples.[37] The theology of Herrmann, the Marburg theologian, is the attempt to see Christianity, especially Christian ethics, from a Kantian perspective, which means, in the end, to place revelation on a rational basis. Now, it should not be forgotten that Herrmann's chief dialogue partner in his years at Marburg was Hermann Cohen. In fact, one can see much more of an influence of Cohen's Kantian rationalism on

Herrmann than vice versa.[38] For Barth, I would speculate, that meant that, if there were to be a natural law theory, it had to be formulated *à la* Kant-Cohen-Herrmann, and that would mean ultimately reducing revelation to reason and thereby making it lose its absolute primacy. This would explain his famous "Nein!" to the attempt of his fellow Swiss Reformed theologian, Emil Brunner (truth be told, a much less impressive theologian than Herrmann), to propose an ethic that recognized "orders of creation," which is a Protestant synonym for natural law.[39] As for Thomistic natural law theory, Barth recognizes that it has greater theological integrity than that of neo-Protestantism, but it is still a theology that seems to be unable to place divine command at the foundation of all theology, the queen of the sciences. Thomistic natural law theory seems founded upon a metaphysics that Barth is convinced is incompatible with Christianity.[40] In some important ways, I wish Barth had been more of a Calvinist in his treatment of law.[41] As such, he might have been able to make better use of the natural law-type thinking of some other modern Calvinists.[42] Finally, I might add, reflecting on my own community, that there are Jewish opponents of natural law who employ an almost identical logic to that of Barth in rejecting any Jewish natural law theory.[43] In other words, my philosophical difference with Barth is one I also have with some of my fellow Jewish thinkers, and some of his fellow Christian thinkers have this disagreement with Barth. So, there are Jews who would agree with Barth, not me; and there are Christians who would agree with me, not Barth.[44]

Nevertheless, I think that if Barth had attempted to rethink the idea of natural law along theological lines, and had not assumed that it had already been exhausted by theories he found theologically dangerous, he might very well have been able to do with the idea of natural law some of the things he was able to do with other traditional ideas that he masterfully reworked and redirected.[45] If Barth had done that, he would have employed philosophy more effectively in his theology, and his theological ethics would have fitted more authentically into current ethical discussions that have no choice but to be held in essentially secular space. Nevertheless, some of us who have learned from Barth—both Christians and Jews—can employ many of his extraordinary insights and formulations in travelling in directions that, for whatever reason, he himself did not care to go. Along those lines, Barth's magnificent discussion of divine command can help us to remain modest in the claims we make for a natural law theory, be it Christian or Jewish. For Barth, the idea of natural law said too little; we who respect him and have learned from him should not let it say too much.[46]

Notes

1 For the best current study of Barth on Jews and Judaism, see Katherine Sonderegger, *That Jesus Christ Was Born a Jew: Karl Barth's Doctrine of Israel* (University Park, PA: Pennsylvania State University Press, 1992).

2 Karl Barth, *Church Dogmatics* [hereafter *CD*] II/2, ed. G.W. Bromiley and T.F. Torrance; trans. G.W. Bromiley et al. (Edinburgh: T. & T. Clark, 1957), 698, where he calls Buber a "neo-Pharisaic Jew." In *CD* I/2 (1956), 80, Barth refers to Buber (and H.J. Schoeps and E.B. Cohn, two other Jewish theologians) as those who "are instructive to listen to on our question [the meaning of the Old Testament, which Barth defends against the attempts of Schleiermacher et al. to denigrate its importance for the church], both in what they say as earnest Jews, and what they cannot say as unconverted Jews." In *CD* III/2 (1960), 277-78, Barth distinguishes his theological anthropology from that of Buber (and some other non-Christians). See also E. Busch, *Karl Barth*, trans. J. Bowden (Grand Rapids, MI: Eerdmans, 1976), 272, 368-69 for some epistolary connections of Barth to Buber.

3 Nevertheless, for Barth's opposition to anti-Semitism, both theological and political, throughout his career, see Busch, *Karl Barth*, 234-35, 247-48. For various Jewish engagements of Barth's thought, see David Novak, "Before Revelation: The Rabbis, Paul, and Karl Barth," *Journal of Religion* 71 (1991): 50-51, n. 2.

4 See, for example, David Novak, "Theology and Philosophy: An Exchange with Robert Jenson," in *Trinity, Time, and Church: A Response to the Theology of Robert W. Jenson*, ed. C. Gunton (Grand Rapids, MI: Eerdmans, 2000), 42-61. Jenson is one of Barth's most important contemporary students. I do not think my conversations with Robert Jenson over the years would have been as illuminating had it not been for what we both have learned, *mutatis mutandis*, from Karl Barth who, even when not explicitly present, is always in the background.

5 These commandments are always in a dialectical relationship with the commandments that pertain to what is "between humans and God" [*bein adam le-maqom*]. See Mishnah: *Yoma* 8.9; Maimonides, *Commentary on the Mishnah*: *Peah* 1.1.

6 See *CD* II/2, 515-16.

7 See Busch, *Karl Barth*, 44, 56, 69. For the integration of Judaism and philosophy in Hermann Cohen's person and thought, see Simon Fisher, *Revelatory Positivism?: Barth's Earliest Theology and the Marburg School* (Oxford: Oxford University Press, 1988), 80-122.

8 *CD* II/2, 757.

9 See David Novak, "Introduction," *Christianity in Jewish Terms*, ed. T. Frymer-Kensky et al. (Boulder, CO: Westview Press, 2000), 1-6. For a longer version of this argument, see David Novak, "Avoiding Charges of Legalism and Antinomianism in Jewish-Christian Dialogue," *Modern Theology* 16 (2000): 275-89.

10 *Kirchliche Dogmatik* [hereafter *KD*] II/2, (Zurich: Evangelischer Verlag, 1948), 847.

11 *CD* II/2, 511.

12 See Karl Barth, *Dogmatics in Outline*, trans. G.T. Thompson (New York: Harper, 1959), 50.

13 See Alasdair MacIntyre, *After Virtue* (Notre Dame, IN: University of Notre Dame Press, 1981), 23-34.

14 *CD* II/2, 514. Note Cohen himself in his major work in ethics, *Ethik des reinen Willens*, 5th ed. (Hildesheim and New York: Georg Olms Verlag, 1981), 70: "Das Recht des Rechts ist das Naturrecht oder die Ethik des Rechts." Barth was undoubtedly familiar with the first edition of 1904. According to Fisher, *Revelatory Positivism?*, 341, Barth purchased his copy of this work for his library in Geneva in June 1910.

15 For the great modern phenomenology of the experience of Sabbath observance, see my late revered teacher, Abraham Joshua Heschel, *The Sabbath*, 2nd ed. (Cleveland and New York: Meridian Books, 1952).

16 See Palestinian Talmud: *Nedarim* 9.4/41c, where this commandment is designated by the greatest of the sages in the Talmud, Rabbi Akibah, to be "the most inclusive commandment [*kelal gadol*] in the Torah." See, also, Maimonides, *Mishneh Torah*: *Mourning*, 14.1.

17 *CD* II/2, 548=*KD* II/2, 608.

18 Martin Buber, *I and Thou*, trans.W. Kaufmann (New York: Scribner's, 1970), 157-58=*Ich und Du* (Heidelberg: Verlag Lambert Schneider, 1962), 110-11, 113.

19 See David Novak, *Jewish-Christian Dialogue* (New York: Oxford University Press, 1989), 80-86.

20 "The Builders," in Franz Rosenzweig, *On Jewish Learning*, ed. N.N. Glatzer; trans.W. Wolf (New York: Schocken, 1955), 115.

21 Ibid., 85.

22 For Rosenzweig's recognition of the early Barth, see N.N. Glatzer, *Franz Rosenzweig*, 2nd ed. (New York: Schocken, 1961), 278. Rosenzweig concentrates on Barth's early notion of God as *ganz Anders*, famously expressed in his 1919 commentary on the Epistle to the Romans. Rosenzweig contrasts that with the nearness of God emphasized by the eleventh-century Jewish theologian/poet Judah Halevi. But, I suspect that Rosenzweig would have resonated much more favourably to Barth's later theology, which also emphasizes the nearness of God. Along these lines, see Randi Rashkover, "Covenantal Ethics in Theologies of Revelation: A

Comparison of Franz Rosenzweig and Karl Barth" (Ph.D. diss., University of Virginia, 1999).

23 *CD* II/2, 655=*KD* II/2, 729.

24 *CD* II/2, 663=*KD* II/2, 739.

25 See David Novak, *Natural Law in Judaism* (Cambridge: Cambridge University Press, 1998), 142-48.

26 See Maimonides, *Guide of the Perplexed*, 1.26; also, 2.40.

27 Cf. John Calvin, *Institutes of the Christian Religion*, ed. John T. McNeill (Philadelphia, PA: Westminster Press, 1960), 1.2.1-3; 1.3.1. I disagree with Calvin that our intuition of God is a causal inference. Instead, it is a phenomenological trace of the divine behind the human presence. Cf. Emmanuel Levinas, *Of God Who Comes to Mind*, trans. B. Bergo (Stanford, CA: Stanford University Press, 1998), 75.

28 Barth himself makes this distinction between what is direct and indirect in theologically justified ethics. See *CD* II/2, 541-42.

29 In Scripture, it seems that the universal recognition of prime divine authority is designated *elohim* ("God," but perhaps better translated "divinity") in distinction from YHWH ("Lord"). See, for example, Gen. 20:11; Exod. 1:17; cf. Exod. 3:13-14; 5:2. As *elohim,* God need not be experienced as person.

30 See David Novak, *Covenantal Rights* (Princeton, NJ: Princeton University Press, 2000), 3-25.

31 One could certainly say that in the Hebrew Scriptures all love (*ahavah*, *hesheq*, etc.) is eros. See esp. Deut. 7:7-9. The Lutheran theologian Anders Nygren, who in his *Agape and Eros*, trans. P.S. Watson (Chicago: University of Chicago Press, 1982), sees eros as "egocentric" (722), built on "the foundation of self-love" (723) and being "after the pattern of human, acquisitive love" (ibid.), is mistaken about eros phenomenologically. Instead, true eros is ecstatically self-giving, so much so that the true lover allows himself or herself to be radically affected by his or her beloved. That is why God, as the exemplar of all eros (see Exod. 34:6; Babylonian Talmud: *Shabbat* 133b re Exod. 15:2), allows us to love him wholeheartedly and erotically in response (see Deut. 6:5; Mishnah: Berakhot 9.5). That is why, in both Jewish and Christian traditional exegesis, the mutual love between God and his people is best expressed in the palpably erotic imagery of the Song of Songs. True eros is not lust, which inevitably turns into violence (see 2 Sam. 13:1-19; Novak, *Natural Law in Judaism*, 36-39).

32 See Maimonides, *Mishneh Torah*: Benedictions, 11.2, and Karo, *Kesef Mishneh* thereon.

33 See Novak, *Natural Law in Judaism*, 16-26.

34 *CD* II/2, 541.

35 Ibid.

36 For the original philosophical use of these important terms, see Aristotle, *Metaphysics*, 1022a14.

37 See *CD* II/2, 520-28, 543-51.
38 For Cohen's influence on Herrmann, see Fisher, *Revelatory Positivism?*, 124-26, 153-63. For Herrmann's uneasiness with that influence, however, see ibid., 133-40.
39 See *Natural Theology: Comprising "Nature and Grace" by Emil Brunner, and the Reply "No" by Karl Barth*, trans. P. Fraenkel (London: G. Bles, 1946).
40 See *CD* II/2, 528.
41 For Barth, in the context of Lutheran-Calvinist debates about law, see J. van Dijk, *Die Grundlegung der Ethik in der Thelogie Karl Barths* (Munich: Manz Verlag, 1966), 262-63, nn. 95-99.
42 Even though he was certainly not in Karl Barth's theological league, it is still useful, along these lines of inquiry, to look at the work of the Dutch Calvinist theologian/statesman Abraham Kuyper. See J.D. Bratt, ed., *Abraham Kuyper* (Grand Rapids, MI: Eerdmans, 1998). I think that Reinhold Niebuhr, who certainly was in Barth's theological league, has a theological anthropology, upon which he bases his political theory, closer to Calvin than that of Barth. See Reinhold Niebuhr, *The Nature and Destiny of Man*, vol. 1 (New York: Scribners, 1941), 158-59. Indeed, despite Niebuhr's criticisms of natural law theory as represented by the Roman Catholic moral theology of his day (ibid., 278-97), his own critiques of the pretensions of human culture and politics can now be seen as akin to the minimalist natural law theory being suggested here. For a comparison of Barth and Niebuhr favourable to Niebuhr as having a more politically adequate theological position, see Will Herberg's introductory essay, "The Social Philosophy of Karl Barth," in *Karl Barth, Community, State, and Church*, ed. Will Herberg (Garden City, NY: Doubleday, 1960), 55-67.
43 See Marvin Fox, "Maimonides and Aquinas on Natural Law," in *Interpreting Maimonides* (Chicago and London: University of Chicago Press, 1990), 24-51. Cf. David Novak, *Jewish Social Ethics* (New York: Oxford University Press, 1992), 25-29.
44 See Stanley Hauerwas, "Christian Ethics in Jewish Terms: A Response to David Novak," in *Christianity in Jewish Terms*, ed. Tikva Frymer-Kensky et al. (Boulder, CO: Westview Press, 2000), 135-140.
45 Barth accepted the idea that there is a law of God pertaining to universal human nature, but he denied that this commandment could be known universally, except by direct divine revelation. For Barth, there only seems to be specific revelation, which, without a reference to general revelation, becomes a singularly exclusive revelation. See Karl Barth, *Ethics*, ed. D. Braun; trans. G.W. Bromiley (New York: Seabury Press, 1981), 209-10.
46 See Novak, *Natural Law in Judaism*, 174-78.

4

NOT MORAL HEROES

The Grace of God and the Church's Public Voice

HAROLD WELLS

In this essay, I explore the foundation of the church's public proclamation and mission for social justice in the grace of God, disclosed in the life, death and resurrection of Jesus Christ. That is, the church's social ethic is fundamentally not a matter of law, but of "gospel." The church, I will argue, should not present itself as the national "conscience," a righteous community of moral heroes, calling others to imitate its moral goodness. We are, at any rate, less than credible in such a role. Rather, we are people who have received love beyond measure, and so, in response, wish to live in a society marked by generosity, loving cooperation and friendship. The church's vision of human social order must flow from its vision of a generous God who loves all alike, but has a special bias for the marginal, the oppressed and the poor—a God who has suffered for us, and suffers with us in all the vicissitudes of our needy finite existence.

Basic to a Christian theology of grace is the doctrine of atonement. In a recent book, Timothy Gorringe[1] points out the relationship between religious doctrines and cultural attitudes at various periods of history. He suggests that theologies of atonement, which emphasize retribution for sin, are associated with harsh retributive practices toward criminals; at the same time, attitudes of compassion and rehabilitative

Notes to chapter 4 are on pp. 96-98.

efforts on behalf of criminals make retributive and "satisfaction" theories of atonement untenable. My interest here is the significance of the grace of God not only for the area of criminal justice, but for social justice in general, and the reciprocal relationship of doctrine to social ethics and the church's public voice. This seems an appropriate discussion for a volume in honour of Roger Hutchinson, principal of Emmanuel College and professor of church and society, whose commitment to the United Church of Canada, and to the integrity of its advocacy for social justice, is well known.

What Does the Public Hear?

The "public" is, of course, a complex concept. The public is not one monolithic reality, but consists of elites and of "underclasses," of a dominant public, of sub-publics and counter-publics.[2] We can also distinguish between Christian and secular or "unchurched" publics, as well as "Catholic," "evangelical" and "liberal Protestant" publics. Space prohibits a thorough analysis of the concept, but this complexity must be kept in mind as we consider what the "public" hears from the church's "public" voice.

What is the church's voice in North America, and especially in Canada, in our time? What do the "unchurched" actually hear from public "Christianity"? Anyone who surfs the channels knows that "TV evangelists" are featured prominently for hours every day on American, but also on Canadian, television.[3] Secular young people, for example, who have never been part of a Christian congregation, will have paused for a few minutes, if only for amusement, to hear this very public Christian voice. They will have seen some spectacular scenes of miraculous healing, and heard a good deal of apocalyptic eschatology and of the "prosperity gospel" (if you are a believer, it pays off financially), as well as a certain widespread version of the doctrine of atonement: the grace of God revealed in the cross of Jesus is presented as payment to a stern, demanding deity to cover the cost of our moral failures. We benefit from this transaction if we believe in it. Failure to believe in it will result in eternal damnation. This is what Gorringe would call a highly "retributive" doctrine of atonement: God needs retribution for our sins and we are rescued from this because the torture and death of Jesus has "paid the price" and God is "satisfied." One can only surmise that, to the secular ear, this is bizarre indeed. Yet, discerning secular ears may well have noticed that this doctrine of atonement, or something like it, is usually associated with a virulent rejection of abortion, gun control and homosexuality, together with a blessing, implicit or explicit, of the values of competitive capitalism. Christianity also appears to stand for capital punishment and retributive attitudes toward youth crime, for lower taxes and curtailment of the welfare state: hard-working citizens deserve to benefit economically from their success and should not be overly burdened with the needs of the unsuccessful. In the United States, these views are held especially by the "religious right,"[4] but they are very much present in Canada as well. A prominent Canadian political leader who espouses this social philosophy is highly visible as a Christian who does not work on Sundays! To many, he has rapidly become the most visible symbol of Christianity's public voice.[5]

The secular public may occasionally be aware of other voices of Christianity. The Roman Catholic Church is well known for its firm opposition to abortion, homosexual practice and contraception. Yet, in Canada, we sometimes hear from Catholic bishops a voice of concern for the victims of economic injustice, and this is capable of winning considerable media attention and even responses from government leaders.[6] The Catholic Church also supports the Jubilee campaign for the forgiveness of Third World debt. The high international visibility of the pope, together with the authority structure of the Catholic Church, ensures that at least the Catholic public hears its public voice.

The public also hears occasionally, in the utterances of United Church moderators, the voice of a "religious left."[7] This voice denounces the government's "war against the poor,"[8] but we would have to be looking carefully to find this in the back pages of our newspapers. The message may not be heard (or welcomed) even by many United Church folk in their pews. The recent moderator, Bill Phipps, is quite well known for his passionate indignation about corporate power in our globalized world, and the failure of governments to stand up for the interests of the poor. But he truly hit the headlines, radio talk shows and magazine front covers when he was coaxed to pronounce on a "religious" question: whether Christ is God. Thus, the capitalist media managed to divert attention from his message about economic justice. One can hope that the moderator's consultation on the economy, conducted on the Internet, has had some significant impact on the political awareness of many church members.[9]

However difficult it is to measure such influence, it is evident that church stances and church-based campaigns are still able to have a visible effect on public attitudes. In 1988, the United Church recognition of homosexuals as eligible for ordered ministry attracted enormous public attention, capturing the top spot on the CBC and CTV national newscasts. The whole country was talking about homosexuality for weeks. This public debate has, especially for a substantial United Church public, increased knowledge and understanding of sexual orientation, and helped to legitimize homosexual relationships in the minds of many mainstream people. In this way, the United Church has exercised an option for one marginalized group and has accompanied its public voice with public action. Public statements of other churches and of ecumenical coalitions are also sometimes heard in public places. For example, as already mentioned, the Jubilee Initiative, campaigning for forgiveness of Third World debt, though limited in its success to date, has demonstrated the capacity of the church's public voice to capture the imagination of large numbers of people and to influence government for the sake of human generosity and justice.[10]

It is my premise, then, that even in our present post-Christendom era it is still possible in Canadian society for the church to assert an effective public voice. "Christianity" in its various forms is still an influential presence in Canada, but its social influence is varied and ambiguous. That is why it is so important for the church to do its social analysis in a careful, professional manner and to present well-informed criticism and well-reasoned alternatives for public consideration. The church can do this, even in our "postmodern" times, recognizing that others too may be instruments of the divine Spirit and acknowledging that other religious or secular voices also make their legitimate contributions to public debates. Theologians and preachers, then, should care very much about the church's public voice—not only about its explicit social ethic, but also about the doctrines that accompany it and underlie it.[11]

We may ask whether the general public hears anything in our time from the "liberal" churches[12] about the grace of God that counters the doctrines of TV evangelism. The grace of God is central to any construal of the Christian faith, and a component of it is the doctrine of atonement. In view of the continuing popularity of TV evangelists and the strength of the evangelical churches, it is evident that this latter concept continues to hold great power. Yet, for many, especially in liberal Protestant churches, the doctrine that "Jesus died for us" has become simply meaningless.

The "Bottom Line" Is Grace

If the church's public voice is to be effective, the church must win the support and engagement of its own membership. Yet, the broad membership of the United Church (and, one suspects, of other mainline churches) is often not onside with what may be seen as the enlightened stances of the official church's public voice.[13] The reasons for this are, no doubt, complex. But could it be that many of our members need to be persuaded that these public stances are firmly based in faith—in Christ and in Scripture? Could it be that they hear church policies as expressions of an ideology which seems to them extraneous to their faith, and which at the same time does not serve their interests? Prosperous people in our congregations are told that they ought to oppose tax cuts and support a generous welfare state; that they should oppose the structures of globalized capitalism and support a more cooperative economic system, nationally and globally. I believe these are appropriate calls to Christian political discipleship. But perhaps many church people hear these calls to self-sacrifice and social solidarity as a kind of moral law being heavily imposed upon them from on high. What will inspire and motivate people—people who are not naturally moral heroes—to think and act graciously, even to act against their own perceived class interests? We may guess that the preaching of a kind of moral law will not accomplish this.

But we know that the call to discipleship is not the proclamation of a moral law. Biblically, care for the poor and commitment to social justice are rooted in the love and grace of God. To follow Jesus is a free and joyful allegiance to one who serves, who lived and died for us. We do not live under a threatening, domineering lawgiver, who alienates our freedom and humanity by the enforcement of his omnipotent will. To live not "under the law" (Rom. 2:12) but under grace is the way of true freedom.

If we explore the biblical sources, we find that nothing is more basic to our whole faith tradition. Looking back to our Hebrew roots, to the events of Exodus and Sinai, we find that the Torah is deeply founded in God's love and grace. The Decalogue begins with what Yahweh has done for the people: "I am the Lord your God who brought you out of the land of Egypt, out of the house of slavery" (Exod. 20:2). God's salvation here is the political liberation of a people. Obedience arises out of gratitude to the compassionate God who has loved them and calls them to love and serve one another. In later centuries, the prophets, in their calls for justice and love, typically based their ethical message in God's steadfast loving-kindness. While God is also wrathful, and judges the people, it was the prophets' intense awareness of Yahweh's generous, passionate love reaching out to Israel that inspired their moral denunciations and declarations of divine judgment, as well as their hope for the messianic reign of universal peace. It was not, then, a break with his own Jewish tradition when Jesus proclaimed a radical gospel of his gracious *Abba*, who calls his hearers to love not only those who love them, but their enemies also, because God "makes his sun rise on the evil and on the good, and sends rain on the righteous and on the unrighteous" (Matt. 5:45). The gospel of free grace did not await the theology of Paul. We hear it dramatically on the lips of Jesus, especially in the parables of the Synoptic Gospels. We hear of a loving father who, having been offended and hurt by his son, is constantly on the lookout for his return and who, then, seeing him on the horizon, runs out to meet and welcome him. The father requires no retribution of any kind; his generous love is lavished upon his son with no strings attached, and with no "payment" or punishment required.

We find grace in Jesus' own actions as well, offering friendship to "tax collectors and sinners," accepting them, eating with them, without regard for their deservingness or moral respectability. The story of Zacchaeus (Luke 19:1-10) is about the turnaround of a man's life toward just economic relations, not because someone preached a moral law to him, but simply because Jesus accepted him, went to his house and treated him as a friend. The story of the woman "who was a sinner," who anointed Jesus' feet, is also one of grace. In response to the condemnation of the woman, Jesus replies that "her sins, which were many, have been forgiven; hence she has shown great love. But the one to whom little is forgiven, loves little" (Luke 7:47).

It is difficult to imagine a clearer affirmation than this, that the foundation of Christian agape is a dynamic, personal response to the freely given agape of God. Again, Jesus is compassionate to the woman caught in adultery, defending her against a cruel execution by stoning (John 8:3-11). Jesus' profound dictum, "Let the one who is without sin cast the first stone," asserts our universal solidarity in sin, and therefore calls us not to retributive punishment, but to gratuitous mercy toward one another.

At the same time, anger and judgment are not absent from the words of Jesus, as reported in the gospels. Despite his overwhelming graciousness, Jesus seems ruthless in his denunciation of those who, insisting upon the letter of the law, "lay heavy burdens, hard to bear" upon the backs of the people, while neglecting "justice, mercy and faith" (Matt. 23:23).[14] In contrast to them, Jesus announces the presence of a compassionate God whose forgiving love is inexhaustible.

Of course, it was Paul's theology of grace that was so formative for the Protestant tradition. Paul's message carries a high degree of continuity with that of Jesus, but Paul lived and wrote in "post-resurrection" mode. He proclaims not only the loving *Abba* of Jesus, and the coming reign of God and new creation, but also Jesus the Christ, crucified and risen. It is not simply Jesus' teaching about the gracious God, but Jesus' own death and resurrection that are foundational for Paul's theology of grace. We are "justified," acquitted of our offences and set right with God, says Paul, not by doing good works of the law, but by grace through faith—i.e., accepting the unconditional love that is offered through cross and resurrection, and entering into reconciliation. Paul states the contradiction of grace and law in dramatic terms:

> We know that a person is justified not by the works of the law but through faith in Jesus Christ. (Gal. 2:16)
>
> We hold that a person is justified by faith apart from the works of the law. (Rom. 3:28)

The Pauline author of Ephesians links grace and faith clearly: "For by grace you have been saved through faith, and this is not your own doing; it is the gift of God, not the result of works, so that no one may boast" (Eph. 2:8-9).

We know how basic Paul's theology of grace was for Luther and the Reformation, and also for the Wesleyan revival of the eighteenth century. Neglect of this Pauline message of grace calls into question the whole Protestant and Methodist identity and saps the dynamism that lies at the root of their spiritual tradition. Paul's ethic flows entirely from grace. God's agape love toward us is the root of our Christian love, and without love everything else is worthless (1 Cor. 13). Because God has loved us so generously in Christ, Paul enjoins us: "Do not repay anyone evil for evil....If your enemies are hungry, feed them" (Rom. 12:17, 20). Thus, grace abolishes all retribution.

The Johannine literature conveys the same central logic of grace. Where Paul contrasts grace and law, John contrasts love and fear: "There is no fear in love, for love casts out fear" (1 John 4:18); "We love because God first loved us" (1 John 4:19). Again, in one of the most eloquent of biblical texts, John proclaims:

> Beloved, let us love one another, because love is from God; everyone who loves is born of God and knows God. Whoever does not love does not know God, for God is love. God's love was revealed among us in this way: God sent his only Son into the world that we might live through him. (1 John 4: 7-9)

These Scriptures remind us that the dynamism of Christian love for our neighbour is rooted in God's grace. If we merely enunciate a "conscience," or "high moral ideals" for society, our hearers can be forgiven if they see us as the proponents of a demanding moral law, one that calls for a moral heroism that we ourselves fail to demonstrate.

Was Jesus' Death a Sacrifice for Our Sins?

However, a major problem exists today in the doctrine of grace. Perhaps much of the liberal Protestant discomfort with the theology of grace, as it is found in Paul, the Synoptic Gospels, John, Hebrews and so on, is the way it is linked to the teaching that Jesus *died for us* and *for our sins* (Rom. 5:8; 1 Cor. 15:3) and as *an atoning sacrifice for our sins* (1 John 4:10). If we preach the grace of God, and derive our personal and social ethic from it, are we thereby implicated in a "retributive" doctrine about a God who insists on being paid in blood as the price of grace? Does grace, then, cease to be grace?

Without doubt, Jesus died because of the way he lived[15]—that is, he died a political death, which was the cost of his loyalty to God and his courageous solidarity with the poor and sinners. It was a vicious and brutal act of political violence. No theory of atonement should be allowed to obscure the human hatred and cruelty that put Jesus on the cross. But just what is the connection between Jesus' cross and the extravagant grace of God about which he spoke with such passion? What does it mean to say that the Son of Man "came not to be served but to serve, and to give his life a ransom for many" (Mark 10:45); that God "did not withhold his own Son, but gave him up for all of us" (Rom. 8:32)? Is Jesus indeed the "merciful and faithful high priest in the service of God, [who made] an atonement for our sins" (Heb. 2:17)? Texts of this kind are so ubiquitous in the New Testament that they cannot possibly be ignored or discarded. Since it is impossible here to offer a detailed exegesis of all these texts, my intention is to consider the basic concept of the sacrifice of Christ, and its viability today.

To appreciate these texts, we must know something of their conceptual background for the early Christians. First, it is evident that the earliest Christians interpreted the event of Jesus in terms of the categories available to them, and sacrifice was a major part of their tradition. Blood sacrifice was part of many ancient religious traditions as a means of "propitiation" (appeasement) of an angry deity and of "expiation" (cleansing the stain or impurity of sin).[16] For the Jews, blood had the power of expiation "because the life of the flesh is in the blood; and I have given it to you for making atonement…for, as life, it is blood that makes atonement" (Lev. 17:11-12). The causal connection between sin and resulting calamities was thought to be broken by the bloody sacrifice of animals, and sometimes other offerings as well. In addition to blood sacrifices, the scapegoat ritual of the Day of Atonement symbolically placed the sins of the people on the head of a goat, which was then driven into the wilderness, bearing the sins of the people (Lev. 16: 20-22). Sacrifice could be a sacramental indication of moral seriousness, expressing thanksgiving (Lev. 7:11-15), or genuine repentance and commitment to God's will.[17] Or it could be part of a taboo mentality, a system of self-protection for the individual or the community from the effects of defilement.[18]

Aside from ritual sacrifice as such, but closely related conceptually, was the belief that innocent suffering and death had atoning power for the people.[19] This concept appears in the famous servant song of Isaiah 52:13-53:12: "He was wounded for our transgressions, crushed for our iniquities; upon him was the punishment that made us whole…he bore the sin of many, and made intercession for the transgressors." We need not enter the long debate about the identity of the servant. The text was used by the first Christians to interpret the death of Jesus (for example, Matt. 8:17; Luke 22:37; 1 Pet. 2:24; Acts 8:32). We also find background to New Testament concepts of atonement in Jewish literature contemporary with Paul (first century CE). In 4 Maccabees, a dying martyr prays: "Be merciful to your people and let our punishment be a satisfaction on their behalf. Make my blood their purification, and take my life as ransom for theirs" (4 Macc. 6:28-29). The author declares, "Through the blood of those righteous ones and through the propitiation of their death, the divine Providence rescued Israel" (4 Macc.17:22).[20] Such concepts provide the conceptual equipment for Paul's declaration that we are "justified by his grace as a gift, through the redemption that is in Christ Jesus, whom God put forward as a sacrifice of atonement by his blood, effective through faith" (Rom. 3:25) and the teaching of Hebrews that "Christ…through the eternal Spirit offered himself without blemish to God" (Heb. 9:14).

These thoughts are not without human nobility of spirit. But what do they say about God? Is God pleased and satisfied by human violence? Will God forgive only if someone dies?

Even more dramatic and profound is the ancient story of the sacrifice of Isaac, required by God of Abraham: "Take your son, your only son Isaac, whom you love, and go to the land of Moriah, and offer him there" (Gen. 22:2). Abraham assures his son that "God himself will provide the lamb" (Gen. 22:8). Yet, the lamb provided by God will not be Abraham's son Isaac, for, when Abraham has shown his faith in his intention to obey God's terrible instruction, God commands the sacrifice to cease and provides instead the lamb caught in a thicket. New Testament authors see Abraham in this story as "a type of God," who provides "the lamb of God who takes away the sin of the world" (John 1:29), who "did not withhold his only Son, but gave him up for us all" (Rom. 8:32; see also Heb. 11:17).[21] This story of a God who does not require sacrifice, but provides it, may well be read in view of the sharp prophetic criticism of sacrifice:

> Will the Lord be pleased with thousands of rams, with ten thousands of rivers of oil?…What does the Lord require of

> you but to do justice, to love kindness, and to walk humbly with your God? (Mic. 6: 7-8)
>
> I desire steadfast love and not sacrifice, the knowledge of God rather than burnt offerings. (Hos. 6:6)

Similar rejections can be found in the Psalms:

> Sacrifice and offering you do not desire…Burnt offering and sin offering you have not required. (Ps. 40:6)

It is improbable that the prophets actually called for the abolition of sacrifices; their rhetoric of rejection was almost certainly meant to "ethicize" sacrificial practice.[22] Whatever the prophets' intention in their time, profound texts have a life of their own (as Paul Ricoeur has taught us), and we must listen for a living word for our own time. In both Reformed and Wesleyan traditions of *sola scriptura*, Scripture must interpret Scripture, and Scripture criticizes Scripture. Texts of both testaments that affirm sacrifice appear to be questioned by other scriptural texts. Today, we may well hear these prophetic texts as encouragement to question the vision of God as one who demands ritual sacrifice. Moreover, if God did not need animal sacrifices as a condition of forgiveness, presumably God did not need the "payment" of Jesus' death as expiation for our sins. God is not blood-hungry. We are encouraged in this direction by the teaching of Jesus himself as he is presented in the gospels. His admonitions never suggest that God demands ritual sacrifice. On the contrary, the parables depict his *Abba* as one who reaches out unconditionally with generous love. Jesus himself pronounces and enacts radical acceptance of sinners without retribution of any kind. According to Matthew, Jesus echoes the prophets' denunciation of sacrifice: "Go and learn what this means: 'I desire mercy, not sacrifice'" (Matt. 9:13).

Nevertheless, a sacrificial theory of atonement has been dominant in the history of the doctrine. There is not space here to peruse the whole history, but we need to take note of the thought of Anselm of Canterbury (1033-1109), who has had such an enormous influence on Western Christian theology, both Catholic and Protestant, and therefore on Western public consciousness even to the present day. Anselm, writing within his eleventh-century feudal context, saw sin as essentially a failure to render to God his due. When a feudal lord was disobeyed, restoration of his honour was necessary in a way satisfactory to himself. The lord must be "satisfied" by due payment or suitable punishment. "God is honoured," said Anselm, "in the punishment of the sinner."[23] The greater the lord, the greater was an offence against him, and the greater the required payment. If the offence was great enough, only the death of the perpetrator could compensate with sufficient satisfaction. Since God's lordship is infinitely high, an offence against his honour could be paid for only by an infinite being. "Only a God-man can make the satisfaction by which man is saved."[24] According to Anselm, this was why God became human. We should note that the love of God is not absent from Anselm's theory. God the Son "died voluntarily" and in that way God has "shown his love toward us."[25]

Anselm's satisfaction theory of atonement is highly unsatisfactory to many today, who simply find it meaningless, since the system of blood sacrifice as well as the feudal system of honour are now so remote from our consciousness. Most notably, a number of feminist theologians (for example, Dorothee Soelle, Elizabeth Johnson, Mary Grey) have protested the concept of God that it implies: an angry male deity who requires the violent sacrifice of his son as the condition for reconciliation is one who legitimizes the worst kind of patriarchal domination and child abuse. They also point out the danger of sado-masochistic pathology in a theology that glorifies suffering and worships a tormented God, and so encourages women and other people to put up with abuse.[26]

Such criticism is not entirely new. In the twelfth century, sacrificial atonement was already criticized by Peter Abelard (1079-1142), a younger contemporary of Anselm. He was influenced by the life of the rising cities of his time, and less tied to the prevailing mentality of feudalism.[27] In his exposition of Romans, he wrote:

> How cruel and wicked it seems that anyone should demand the blood of an innocent person as the price of anything, or that it should in any way please him that an innocent man should be slain. Still less that God should consider the death of his Son so agreeable that by it he should be reconciled to the whole world![28]

All of these considerations, both traditional and contemporary, lead us to abandon the language of "sacrifice to God" as it relates to Christology. The God of Jesus Christ, the gracious one whom we encounter in Jesus, does not demand retribution or payment of any kind, certainly not the violent spilling of blood in exchange for the forgiveness of sins. If we are to preach a credible, empowering message of free grace that inspires a public ethic of compassion and generosity, we must reread the numerous sacrificial texts of the New Testament, and understand the reconciling life, death and resurrection of Jesus in quite other terms.

God's Own Self-Giving

If we leave behind a "satisfaction" understanding of Jesus' death, must we also discard the self-giving agape of God which Christians have always discerned precisely in the cross of the risen Christ? Has the cross really nothing to do with God's grace? If we refuse to speak of it as a sacrifice demanded by God, must we also dismiss entirely the constant connection that the New Testament makes between the death of Jesus and God's generous love? Should we abandon the Eucharistic words, "My body broken for you..., my blood shed for you"? Is Jesus, then, simply one more inspiring moral hero and tragic martyr? If so, then followers of Jesus are also called to be moral heroes, and possibly tragic martyrs, who find self-worth in their own moral goodness and suffering.

Basic to a more satisfactory understanding of the affirmation that Jesus died for us is the doctrine of the Incarnation of God in Jesus Christ.[29] If we read the sacrificial texts of the New Testament in light of it, we realize that it is not that God demands the terrible suffering of his Son, but that, on the contrary, God, in Christ, bears the cost of our reconciliation. According to Matthew, Jesus is Emmanuel, God with us (Matt. 1:23). According to Paul, "God was in Christ, reconciling the world to himself" (2 Cor. 5:19). Jesus is the incarnation of the wisdom (*sophia*) of God (1 Cor. 1:30).[30] The "lamb of God" of whom John speaks (1:29) is none other than (in the same chapter) the word of God who was with God, and was God, and who was in the beginning with God (1:1-2), and who was *made flesh*—that is, fully and truly human—in Jesus (1:14). The divinity, as well as the humanity, of Jesus is basic, then, to any belief that Jesus died for us. John's declaration that "God so loved the world that he gave his only Son" (3:16) has to be understood in a Trinitarian manner—i.e., God's giving of "the Son" is nothing else but God's own agapeic self-giving.

Indeed, the whole identification of Jesus as Saviour implies and depends upon the identification of the human Jesus as the embodiment of the saving God of Israel, the enfleshment of God's own creative and saving wisdom. The first Christians believed that they had found *salvation* in the crucified and risen Jesus: the proleptic (anticipated) inbreaking of God's messianic reign of justice and peace, reconciliation with God, and the overcoming of death in his resurrection, and thus the immediate presence of the eternal. Because they believed that Jesus revealed God, mediated salvation and embodied the divine presence uniquely, they related to him *as to God.* Because they knew him as living *kurios*, risen and present in their midst as sovereign in life and in death, they offered him praise, thanksgiving, obedience and trust. This continues to be true today. Christians everywhere are centred upon Jesus Christ in their worship, ethics and mission in a way that would be sheer idolatry if Christ were not indeed incarnate God. While the theology of Incarnation in Christ flows from our experience of salvation in him, so, also, in circular fashion, the theology of salvation by God's grace in Christ becomes intelligible only in relation to the Incarnation. A Christian theology of grace operates on the premise that God is utterly identified and *one with* the human Jesus, and that the humanity of Jesus is none other than *the humanity of God*!

Our vision of God, then, must be quite different from that of the TV evangelists, and also quite different from that of the dominant Western theological tradition. The key point here, and the most dramatic shift in the Christian doctrine of God in our time, has been the affirmation of the suffering of God. The suffering of Jesus is God's own suffering, and the death of Jesus Emmanuel is "death in God."[31] The early Christian theological tradition almost unanimously insisted upon the *impassibility* of God (God's inability to suffer).[32] Today, following the century of Auschwitz, Hiroshima and Chernobyl, such an untouched and untouchable deity has become unthinkable. The most persuasive objection to Christian faith comes from protest atheism, which finds belief in a God of love absurd in light of the colossal suffering of the twentieth century. In face of this protest, Jürgen Moltmann is notable for his eloquent attestation to the suffering God:

> The only way past protest atheism is through a theology of the cross which understands God as the suffering God in

> the suffering of Christ and which cries out with the godforsaken God, "My God, why have you forsaken me?" For this theology, God and suffering are no longer contradictions, as in theism and atheism, but God's being is in suffering and the suffering is in God's being itself, because God is love.[33]

The Trinitarian feminist Elizabeth Johnson, who, like most feminists, is wary of glorifying suffering and thus strengthening women's potential for victimization, is also critical of substitutionary doctrines of atonement.[34] Yet, she also speaks eloquently of God's suffering in Christ:

> In the human integrity of a broken human being, who prized truth and fidelity above his own safety and loved his friends in an ever-widening circle until the godforsaken end, something of the mystery of God is darkly manifest: Christ crucified, the wisdom and power of God. Here if anywhere it can be glimpsed that Wisdom participates in the suffering of the world and overcomes, inconceivably, from within through the power of love.[35]

The love of the suffering God is revealed as inexhaustible, stopping at nothing to reach out to us. This is emphatically not the God who demands the satisfaction of his "honour," but one who chose to enter into the most dishonourable state imaginable in order to embrace us.

We do well to listen again to Abelard, who, though he rejected Anselm's theory of satisfaction, continued to declare that Jesus died "for all people." In a letter to his beloved Héloïse, he pleads with her to continue in her love for Christ:

> Are you not moved to tears of remorse by the only-begotten Son of God, who for you and for all people, in his innocence was seized by impious men…to die a horrible and accursed form of death?…Look at him going to be crucified for your sake, carrying his own cross.…He suffered truly for your salvation, on your behalf, of his own free will.[36]

Abelard's doctrine is sometimes named (and perhaps misnamed) the "moral influence" theory because of what he wrote in his exposition of Romans:

> Our redemption through Christ's suffering is that deeper affection in us which not only frees us from slavery to sin, but also wins for us the true liberty of sons of God, so that we do all things out of love rather than fear.[37]

But more than that, God has freed us, says Abelard, because he has "bound us to himself by love."[38] Abelard's doctrine has been criticized as unduly subjective, and has sometimes been labelled a "liberal" doctrine, [39] appearing to suggest that atonement is merely an impression made upon human beings and not a reality in itself.[40] But in fact he affirms the full divinity of the "only begotten Son of God," the reality of the love of God poured out for us in the death of Jesus, and the free grace and pardon that God offers to us in and through Jesus. Though Abelard's account is not entirely adequate, his claim that by Christ's death God has "bound us to himself by love" suggests another way of looking at atonement. We may speak of our "unity" with Christ and of our "inclusion" in him. Because Christ is incarnate in our flesh, and even dies our death, we are included "in him," and therefore we are given a share in his resurrection and in his divine life. The Spirit, which is the Spirit of Christ, dwells in us, and we dwell "in the Spirit," revealing that the Trinity is not a closed circle in heaven, but open to humanity and creation.[41] Thus, we are given a share in the eternal life of the triune God! (See Pauline and Johannine texts about our mutual indwelling with Christ, and our inclusion in the divine life: Rom. 8:9-11; John 15:5, 17:21.)

That God has "bound us to himself by love" also speaks of reconciliation. This, rather than "satisfaction," I suggest, is the key biblical concept that clarifies what it means to say that Jesus died "for our sake" and "for our salvation." We know from human experience that reconciliation is costly. When grave offence and deep hurt have occurred among people (whether between individuals, or among nations, races or classes), reconciliation is never cheap or easy. The overcoming of alienation is painful, but the one who forgives does not get "paid." Rather, the one who forgives "pays," or bears the cost, by taking the hurt into himself or herself. The story of Jesus as the story of God incarnate is such a story of reconciliation. We are told that Jesus Emmanuel came among us preaching repentance, offering forgiveness freely, and calling us to participate in God's reign of justice, peace and wholeness. As we noted above, his teaching and preaching, his healing work and relationships were marked by extraordinary grace. His parables about his forgiving *Abba*, his remarkable fellowship with disreputable people, his solidarity with marginalized women, the lame, blind and poor all speak of God's outreaching love for "sinners." With hindsight, we can say that it was surely inevitable that Jesus would have to suffer. "The cross," writes Jon Sobrino, "is the outcome of an incarnation situated in a world of sin."[42] This estranged world could not stand his holy innocence, his strong freedom, his utter generosity or, especially, his courageous challenge to injustice and hypocrisy. Powerful forces of his society and of the occupying imperial power combined to get rid of him. He died asking his *Abba* to "forgive them, for they do not know what they are doing" (Luke 23:34).

We cannot say that the salvation Jesus brings is through his death only. Rather, his death was the culminating point of his whole outreaching ministry of grace. Nor can we say that God willed this cruel event, for the gracious *Abba* of Jesus does not will that human beings should be vicious and hateful, or that anyone should suffer such degradation and despair. God did not demand a sacrifice, but *God, in Christ, did will to give Godself utterly, bearing the cost of reconciliation.* God has not taken our sin lightly, but, appealing for our repentance, has taken the judgment and consequence of sin and the cost of reconciliation into Godself. The event of God's self-giving in Jesus' life and death was the exact opposite of "retribution." Retribution is entirely set aside by the freedom of grace. No one is "punished" as a substitute for others. Yet, the pain and cruelty of human sin, with all its horrendous consequences, fall upon Christ and, in Christ, upon God, with whom he is wholly one. Sobrino says it eloquently:

> On the cross of Jesus God himself is crucified....The Father suffers the death of the Son and takes upon himself all the pain and suffering of history. In this ultimate solidarity with humanity he reveals himself as the God of love, who opens up a hope and a future through the most negative side of history.[43]

In total solidarity with us, Jesus did indeed *die for us and for our sins.* He did truly bear the sins of the world, and is indeed the "lamb of God who takes away the sin of the world." God, like Abraham, did not withhold his Son, his only Son (Gen. 22:12; Rom. 8:32; John 3:16). Jesus' cross stands for us as the supreme sign of God's inextinguishable love.

But no account of the cross is complete without the resurrection. Another major historic theory is *Christus victor,*[44] which emphasizes Christ's victory over the evil powers of sin and death. The truth in this is that the cosmic and salvific meaning of Jesus' life and death become clear only in the event of the resurrection. In its light, Jesus' death and his whole life of grace came to be seen as a saving event of God-with-us. It is an eschatological event, the decisive in-breaking of God's reign. It is an all-inclusive event, effective for all creation. In light of the resurrection, Paul could say, "God was in Christ reconciling the *kosmos*" (2 Cor. 5:19). In light of the resurrection, the cross of Jesus can be seen as an event of cosmic salvation, of God's self-giving agape for the reconciliation of all things: "For in him all the fullness of God was pleased to dwell, and through him, God was pleased to reconcile to himself all things, whether on earth or in heaven, by making peace through the blood of his cross" (Col. 1:20).

The sacrificial texts must be taken seriously, then, even if today we read them differently than ancient people did, and differently from most of our Western tradition. They speak of God's own suffering for us within our human flesh. Linked to Jesus' deeds and teaching, and to the victory of his resurrection, the story of the cross is a good-news story of God's unending love for the world. In the cross of the risen Christ, we have encountered the holy one whom we can worship, love and trust.

Again: The Church's Public Voice

It may seem to the reader a long way from a theology of atonement to social policy. No doubt our politicians would be amused. Nevertheless, as I suggested at the beginning of this essay, together with Gorringe, doctrines and social ethics are reciprocally related, and together may have great long-term influence on public consciousness and, therefore, on politics, economic life and culture. We have seen that certain construals of Christian doctrine are associated today with certain social, political and ethical attitudes. I argued at the outset that various Christian public voices are still significant in our secular, pluralistic culture, and that we need to be aware of the long-term political and social significance of the *theological* messages we propagate.

Just what vision of God do the liberal Protestant churches communicate to the public? Or more to the point: Does the secular public hear *anything at all* about God from those churches to challenge the clamorous public voice of the TV evangelists? When our public spokespersons are asked "religious" questions, do they have a *theological* message to communicate, or do they return as quickly as possible to moral comment on social ethics and public policy? The challenge is that the espousal of certain social and political stances rather than others must be seen to arise out of faith and theology. And they must arise out of grace.

I have pointed out that *grace*, not law or morality, is the "bottom line" for the Christian tradition—not only the Reformed and Methodist confessional family, but our biblical traditions, stretching far back to their early Hebraic roots. The God of Israel is, from the beginning, the God of compassion, liberation and reconciliation. The message of Jesus, as well as the church's witness to him, is primarily one of grace. Not only his cross, but also his teaching and practice are depicted in the New Testament as replete with the grace of God. While judgment is not absent from either of the testaments, the overwhelming message is about a God who is to be thanked and praised for sheer goodness and love. We need to be suspicious of any doctrinal expression that obscures the goodness of God, and must miss no opportunity to speak—even publicly—about God's self-giving love in Christ, and about God's resurrection victory over all the powers of darkness and death. Our political public voice will then be, persistently, one of generosity and hope, whether we speak of criminal justice or of economic, social or international affairs.

If church members are to be "on board" with their leaders for a politics of generosity, and even support attitudes that are contrary to their own class interests, they will have to be built up and nourished in a theology of grace. Constant moral exhortations, not rooted in grace, will fail to motivate and inspire. Personal transformation in the Holy Spirit, within the faith community—not under law, but under grace—is the base from which a strong Christian public voice must proceed.[45]

Above all, we will not present ourselves as moral heroes. We are not better people than others. But we believe that we have received love beyond measure—a love that is offered and effective for all.

Notes

1 Timothy Gorringe, *God's Just Vengeance* (Cambridge: Cambridge University Press, 1996). I am indebted to Roger Hutchinson for bringing this book to my attention.

2 See a helpful discussion of this concept by Rebecca Chopp, "Reimagining Public Discourse," in *Black Faith and Public Talk: Critical Essays on James H. Cone's* Black Theology and Black Power, ed. Dwight N. Hopkins (Maryknoll, NY: Orbis, 1999), 150-64.

3 See, for example, *100 Huntley Street.*

4 Some examples of writing from the religious right that exhibit these attitudes are: Ralph Reed, *Active Faith: How Christians Are Changing the Soul of America* (New York: Free Press, 1996) and David E. Duke, *My Awakening: A Path to Racial Understanding* (Covington, LA: Free Speech Press, 1998). For an early critical assessment of the religious right, see Robert E. Webber, *The Moral Majority: Right or Wrong?* (Westchester, IL: Cornerstone, 1981).

5 See "The Great Divide," an article on the religious attitudes and public policy stances of Stockwell Day in *The Toronto Star,* 11 November 2000, B4.

6 See Episcopal Committee for Social Affairs, Canadian Conference of Catholic Bishops, "Ethical Reflections on the Economic Crisis" (1983) in *Ethics and Economics*, ed. Gregory Baum and Duncan Cameron (Toronto: James Lorimer, 1984), 3-18.

7 See Harold Wells, "Limitations of the Liberal Spirit: The Need for a Religious Left in the Year of Grace 2000," in *Genesis and the Millennium*, ed. Derek H. Davis (Waco, TX: J.M. Dawson Institute for Church-State Studies, Baylor University, 2000), 69-75.

8 A pastoral letter of Moderator Marion Best, supported by thirteen Conference presidents, called for congregational action to oppose the "war against the poor" (17 December 1995).

9 See a discussion of the United Church moderator's consultation on the economy in Ted Reeve ed., *God and the Market: Steps Toward a Moral Economy* (Toronto: United Church Publishing House, 2000).

10 The petition for the relief of Third World debt was signed by an estimated 640,000 Canadians, and 24,000,000 people worldwide (*Toronto Star,* 26 December 2000, A22). See the Canadian Ecumenical Jubilee Initiative (CEJI), *Making a New Beginning: Biblical Reflections on the Jubilee* (Toronto: CEJI, 1998); also *Sacred Earth, Sacred Community* (Toronto: CEJI, 2000).

11 See Roger Hutchinson's exploration of the role of religious conviction in public choice, as an exercise in comparative religious ethics in *Prophets, Pastors and Public Choices: Canadian Churches and the Mackenzie Valley Pipeline Debate* (Waterloo, ON: Wilfrid Laurier University Press, 1992).

12 Although the labels "mainline" and "liberal" are rather ambiguous and unsatisfactory, I use them in this essay for want of a better term to identify the historic Protestant churches in Canada, especially Presbyterian, Lutheran, United and Anglican which, together with the Roman Catholic Church, make up the so-called PLURA churches that work together in ecumenical coalitions.

13 Evidence of this would be, for example, the high vote in the 905 suburban areas around Toronto for the provincial Conservative government of Mike Harris. This is an area with a large Anglo-Saxon Protestant population, which overwhelmingly voted twice for Harris's "common sense revolution" in spite of the obvious antipathy of the churches to his policies.

14 I discuss this more fully in my article, "Theology for Reconciliation," in *The Reconciliation of Peoples: Challenge to the Churches,* ed. Gregory Baum and Harold Wells (Maryknoll, NY: Orbis, 1997).

15 Jon Sobrino, *Christology at the Crossroads,* trans. J. Drury (Maryknoll, NY: Orbis, 1976), 201-04.

16 The distinction between propitiation and expiation is challenged by some scholars. See the discussion by Gorringe, *God's Just Vengeance*, 38.

17 See a positive account of sacrifice by Jewish theologian Abraham Heschel in *The Prophets*, vol. 1 (New York: Harper and Row, 1962), 195-98.

18 An Old Testament example of this is the story of David's vengeance for the Gibeonites on the sons of Saul, in 2 Sam. 21. See the discussion of defilement by Paul Ricoeur, *The Symbolism of Evil,* trans. E. Buchanan (Boston, MA: Beacon Press, 1967), chap. 1.

19 See the discussion by Gorringe, *God's Just Vengeance,* 69-71.

20 J.H. Charlesworth, ed., *The Old Testament Pseudepigrapha,* vol. 2 (New York: Doubleday, 1985).

21 See Søren Kierkegaard's profound treatment of Abraham's faith in *Fear and Trembling* (Princeton, NJ: Princeton University Press, 1941).

22 Some other prophetic texts criticizing the sacrificial system are: Amos 5:21-24; Isa. 1:11-17, 43:22-24, 66:1-3; Jer. 7:22-23, 9:10; Ps. 50:8, 13, 23 and 51:16-17. C.F. Whitley in *The Prophetic Achievement* (London: A. R Mowbray, 1963) 63-92, argues, citing many other scholars, that the canonical prophets repudiated the sacrificial cult entirely. However, Abraham Heschel strongly argues the opposite in *The Prophets,* vol. 2, chap. 11.

23 Anselm of Canterbury, "Why God Became Man," in *A Scholastic Miscellany: Anselm to Ockham,* ed. and trans. Eugene R. Fairweather (Philadelphia: Westminster, 1956), 122.

24 Ibid., 150-51.

25 Ibid., 106, 112.

26 Dorothee Soelle, *Thinking About God: An Introduction to Theology* (Philadelphia: Trinity Press International, 1990), 120. See also Elizabeth Johnson, *She Who Is: The Mystery of God in Feminist Theological*

Discourse (New York: Crossroad, 1992), 208 and Mary Grey, *Redeeming the Dream: Feminism, Redemption and the Christian Tradition* (London: SPCK, 1989), 11-14.

27 See comment on Abelard by Gorringe, *God's Just Vengeance,* 108-17.

28 Peter Abailard, "Exposition of the Epistle to the Romans" in Fairweather, *A Scholastic Miscellany,* 283.

29 This connection is fundamental to the soteriology of the theologians of the early church and the Nicene Creed. It is spelled out massively in the twentieth century by Karl Barth, when he speaks of "the Judge judged in our place." Karl Barth, *Church Dogmatics,* IV/1, ed. G.W. Bromiley and T.F. Torrance; trans. G.W. Bromiley et al. (Edinburgh: T. & T. Clark, 1957), 211-83.

30 See Johnson on incarnate *sophia* in *She Who Is,* 150-69.

31 "Death in God" is the expression of Jürgen Moltmann in *The Crucified God,* trans. R.A. Wilson and J. Bowden (London: SCM Press, 1974), 207.

32 See a classic study of impassability by J.K. Mozley, *The Impassibility of God* (Cambridge: Cambridge University Press, 1926). For a thorough discussion of the question, see Catherine Mowry LaCugna, *God for Us: The Trinity and the Christian Life* (San Francisco: HarperSanFrancisco, 1991).

33 Moltmann, *The Crucified God,* 227. See his discussion of protest atheism, 219-27.

34 Johnson, *She Who Is*, 254.

35 Ibid., 263.

36 Quoted by Gorringe, *God's Just Vengeance,* 111.

37 Ibid., 110.

38 Abailard, "Exposition of the Epistle to the Romans," 283.

39 See the comment of Daniel Migliore, *Faith Seeking Understanding* (Grand Rapids, MI: Eerdmans, 1991), 153.

40 See, for example, Bernard of Clairvaux, quoted by Gorringe, *God's Just Vengeance,* 113-17.

41 Jürgen Moltmann discusses the concept of "open Trinity" in *The Trinity and the Kingdom,* trans. M. Kohl (San Francisco: Harper and Row, 1980), 94.

42 Sobrino, *Christology at the Crossroads*, 202.

43 Ibid., 224.

44 This approach is perhaps the oldest, being the view of a number of early theologians of the church, who spoke of Christ's victory over the devil in the cross and resurrection. It is championed by Gustaf Aulen in his book *Christus Victor,* trans. A.G. Hebert (New York: Macmillan, 1931).

45 The point is made eloquently by Ian Manson, "The United Church's Social Witness Over Seventy-Five Years," in *Touchstone* 18/3 (September 2000): 32-43.

5

"O DAY OF GOD, DRAW NIGH"

R.B.Y. Scott, the Church and the Call for Social Reconstruction

IAN MANSON

Throughout his career as professor of church and society, Roger Hutchinson has demonstrated that the work of the Christian church deserves serious study. In his classes on Christian ethics, he has consistently encouraged his students to examine the various reports and documents that different ecclesiastical commissions and councils have produced on a wide assortment of topics. In his published writings, he has analyzed the ways in which the institutional church has responded to the Great Depression of the 1930s, the Mackenzie Valley Pipeline debate and a host of other issues. As principal of Emmanuel College, he has ably administered an institution that educates a significant number of men and women for ministry in the United Church of Canada. And in his personal life, he has long been an active member of Trinity-St. Paul's United Church in Toronto. As teacher, scholar, educator and Christian, Hutchinson has constantly affirmed that the church's work is of critical importance, and he has contributed much to its life and witness.

In his conviction that the church's life is important and that its reflections on issues of public policy are deserving of critical attention, Hutchinson continues the work of a distinguished line of teachers and writers who have helped to build bridges between the church and the academy. Indeed, he stands clearly in the tradition of those members of

---

Notes to chapter 5 are on pp.109-11.

the Fellowship for a Christian Social Order (FCSO) featured in his dissertation who continued to remain active in the church after the organization's demise.[1] One such individual was R.B.Y. Scott, the noted biblical scholar who was national president of the FCSO between 1935 and 1938. Throughout his career in this country, Scott devoted significant time and energy to the work of the United Church of Canada. He taught in two of its colleges, wrote frequently for its denominational paper, participated actively in its courts, authored some well-loved hymns, and helped to write and develop several important reports. Scott believed that the church had an important contribution to make to the social and intellectual life of society, and he helped the United Church to respond with creativity and passion to a host of social, economic and intellectual challenges during the 1930s and 1940s.

Robert Balgarnie Young Scott was born in Toronto and graduated in theology from Knox College after earning a Ph.D. in oriental languages from the University of Toronto. He was ordained to the United Church ministry in 1926, and served the Ontario parish of Long Branch for two years before being appointed professor of Old Testament languages and literature at Union College in Vancouver. In 1931, Scott was chosen to be professor of Old Testament literature and exegesis at the United Theological College in Montreal, where he also served as registrar and dean of residence. When McGill University established its faculty of divinity in 1948, he became its first dean as well as professor of Old Testament. In 1955, he accepted the position of Danforth Professor of Religion at Princeton University, where he remained until his retirement in 1968.[2] Described by the United Church's first moderator, George Pidgeon, as a man who was "frank and open in his approach" with others, Scott combined a profound and detailed knowledge of the Old Testament with a passionate commitment to the United Church. For these reasons, Pidgeon urged his brother Leslie to encourage Principal James Smyth of Montreal to hire Scott to fill the vacant Old Testament position at United in 1931.[3] W.R. Taylor of the University of Toronto's Department of Semitics also recommended Scott for this appointment. He wrote that "Scott is probably the most outstanding man of the younger teachers in Britain and Canada in this field, and that therefore he would be the very best choice as successor to the late Professor A.R. Gordon." Furthermore, Taylor asserted that Scott "combined in a very remarkable way evangelical warmth with scholarly instincts and ambitions."[4] History shows that this faith in Scott was not misplaced. According to his long-time friend and colleague Wilfred Cantwell Smith, Scott was elected to membership in the Royal Society of Canada because of his "pre-eminence as a scholar, in the field of classical Hebrew and Biblical studies." In addition, he noted, Scott's "contribution in other related areas was also of high distinction—ranging from the cause of social justice in Canada, particularly during the Depression years, to Christian devotional life."[5]

The son of a Presbyterian minister, R.B.Y. Scott grew up in the church and was steeped in its heritage. From the outset, he understood the church to be "a special grouping of society" that was committed to "the nourishment and spread in mythological, dramatic, ideal and practical forms, of the fundamental affirmations about spiritual reality, and about the nature, meaning and goal of personal and social life," which were revealed through the biblical story and ultimately through Jesus Christ.[6] For Scott, the church served to enable people to experience God's presence so that they would be empowered to follow Jesus' way, resist the worldly forces of evil and live according to God's will for the world.

Scott clearly understood that the church faced serious challenges in undertaking this work. "If Jesus had confined Himself to a ministry to individuals and to preaching social salvation only in vague and general terms, He would never have been executed by the rulers of His people as a menace to the status quo," Scott suggested.[7] Because this path is full of dangers, throughout its history the church has "often acquiesced in the resistance to change offered by those elements in society whose power is threatened by social and ethical advance." Therefore, Scott believed that "regenerative forces" must constantly arise within the Christian community to demand "that the Church abandon her complacency and move forward toward the ideal society which it is one of her tasks to establish."[8] He contended that this calling was central to the mission of the FCSO.

Throughout his career, Scott worked to enable the church to ground its life more clearly in the revelations about God, humanity and human society found in the Bible. In his view, Scripture affirms that God is an active presence in the world, and has been from the beginning of time. In 1945, Scott wrote: God is "a living personal Being of unique ethical character, not a static or abstract Being but a 'Doer,' Lord of nature and history, whose good purpose for humanity leads to his concern for man's character and behavior, and to his participation in man's historic experience."[9] Scott believed that the biblical writers saw God as being present throughout history, and he condemned as false the view that God is a benign deity who has abandoned creation and left the world to its own devices. Instead, he constantly affirmed that "God's essential Nature is Justice, Mercy, Truth, Beauty, Peace, Creative and Redemptive Love."[10]

Scott asserted that these understandings permeated the Old Testament and received their most complete expression through the pronouncements of the biblical prophets. They embodied the true "spiritual essence" of Old Testament faith and continued the religious heritage that had originated with Moses and that was later given most complete expression by Jesus. "In the prophets themselves is found the clearest expression of what is distinctive and creative throughout the religious experience and tradition of Israel," he stated.[11] Isaiah, Amos, Hosea, Jeremiah and other prophetic figures had shared some "extraordinary religious experiences" whereby they had encountered Yahweh, the one true living God. These moments "were not only emotional," but also involved "an irresistible compulsion to deliver a message which they had received" from God.[12] Theirs "was a mysticism of faith, of understanding and of action" that left them acutely conscious "of the mind of God."[13] Each prophet was "awed by a majesty" and touched by "a personal will that called for his own surrender and obedience." They had all known a great "intensity of feeling associated with the realization of the divine presence" and understood that Yahweh "is an active and interested party to what happens" in the world.[14] Thus, the prophets "were conscious instruments of an immediate divine commission and demand" and gave voice to God's eternal word.[15]

Scott challenged the church to take the prophetic tradition seriously, and to recognize that the prophets believed that loving and serving God involves living in social relationships that are consistent with Yahweh's teachings and commandments. Through Moses, God had made a covenant with Israel that had established the basis for the type of life that God intended. As understood by Moses, this covenant affirmed "that the nation is constituted in terms of religion and social ethics, that God and people, a man and his neighbour, are linked by a single covenant in a single living structure of relationships."[16] In Moses' day, this impulse was reflected in the fact that "economic wealth was in flocks and herds, held in common, or by the head of the family in trust for the family and its dependents." Even in later days, when agriculture became the principal base of subsistence and families began to own their fields and vineyards, "the 'rights' of private property" remained "subordinate to the human and social good." However, leaders later departed from this egalitarian approach to economic organization. "Solomon (and probably David himself in his later reign) forsook the principle of share-and-share-alike" that had long characterized Israelite life. Solomon's magnificent court, huge army and great building program were paid for by his loyal subjects, "who were supposed to be his brethren and were in fact his slaves." His cruel "conscription of labour crippled their efforts at self-support, and a crushing weight of taxation drove them to mortgage their land and their persons."[17] Through these and other oppressive practices, Israel had become full of "treachery, exploitation, oppression, cruelty, anger, strife, greed of money, luxury and power; dishonesty, venal justice, lying, violence, murder."[18] Because of humanity's ongoing proclivity to sin, the covenant between God and Israel had been shattered. "The fabric of the covenant was rent in twain when enslaved Israelites and a landless proletariat confronted the *nouveaux riches* on their great estates," Scott contended. "Property had lost its religious sanction as the instrument of the common life, and, being equated now with private wealth, had become instead a barrier to neighbourhood."[19] The prophets' task was to call upon the people of Israel to repent, turn away from their sinful ways, open themselves anew to God's presence, and embrace a new covenant in which God would write on human hearts "the law those hearts refused when it was imposed from without."[20]

Therefore, the prophets asserted that only a widespread spiritual and religious reawakening was capable of lifting Israel from bondage and re-establishing its covenant with God. In their view, such a renewal would uphold the "genuine conviction that the Supreme Power in the beginning, now and in the end, is a God who seeks to realize his goodness in the life-experience of individuals and of a people."[21] Their message "contains an imperative that society be so ordered as to make possible and to support a way of life which is *good* in the eyes of Yahweh."[22] In prophetic understanding, the "realization of Yahweh's will is pictured in a state of social life where there is an end of war and economic privation, and where social corruption and oppression is ended."[23]

Scott maintained that Jesus' life and teachings continued this legacy, and that Jesus' followers in the church are to embrace this heritage as theirs. Through Jesus, God's very essence is revealed to the world, in that "what Jesus was, God eternally is."[24] In Jesus, one finds "the same insistence as in the prophets, that the institutions of society must foster man's highest life in harmonious ethical relationship with his fellows and with God."[25] Like his ancestors, Jesus did not "simply preach a spiritual message in the confidence that as a result, somehow, eventually, His hearers would attack the evils and heal the pain of their society." Rather, Jesus himself "went about teaching, preaching and healing; for, to attack the evils and to heal the pain was precisely to preach the Gospel of the Kingdom in concrete terms."[26] In these ways, Jesus carried forward the prophetic heritage and gave it new expression. Jesus revealed that "ignorance, sickness, hunger and cold are not part of God's good purpose" for any person. Instead, God's "abundant gifts, through a right economic organization of society, should be used to provide for all His children the necessities and amenities of daily life." For these reasons, Jesus offered the "good news" of the gospel "specially and specifically to toilers and sufferers, to the poor, the weak, and the oppressed."[27]

Clergy and laity alike were encouraged to share this message with passion and intelligence, and to make this work central to ecclesiastical life. Although Scott admitted that the church's historic identification with society's political and economic elite posed some "serious obstacles" to this work, he believed that the church's "prophetic minority" could help it overcome its resistance. In his view, the gospel demands "that the Church abandon her complacency and move forward toward the ideal society which it is one of her tasks to establish." Although "the mass of Christians may not feel the same urgency in the matter, they have not the same interest in maintaining the status quo as the groups in power, and therefore provide the advancing minority with a potentially responsive constituency, since they can be appealed to from basic Christian premises."[28]

Thus, it was important for the church to critique a wide range of commonly held assumptions from the perspective of "the bar of Christian conscience." While Scott was not prepared to "say outright that private property is wrong," he believed "property has no sacredness comparable to the sacredness of human life" and that "no vested interests shall withstand the concern of the Christian community to secure the conditions of the good life for all." Furthermore, he affirmed, "the concern of Christ is with the whole of life," so "we must look critically at the working of the profit motive in our commercial life, at the conditions by which power and privilege are obtained in our society, at our political life, at our international relations, at the basis of our cultural establishments, at our own personal, habitual manner of living."[29]

To demonstrate that such concerns are central to Christian theology, in 1936 Scott and Gregory Vlastos of Queen's University edited a volume of essays contributed by various FCSO members entitled *Towards the Christian Revolution*. In it, John Line discussed both the theological and the philosophical grounds for this approach to faith, while Vlastos outlined the ethical aspects of this argument. Eugene Forsey related these insights to the contemporary economic situation, J. King Gordon addressed the political tensions of the day and Martyn Estall (under the pen name "Propheticus"[30]) compared the FCSO approach to social reconstruction with modern Marxism. In addition to co-editing the volume, Scott contributed a chapter on the Bible and a discussion of how Christian worship can fuel and sustain this venture.

The book generated a good deal of public discussion, and Scott was not afraid to offer a spirited defence of their work. For example, in 1940 he challenged a statement that appeared in a letter to the editor of *Saturday Night* magazine claiming that Eugene Forsey and all the other authors of *Towards the Christian Revolution* (including himself) had abandoned the church in favour of Communism. According to this correspondent, these writers had substituted "faith in Marx for faith in the Founder of Christianity as a prerequisite to Christian salvation."[31] Scott firmly rejected this claim. Their critic ignored and "does not challenge the argument in the first four chapters of the book which lay the foundation in distinctively Christian theology and ethics, and in the light of which the subsequent discussion of the economic problem must be understood." The writer had failed to recognize that the book was written by "ministers and members active in the work of the Christian Church." Furthermore, Scott declared, "no one of the contributors to this volume is a communist" and the book's "basic premises and conclusions would be unacceptable to any thoroughgoing Marxist."[32] Instead, he concluded, the book demonstrated how "the faith of the prophets and Jesus" was "a disturbing revolutionary force" and that, in modern times, "our historic faith has revolutionary resources" for the economic crisis.[33]

Scott believed that this basic theme permeates the biblical story, but suggested that the vagaries of scriptural translation often prevented the church's leaders from grasping its true meaning.[34] In an article for *The Expository Times*, Scott demonstrated the importance of linguistic analysis by looking at the parable of the unjust steward in Luke 16. He analyzed a popular translation of verse 9 of that passage, which read: "And I say unto you, make to yourselves friends *by means of* the mammon of unrighteousness, that when it shall fail, they may receive you into the eternal tabernacles." In this form, Scott believed, the passage "suggests a cynical worldly-wisdom foreign to the Gospels" and also "to the moral teaching of Israel's sages." However, an examination of the Greek text reveals that this discrepancy was due to the mistranslation of the word *ek*.[35] Thus, Scott suggested that a more accurate translation of Luke 16:9 is: "Make to yourselves friends *without* (or, apart from) unrighteous mammon, that, when it fails you (as it is bound to do), they may receive you into the eternal abodes." Scott maintained that this version readily corresponded with other Synoptic sayings, such as "you cannot serve God and mammon," "a person's life consists not in the abundance of the things which they possess" and "lay not up for yourselves treasures upon the earth." Jesus' true message can therefore clearly be seen in this passage.[36]

With this message clearly in place, the church was called to relate these tenets to some of the central social and political questions of the time. One of these initiatives was the Commission on Church, Nation and World Order, which the 1942 General Council of the United Church established in order to develop a plan for a postwar Canadian society based on Christian principles. Scott served as the commission's research director and also wrote several drafts of its report. The final document identified some "basic Christian beliefs concerning man and society," offered a "Christian charter for man and society" and then focused on how these principles might be applicable to the realms of Canadian economics, politics and social affairs. In it, the United Church endorsed the development of a comprehensive plan for a full welfare state. It emphasized that the objectives of "full employment, adequate production of goods serving basic needs, wise and just distribution, and basic security for all" should guide Canadian public policy.[37] Human well-being was deemed more important than the quest for profit, and the state had an important role to play in protecting the public interest. To this end, the report encouraged the federal government to develop policies concerning health, education, employment, housing, labour relations, social insurance, social security and taxation to ensure that everyone's basic human needs were met. By taking control of selected economic sectors through the establishment of Crown corporations, the state could help protect the weak and vulnerable from the vagaries of free-market economics and ensure that basic levels of food, clothing and shelter would be the right of all Canadians. The report also urged the government to develop a publicly funded, universal medicare system, an unemployment insurance program and a full employment strategy.[38]

Scott fully endorsed these proposals and affirmed the church's right to make such suggestions. However, he also recognized that, in working to establish a new social and economic order, the church must *not* neglect the spiritual dimensions of faith. Indeed, he believed that radical social transformation was impossible without a corresponding spiritual rebirth. The gospel of Jesus Christ does not provide "any ready-made economic, political and cultural alternatives," Scott informed the 1936 annual meeting of the United Church's Board of Evangelism and Social Service. "Always the Kingdom of God stands over against any given human situation; always the relativity of ethical achievement remains; always we are sinners standing in need of the Divine forgiveness."[39] Nevertheless, he affirmed that "God is already at work in the turmoil of our time, using refractory human material" to remould and reshape persons and communities to reflect God's will more closely. What sinful and self-sufficient humanity cannot do, "God is waiting to do through those who will discern His presence, surrender to His forgiveness and believe in His creative power. This is a historic moment, and we must choose whom we shall serve."[40] Therefore, God's call is "for instant response, for decision....Repent and believe!"

In Scott's opinion, the regular practice of Christian worship is necessary to bring about the type of personal and social transformation God wills. Through public worship, the church provides Christians with the language and symbols through which they can give expression to the meaning in which their lives are rooted. A Christian "must have some symbol of the Kingdom, some symbol worthy to express his reverence and his hope, some authentic voice of the human spirit refusing to be the slave of economic processes and aspiring to the liberty of the children of God," Scott noted. Therefore, the regular practice of Christian worship is an integral part of transforming any social order. "Christians who see the necessity of economic change because of capitalism's denial of the first principles of our religion should be the first to see also that the forms of public worship must make those principles clear and compelling."[41]

Scott also believed that the singing of appropriate hymns is key to this type of transformation. In a *New Outlook* article entitled "A Call for New Hymns," Scott told of a men's group that had listened enthusiastically to a message calling for significant social change, but that concluded its meeting "with a hymn announcing with solemn reiteration that it was well, it was well, with each man's soul." Although he realized that hymns that cultivate personal piety have their place, he felt that "this ancient ditty" clearly illustrated how "forms of worship become a hollow sham when they are only words and sounds from which all meaning and relevance have evaporated." Thus, it is important to develop new hymns that are "appropriate to a changing intellectual and spiritual climate" and that also express the "convictions and aspirations" of the present age.[42]

Throughout his career, Scott maintained that the Christian church can be an important force for social reconstruction. By focusing on the biblical record, paying particular attention to the prophets, and heeding the word and way of Christ, the church has the resources to overcome human sin and transform human attitudes so that a new type of society can be created. Scott believed that even though the church would encounter frequent resistance in pursuing this course, a new day would dawn and a new realm of justice would come upon the land. As he put it in his well-known 1937 hymn:

> O day of God, draw nigh
> In beauty and in power,
> Come with your timeless judgement now
> To match our present hour.

Bring to our troubled minds,
Uncertain and afraid,
The quiet of a steadfast faith,
Calm of a call obeyed.

Bring justice to our land,
That all may dwell secure,
And finely build for days to come
Foundations that endure.

Bring to our world of strife
Your sovereign word of peace,
That war may haunt the earth no more
And desolation cease.

O day of God, draw nigh
As at creation's birth;
Let there be light again,
And set your judgments in the earth.[43]

Roger Hutchinson, I believe, would agree.

Notes

1 Roger Hutchinson, in "The Fellowship for a Christian Social Order: A Social Ethical Analysis of a Christian Socialist Movement" (Th.D. diss., Victoria University, 1975), explains the split that eventually occurred in the FCSO between those who felt that the organization should continue to work within the church and those who felt that the group must become independent of all external organizations.

2 R.B.Y. Scott biographical file, United Church of Canada Archives, Toronto.

3 Letter from George Pidgeon to Leslie Pidgeon (23 March 1931). George Pidgeon Papers, box 14, file 261, United Church of Canada Archives, Toronto.

4 Letter from W.R. Taylor to George Pidgeon (7 March 1931). George Pidgeon Papers, box 14, file 261, United Church of Canada Archives, Toronto.

5 Wilfred Cantwell Smith, "Robert Balgarnie Young Scott, 1899-1987," *Transactions of the Royal Society of Canada* 5/4 (1989): 431.

6 R.B.Y. Scott, *The Gospel of the Kingdom* (Montreal: FCSO, 1936), 11.

7 R.B.Y. Scott, "Concrete Evangelism," *The New Outlook*, 16 September 1936, 860.

8 R.B.Y. Scott and David MacLennan, "The Christian Contribution to Rebuilding of Society," *The New Outlook*, 6 March 1935, 244.

9 R.B.Y. Scott, "Prophets, Prophecy," in *An Encyclopedia of Religion*, ed. Vergilins Ferm (New York: The Philosophical Library, 1945), 615.

10 R.B.Y. Scott memorandum, "Christian Standards and Principles Which Should Govern the Social Order." George Pidgeon Papers, box 9, file 177, United Church of Canada Archives, Toronto.

11 R.B.Y. Scott, *The Relevance of the Prophets* (New York: The Macmillan Company, 1944), 180.

12 Ibid., 84.

13 Ibid., 88.

14 Ibid., 107-09.

15 Ibid., 104.

16 Scott, *The Gospel of the Kingdom*, 2.

17 R.B.Y. Scott, "The Biblical Basis," in *Towards the Christian Revolution,* ed. R.B.Y. Scott and Gregory Vlastos (Chicago and New York: Willett, Clark & Company, 1936), 84-85.

18 Scott, *The Relevance of the Prophets*, 124-25.

19 Scott, "The Biblical Basis," 85.

20 Scott, *The Relevance of the Prophets*, 130.

21 Scott, "Prophets, Prophecy," 615.

22 Scott, *The Relevance of the Prophets*, 158.

23 R.B.Y. Scott, "The Real Significance of the Hebrew Prophets," *Christian Social Action* 2/4 (October 1940): 1.

24 R.B.Y. Scott, G.R. Craig and G.G.D. Kilpatrick, "Statement of Faith (First Draft), typescript dated December 1939 and prepared for the United Church's Commission on Christian Faith, Commission on Christian Faith Papers, box 2, file 18, p. 2, United Church of Canada Archives, Toronto.

25 Scott, "The Biblical Basis," 82.

26 Scott, "Concrete Evangelism," 860.

27 R.B.Y. Scott, "What Has Christianity to Say on Social and Economic Questions?" *The New Outlook*, 11 April 1934, 267.

28 Scott and MacLennan, "The Christian Contribution," 244.

29 Scott, "What Has Christianity to Say on Social and Economic Questions?" 267.

30 "Propheticus" is identified in Hutchinson, "The Fellowship for a Christian Social Order," 58.

31 Letter to the editor, *Saturday Night*, 6 January 1940, 4.

32 R.B.Y. Scott, "Christian Revolution," *Saturday Night*, 20 January 1940, 5.

33 Scott and Vlastos, Preface to *Towards the Christian Revolution*.

34 R.B.Y. Scott, "The Case for Hebrew," *Canadian Journal of Religious Thought* 4/2 (March-April 1929): 107.

35 To mean "by means of" rather than "without" or "free from."

36 R.B.Y. Scott, "The Parable of the Unjust Steward," *The Expository Times* 49 (October 1937-September 1938): 235.

37 *A Report of the Commission on the Church, Nation and World Order* (Toronto: Board of Evangelism and Social Service of the United Church of Canada, 1942), 19.
38 *A Report of the Commission on the Church, Nation and World Order*, 20-24.
39 R.B.Y. Scott, "The Evangel of God," in *Play the Man*. Twelfth Annual Report, United Church Board of Evangelism and Social Service of the United Church of Canada, 1936, 42.
40 Ibid., 40.
41 R.B.Y. Scott, "The Cultus of the Community," in *Towards the Christian Revolution*, 195-96.
42 R.B.Y. Scott, "A Call for New Hymns," *The New Outlook*, 27 May 1936, 505.
43 R.B.Y. Scott, "O Day of God, Draw Nigh," in *Voices United: The Hymn and Worship Book of the United Church of Canada* (Toronto: United Church Publishing House, 1996), 688.

6

ETHICAL VALUES AND CANADIAN FOREIGN POLICY

CRANFORD PRATT

Introduction

Roger Hutchinson has written extensively and in depth of the efforts of Canadian churches to make public policy more ethically responsible. He has sought to clarify the relationship of this social-activist work of Canadian churches to their Christian faith. He has studied in detail the basis and dynamics of the cooperation that the Canadian churches have achieved as they pursue these objectives. He has recurrently warned that such inter-church cooperation is more likely to be sustained if it is based on a close examination of the specifics of the injustices to which the churches are responding, rather than on a search for either a shared theological foundation for the proposed social action or a common understanding of the underlying systemic causes of the social harm they are seeking to erase. He has been concerned with the quality and adequacy of the policies advocated by the churches and, more fundamental still, with the persuasiveness of the arguments used to advance their claim that government policy ought to be more responsive to ethics.

This essay asks a closely related and somewhat subversive question: What success have the churches and other concerned civil society organizations had in their efforts to promote a more ethically responsive Canadian foreign policy? It seeks to answer this question by look-

Notes to chapter 6 are on pp. 130-33.

ing at the sustained efforts of inter-church groups and non-governmental organizations (NGOs) in Canada over several decades to influence Canadian policies in regard to two major foreign policy issues, on which ethical considerations might, prima facie, be expected to have had significant influence—foreign aid and apartheid South Africa.

Approaches to Canadian Foreign Policy

The scholarly literature on Canadian foreign policy does not encourage hope that ethics have had much impact on Canadian policies. Two theoretical approaches, the statist and the dominant class, have dominated this literature in recent years.[1] Statist analysts emphasize the breadth of the autonomy enjoyed by senior decision-makers in government as they shape Canadian foreign policy. Many of these analysts concede that public opinion sets parameters within which this autonomy can be exercised, but, in their view, these parameters are very broad and have rarely constrained senior decision-makers. Statists do not suggest that decision-makers are totally impervious to lobbying for greater ethical sensitivity in Canadian foreign policy, but they point to the wide range of initiatives available to these decision-makers to win public acceptance of the policies they favour. Typically in statist analyses, these policies encompass an amalgam of objectives, some reflecting their judgment of what will serve the national interest, and others autonomous interests specific to the government itself or to the unit within the department to which the decision-makers are attached.

The dominant class approach shares the statist recognition that senior decision-makers enjoy significant autonomy in the shaping of Canadian foreign policy. However, it offers its own hypothesis on how that autonomous power is often exercised. I have, for example, argued that senior decision-makers constitute a highly professional corps, sharing a common understanding of international politics and a common view that their responsibility is to advance Canadian interests internationally. Central to this cluster of dominant attitudes and convictions, this ideology, is an acceptance that the health of the economic system, on which rests the prosperity of Canadian society, depends on the profitability of capital and the confidence of capitalists. As a result, these decision-makers exhibit a particular sensitivity to the long-term interests of capitalism in Canada. Alongside this structurally determined component of the ideology that is dominant among senior foreign policy decision-makers, dominant class theory identifies a second, central component—a concern to preserve and expand Canadian influence internationally and to contain those states that are seen as potential enemies.[2]

Thus, neither a statist nor a dominant class approach suggests that ethical considerations have been a significant component of the dominant world view of senior Canadian foreign policy decision-makers or that lobbying from within Canadian civil society has forced them to become more engaged with issues such as sustained oppression and severe poverty beyond our borders. Each sees such "soft" policy objectives as promoting human rights or helping the world's poorest peoples as being largely filtered out within the decision-making process. Dominant class theorists emphasize the role of the ideology that is dominant within Canadian decision-making circles in sifting out such objectives, while statist theorists identify the interests that act as this sieve in less ideological and more narrowly bureaucratic terms. However, it is clearly implicit in each that civil society efforts to promote more ethical foreign policies have had but little impact.

A closer look at the development of Canadian foreign aid policies and Canadian policy toward apartheid South Africa—two policies that have long been the focus of sustained ethical lobbying by the Canadian churches, the NGO community and many other civil society public interest groups—suggests that a more nuanced approach may be needed to secure a more ethically responsive Canadian foreign policy.

Ethical Values and Canadian Foreign Aid[3]

The literature on the determinants of Canadian aid policies gives emphatic mention to a surprisingly wide range of influences. These include, for example, the politics of the Cold War, the example and influence of major donors, the importance attached by the Canadian government to Canada's primary alliances, Canada's historic links with the Commonwealth and la Francophonie, bureaucratic politics within the Canadian government, and the government's particular responsiveness to Canadian trade and investment interests. Canadian ethical values, in contrast, are hardly mentioned in this literature.[4]

Certainly at its inception, Canadian development assistance was very much a product of Cold War alliance politics. In the late 1950s and early 1960s, the United States, along with France and Britain, had significant foreign aid programs. As the purpose of this aid was to counter any expansion of Soviet influence, the United States pressed its allies to assume part of this burden. Canadian aid thus began, timidly and somewhat begrudgingly, as an obligation arising from Canada's major alliances rather than issuing directly from the ethical values of Canadian society.

There was then, for at most ten years, an exceptional confluence of factors and events, which produced a very rapid expansion of the aid program and a sustained effort to ensure that it reached and helped the poorest people and countries. The most fundamental of these factors was the upsurge in deep-rooted, public support for strong social welfare programs in Canada.[5] This essentially ethical development within the dominant Canadian public philosophy created an intellectual and ideological environment in Canada that made foreign aid seem almost self-evidently a particularly appropriate way to contain Communism. These ethical values, as Lumsdaine persuasively argues, must be seen as an essential precondition of the foreign aid programs that became a significant feature of the foreign policies of most developed capitalist countries. Without the widely shared conviction that governments must concern themselves domestically with the welfare of the poor, generous foreign aid programs to help citizens of other lands would have been politically inconceivable.

For decades these values shaped the public discourse about foreign aid. Public-opinion polls in Canada, at least until recently, have long confirmed that a substantial majority of Canadians support Canadian foreign aid and that they do so for primarily ethical reasons. Time and again, when asked why they support Canadian foreign aid, Canadians have ranked humanitarian considerations far higher than such narrowly national reasons as advancing Canadian trade and political interests. Ethical values were equally central to the policy recommendations offered by each of the three major parliamentary committees that have reviewed Canadian aid policies since 1975.[6] Finally, ethical considerations were centrally emphasized in each of the official policy statements on Canadian aid policies issued in this era, the first in 1975 and the second in 1987.[7]

Several additional factors specific to those years powerfully reinforced the impact of ethically founded arguments for foreign aid. There was a surge of citizen concern over global poverty and a great increase in the number and strength of Canadian NGOs working on Third World issues. The government, recognizing this, presented the aid program as a humanitarian, rather than a Cold War, enterprise. This in turn enabled supporters of a generous foreign aid program to use the rhetoric of the government to advantage as they sought to lessen the use of foreign aid for the pursuit of commercial and geopolitical objectives. As well, recruitment of many individuals from the NGO community for the newly established Canadian International Development Agency (CIDA) created a core of officials who lobbied for a more ethically responsive aid policy from within the government bureaucracy.

These efforts were aided by a prosperous economy and rising government revenues, which allowed an easy expansion of the aid program. Equally relevant, the Liberal government felt a political need in the late 1960s to demonstrate that, despite its reluctance to criticize the United States' war in Vietnam, it was well able to articulate a foreign policy different from that of the United States. Because of the strength of social idealism in Canada at that time, a major foreign aid policy that was genuinely committed to humane internationalist objectives was seen as a particularly appropriate way to demonstrate this ability.

This confluence of circumstances worked to the distinct advantage of the aid program. For about ten years, from 1966 to 1976, Canadian aid did seem to respond significantly to ethical values.[8] In these years it grew at a quite prodigious rate, rising from 0.20 percent of Canada's gross national product (GNP) in 1965 to 0.55 percent ten years later, and became increasingly focused on genuine development objectives.[9] As well, in 1975, as if confirming and consolidating the humanitarian and developmental focus of Canadian aid, the government endorsed a five-year development assistance strategy that reflected ethical considerations to a far more substantial degree than had any earlier policy statements.[10]

However, the greater centrality of ethical values in the shaping of Canada's aid program did not last. The global economic crisis of the post-OPEC era and long-term structural problems in the Canadian economy, to which it drew attention, crowded out any concern for global equity. Canada became increasingly preoccupied with its relations with the United States and with Canada's membership in the Economic Summit. Those urging that more effective expression be given internationally to Canadian humanitarian values were suddenly seen as naive.

The appointment of Michel Dupuy as president of CIDA in March 1977 signalled a major change in aid policy. In the judgment of most CIDA observers, Canadian international development assistance was, from that appointment on, increasingly subverted to serve Canadian trade and foreign policy interests. Humanitarian and development considerations were not obliterated, but very often they yielded place to self-interested Canadian objectives. Examples of this are many.[11]

The 1975 CIDA strategy paper with its clear humane internationalist thrust quickly ceased to be a major determinant of policy. Instead, CIDA was called upon to give far greater emphasis to Canadian trade and foreign policy interests. In the 1980s, CIDA developed major programs in countries such as Thailand, Indonesia and the Philippines to provide an entree to important and rapidly expanding markets for Canadian exporters. It introduced a range of programs that made Canadian aid dependent on the awarding of contracts to Canadian businesses. Canadian emergency food aid—indeed, all Canadian food aid—remained very narrowly tied to Canadian products, and the value of that aid to the recipients was further reduced by the inclusion of less appropriate products that were, however, in current surplus in Canada. CIDA, in short, had become, in the words of Dupuy's successor, Margaret Catley-Carlson, "a policy-taker not a policy-maker."[12]

With the collapse of the Soviet Union in 1989, the geopolitical reasons for Western aid evaporated. Since then, CIDA's budget has been very severely cut, far more severely than that of most other government departments. Moreover, the government's overwhelming preoccupation with improving Canada's competitive position in the international economic system has eroded the humane internationalist focus of Canadian aid policies. This erosion is easily traced. In 1975, the CIDA strategy paper had stated that "assistance would be concentrated in those countries that are at the lower level of the development scale" and that CIDA would "give highest priority to projects and programs aimed at improving the living and working conditions of the least privileged of the recipient countries."[13] In 1987, the Standing Committee on External Affairs and International Trade stated that "the primary purpose of Canadian official development assistance is to help the poorest countries and people,"[14] a statement of primary purpose that the government's strategy paper for CIDA, *Sharing Our Future,* embodied in CIDA's Development Charter. Seven years later, a Special Joint Committee of Parliament reviewing Canadian foreign policy was equally emphatic. It stated that "the primary purpose of Canadian Official Development Assistance is to reduce poverty by providing effective assistance to the poorest people, in those countries that most need and can use our help."[15]

> In sharp contrast to each of these pronouncements, *Canada in the World* declared that:International Assistance is a vital instrument for the achievement of the three key objectives being pursued by the Government. It is an investment in prosperity and employment. It connects the Canadian economy to some of the world's fastest growing markets…[It] contributes to global security…[and] is one of the clearest international expressions of Canadian values.[16]

The government could hardly have made clearer its resolve that Canada's aid policy was to give priority to trade and foreign policy objectives.

Nevertheless, the humanitarian component within Canada's aid program was not obliterated. Indeed, it retained a resilience that is not easily explained in either neo-realist (i.e., statist) or dominant class terms. Even as the aid budget was cut, the humanitarian thrust of its official objectives diffused and its programs increasingly focused on narrowly national economic objectives, the impact of ethical values could still be discerned. Substantial Canadian aid still continued to be sent to very poor countries of little economic or political interest to Canada. Meeting the basic needs of the poorest was freshly reaffirmed as a centrally important objective of CIDA policies. The NGO community continued to speak out for enduring humane internationalist values. And each time a parliamentary committee reviewed aid policies, it called for a renewal of CIDA's primary commitment to humanitarian objectives. Thus, in the years since 1976, even though the factors that are central to a dominant class perspective regained their predominance, a determined rearguard action from within CIDA and from civil society has been able to lessen the erosion of ethical influences upon the Canadian foreign aid program.

Ethics and Canadian Policy toward Apartheid South Africa[17]

Until well into the 1950s, the sentiments of Canadians toward South Africa and Canadian foreign policy toward that country were in substantial harmony.[18] The dominant public attitude was focused on the white minority and was sympathetic and uncritical. South Africa had been a trusted ally in two world wars. It had evolved, as had Canada, from being a British colony to becoming one of the core members of the Commonwealth. Its internal tensions between its English and Afrikaner populations were in many ways similar to those in Canada between English-speaking and French-speaking Canadians. There was little interest in or knowledge of the black majority. They were seen, if contemplated at all, as untutored wards of the whites, similar to, but more populous than, the Canadian indigenous peoples. Parallel to these dominant sentiments and in no way in conflict with them, Canadian foreign policy toward South Africa was that of a trusting ally and a good international friend.

Beginning in the late 1950s, the overall Canadian view of South Africa shifted. The 1948 South African election (in which the vast majority of those permitted to vote were white) brought the Nationalist Party to power for the first time. It was determined to entrench fully in law and in practice racial segregation and white political supremacy. Leading figures in the United States, Britain and elsewhere condemned the new apartheid regime and organized international protests against it. Gradually, the Canadian consciousness awakened to the fate of South Africa's black majority. An increasing number of Canadians came to recognize that the South African government was in fact a highly repressive regime whose constitution, policies and practices had accomplished a total consolidation of white supremacy over the black majority. Although the older, previously dominant, Canadian attitudes based on ties of race and history with the white South Africans continued to be a political force, by the late 1960s many in Canada had become strongly critical of South Africa's apartheid policies. They began to ally themselves with South African blacks rather than with the ruling white minority, and they pressed for Canadian policies that would reflect these sentiments.

Canadian churches were among the first structures within civil society to voice these sentiments. The inter-church coalition, the

Taskforce on the Churches and Corporate Responsibility, played a leading role within the wider anti-apartheid movements in Canada, as those movements grew in strength and their impact increased.[19] Black resistance to the apartheid regime intensified and, in reaction to it, the regime sought with increasing brutality to block the prospects for any meaningful reform. International support, particularly from the rest of Africa and other newly independent countries, consolidated behind the African National Congress (ANC) and its demand for black majority rule in South Africa. This support was reflected in mounting pressure in the General Assembly of the United Nations for economic sanctions and other vigorous measures against the South African regime. These developments in turn reinforced the commitment of those pressing for stronger Canadian policies and augmented their numbers.

Canadian policy was not entirely impervious to these developments. The most dramatic illustration of this came in 1960-61, before there were significant organized anti-apartheid forces in Canada. Prime Minister John Diefenbaker, rejecting the advice of his Cabinet colleagues and the Department of External Affairs, supported the demand of the newly independent members of the Commonwealth that South Africa should be permitted to remain in the Commonwealth only if it accepted a statement of principle which identified racial equality as a central, unifying principle of the Commonwealth. It was a decision of great importance, for otherwise the Commonwealth would have divided along racial lines on the issue, with Britain and the other three older members standing against a probably unanimous phalanx of non-white members. However, Diefenbaker's decision did not in fact herald any ongoing Canadian leadership on the issue. Over the next twenty-five years, during which both the oppression in South Africa and Africans' demands for international intervention on their behalf very significantly increased, Canadian policy, though marked by rhetorical denunciations of apartheid, included only the most minimal of initiatives.

This is best illustrated by the new policy toward South Africa, which the then Secretary of State for External Affairs, Donald Jamieson, introduced in 1977.[20] Canada at that time, along with the United States, Britain and France, strove to deflect the intense pressure at the United Nations for the introduction of diplomatic and economic sanctions against South Africa because of its illegal occupation of Namibia. Canada needed to improve its image as a convincing opponent of apartheid. The 1977 policy statement was therefore presented to demonstrate Canada's determination to pressure the South African regime into meaningful reforms.

On the surface, it appeared to do so. For example, Jamieson announced that the new policy would be phasing out " all…its Government-sponsored, commercial-support activities in South Africa."[21] It would develop a code of conduct for Canadian companies in South Africa. It would no longer permit the government account of the Export Development Corporation (EDC) to assist any transaction relating to South Africa, and it would review the tax concessions granted to Canadian companies operating in Namibia. However, it swiftly became clear that the claims made by government spokespersons on behalf of these initiatives were much inflated.

The restrictions on the ability of the EDC to assist Canadian trading with South Africa in fact applied only to the government account, which had been largely unused for South African transactions, and not to a second account, the corporate account, which had been in active use. Moreover, the EDC facility most valuable to Canadians trading with South Africa, that which provided export insurance, remained open. There were equally vast gaps between the government's early rhetoric about the new policy and many other features of the policy as it was implemented. The code of conduct, when it finally emerged, was minimal in definition, voluntary and not compulsory, and indifferently administered. There was no change made to tax laws applying to Canadian firms in Namibia. The importance of the withdrawal of the three Canadian trade commissioners was minimized by the simultaneous local appointment by the Canadian ambassador in Pretoria of a commercial officer with experience in Rhodesia in sanction-busting. The 1977 announcement had been made to strengthen Canadian influence at the United Nations. It clearly never was the government's intention to enforce it vigorously, let alone to build upon it.[22] Despite overwhelming evidence of mounting oppression in South Africa, and increasing black resistance to it, and the totally inconsequential character of Canada's "new policy toward South Africa" for the next seven-and-a-half years, Canadian policy underwent no additional change.

Although the older and essentially racist attitudes of friendship toward the white regime in South Africa were still a force within the dominant class, the continued softness of the policy of the Canadian government toward South Africa was primarily a response not to such sentiments, but rather to the "greater than average profits to be made in South Africa,"[23] and to the government's desire not to mar its relations with the United States and Great Britain, which were willing to leave unchallenged the oppression in South Africa. It is a dramatic example of how policy changes that would be at least partially responsive to ethical considerations are filtered out by the greater importance given by senior decision-makers to commercial and geopolitical objectives.

Things changed dramatically in 1985. Under the leadership of Prime Minister Brian Mulroney, Canada joined the Scandinavian countries and the Netherlands as leading champions of concerted and sustained international pressures on the South African regime.[24] On 25 October 1985, in a major speech at the United Nations, Mulroney promised to end diplomatic and trade relations with South Africa if there were not an early and significant dismantling of apartheid. He consolidated and gave leadership to the Commonwealth's anti-apartheid initiatives, rejecting British pressure to temper his opposition and facing down an angry Prime Minister Margaret Thatcher in the process. In July 1985, he introduced an initial range of economic sanctions and other measures to demonstrate Canada's determination to sustain and increase international pressure on the South African regime. Mulroney then escalated these sanctions in September of that year, and again in August 1986.

Mulroney did not have the backing of many Conservative MPs taking these initiatives. As well, he had to set aside the advice of the Department of External Affairs, and offset the skilful endeavours of its senior officials to minimize the significance of the measures that they could not block. Several examples will illustrate how resourceful the department was in its efforts to subvert the introduction and effective pursuit of strong policies, and how attentive Mulroney and Joe Clark had to be to confound these efforts. Mulroney, dissatisfied with the preparatory work on possible policy measures provided for him by External Affairs, moved to the Privy Council Office the task of setting out a more imaginative list of strong policies he might introduce. Clark sought policy recommendations from the Taskforce on the Churches and Corporate Responsibility out of his own frustration with the advice of his officials.[25] Mulroney bypassed the department altogether when making several key appointments crucial to the vigorous pursuit of a stronger policy, including the appointment of Stephen Lewis as Canada's representative to the United Nations and of Roy McMurtry as High Commissioner in London. He named Bernard Wood, director of the North-South Institute, a non-governmental policy research centre, as his special envoy to present his views to the Commonwealth's African political leaders. He overruled the department when Lewis took directly to him the department's refusal to agree that he should be a member of the Canadian delegation to the Commonwealth Heads of Government meeting in Vancouver in October 1987.

Mulroney persevered. For nearly two years, Canada intensified its various measures, including economic sanctions, to apply pressure on South Africa to dismantle its apartheid system. Moreover, at the same time, Canada provided leadership in the Commonwealth, the Economic Summits and the United Nations for an intensification of international pressure on South Africa.

It is difficult to arrive with full confidence at a balanced view of this sustained effort by Mulroney to achieve a much stronger Canadian policy toward South Africa. Canadian policy under Mulroney's direction must surely be judged to have been significantly more responsive to ethical values than earlier policies.[26] Mulroney's policy initiatives, moreover, were politically courageous. They were widely criticized in Canadian corporate circles and brought him into direct conflict with both the British and the American governments.

Mulroney's anti-apartheid initiatives, however, should not be read entirely as a victory of conscience over commerce.[27] Underlying them was shrewd political judgment. By the mid-1980s, there were many signs that black resistance to apartheid was threatening the stability of the country. As a result, there were significant flights of domestic capital from South Africa, withdrawals of foreign investment and a severe lessening of international bank lending. Mulroney's and Clark's initiatives were geared to support significant efforts already underway by leading members of South Africa's business elite to promote a negotiated settlement with the ANC. This envisioned eventual majority rule while safeguarding property rights in South Africa to ensure the security of foreign and domestic investments. Mulroney and Clark defended their major policy innovations mainly in terms of backing what they saw as far-sighted efforts by white industrialists to convince the Botha regime to enter into negotiations with the ANC leadership.

They saw this as the best way to help safeguard the future of capitalism in South Africa.

In mid-1987, Mulroney and Clark retreated from this view and from the Canadian policies that had issued from it. Two key developments explain this. First, P.W. Botha, the South African president, finally and firmly rejected the advice of liberal international capital and instead further intensified the repression in South Africa. With this, the efforts of the liberal capitalist faction in South Africa to win the regime over to a negotiated compromise with the ANC collapsed, and its members backed the imposition by the regime of a series of new and even more repressive states of emergency. With this development, Mulroney and Clark could no longer argue that they were supporting an important and rising liberal force in South Africa. Their isolation was further heightened in 1987 when Mulroney failed to win any support at the Economic Summit meeting in Venice for even the inclusion of a mention of concern over South Africa in its final communiqué, let alone for any heightening of pressures on that regime.

From that point on, the Canadian government was in full retreat from its earlier commitment to increase international pressure on South Africa. Canada was, in Renate Pratt's assessment,

> simply unwilling and unable to transform its shallow commitment to the reform goals of the liberal wing of white South Africa's business elite into a lasting and profound support for the black struggle.
>
> The Canadian government had failed to recognize or had chosen to ignore the powerful role of the many composite parts of the popular resistance in South Africa who were to merge into the Mass Democratic Movement in support of the ANC. A major commitment to these forces would have led Canada to follow the example of the Nordic states, particularly Sweden, with major non-military support for the ANC, a downgrading of its embassy to consular status and an adherence to total sanctions until apartheid was dismantled.[28]

Instead, for the final few years of apartheid in South Africa, Canada brought its policy into line with that of its major allies and, by refusing to support any further economic pressures on the South African regime, it ceased to offend the interests of the dominant class in Canada. The classic dominant determinants of Canadian foreign policy had returned.

Concluding Reflections on the Influence of Ethics on Canadian Foreign Policy

Much legitimates the expectation that ethical values are likely to have had a significant impact over the years on Canadian foreign aid policy, and on Canadian policy toward apartheid South Africa. Values that most Canadians are likely to regard as fundamental—compassion toward those in desperate need and a belief in racial equality—were directly relevant to these two foreign policy issues. Both, as well, were the focus of sustained public interest. Strong organizations within civil society had long been active in each case, advocating more ethically responsive policies.

Nevertheless, our overview of Canadian policy in each case seems to bear out the validity of a dominant class analysis. The necessities of alliance politics in the early years of the Cold War, not a concern for the world's poorest, were the primary reason for the beginnings of the Canadian aid program. With the end of the Cold War in 1989, the program was severely and rapidly cut. Moreover, particularly since 1977, Canada's aid program has been increasingly responsive to government and dominant class pressures to promote Canadian economic and geopolitical interests. A similar pattern emerges from our review of Canadian policy toward South Africa. Geopolitical and commercial interests, rather than Canadian antipathy toward racial oppression, determined Canada's stance for many decades. And when Mulroney finally and dramatically shifted policy in 1985, the Department of External Affairs, responding to the priority it attached to the same determinants, persistently tried to minimize the significance of the prime minister's anti-apartheid initiatives. These same preoccupations, as argued above, also accounted for the retreat from those policies in 1987.

The two case studies thus illustrate that civil society structures seeking to secure a more ethically responsive foreign policy are operating in a socio-political environment that is greatly biased against such policies. However, neither the evolution of Canadian foreign aid policy nor that of Canadian policy toward South Africa suggests that the creation of foreign policy is totally deterministic, with class and geopolitical considerations inexorably overwhelming ethical values. Rather, they suggest that recurrently there are circumstances in which civil society can exercise significant influence to advance the ethical responsiveness of foreign policy. These circumstances are of two kinds: first, when the issues about which there is civil society concern are not seen by senior policy-makers as relevant to Canadian economic or geopolitical interests; and, second, those occasional historic moments (which Linda Freeman has aptly called "strategic conjunctures") "when elements of a situation come together in a new way to override pre-existing limitations."[29]

Issues with Minor Economic and Geopolitical Ramifications

The two issues discussed here, foreign aid policy and policy toward apartheid South Africa, each closely touched the economic interests of the dominant class and had relevance to Canada's perceived geopolitical interests. Decision-makers therefore particularly guarded against pressures seeking to shift the primary focus away from important commercial and geopolitical objectives. However, there are foreign policy issues, even quite important issues, that do not significantly affect the geopolitical interests of the state and are not of much concern to Canadian business interests. In these policy areas, there is far wider scope for senior decision-makers and civil society organizations to secure more ethically responsive policies.

This seems always to have been the case. The recent successful joint initiative of Lloyd Axworthy as minister of Foreign Affairs and committed NGOs to win international support for the Landmine Convention illustrates this, as do the celebrated foreign policy achievements of Lester Pearson in 1956. In these instances, there was space for the promotion of ethically driven policy initiatives, and they were successful.

Two rather different arguments are being offered here. The first is that, in policy areas that are marginal to Canada's economic and geopolitical interests, there are more likely to be initiatives that stem from a genuine engagement of senior decision-makers with ethically founded policy objectives. The second refers to those initiatives within these marginal policy areas in which government perceptions of national self-interest still play a significant role. The argument is that, even where the government's primary motivations have been more complex and have included the pursuit of a more subtly identified self-interest, ethical reflection about these policy options, and advocacy from within civil society for more ethically responsive policies, were important prerequisites to the government's decision to adopt them. As was argued above in regard to the expansion of Canadian foreign aid in the years 1966-76, extensive discussion and strong public advocacy were necessary to bring these options to the public discourse. This ethically rooted contribution from within civil society to policies that were then introduced by government for more traditional self-interested reasons needs to be acknowledged in any comprehensive assessment of the role of ethics in shaping foreign policy.

Strategic Conjunctures

The two cases reviewed here illustrate how the interests of dominant social forces shape the making of foreign policy. They each also contain particular historical moments in which there were major policy initiatives that ignored these interests. Unless these are accommodated, as Linda Freeman points out in regard to one of them, "one could not explain how a Conservative government in a liberal, capitalist country like Canada would choose a program of economic sanctions against a Cold War ally like South Africa which, at the same time, hurt the short-term interests of Canadian exporters."[30] Quite similar questions could also be asked of the ten-year period from 1966 to 1976 in which Canadian foreign aid expanded at a phenomenal rate and became significantly more committed to reaching and helping the poorest.

There thus were moments in the history of each of these policies when decisions were made and policies pursued that seemed responsive to ethical values and defiant of dominant economic and geopolitical interests. These quite dramatic policy changes were possible because of a specific coming together of a wide variety of factors that, for the moment at least, undermined the determining power of the ideology dominating senior policy-making circles. Our analysis above suggests that such a confluence occurred in regard to foreign aid policy in the late 1960s and early 1970s, and in regard to Canadian policy toward South Africa from 1985 to 1987.

But strategic conjunctures such as these only serve to make change possible. For change to become a reality, as these two case studies illustrate, new policy alternatives need to have been already carefully developed and powerfully advocated. There need to be agencies within government that are searching for policies more appropriate to the new circumstances; and strong organizations in civil society must be pressing the government to make public policy more responsive to ethical values.

In the cases of Canada's foreign aid policies and its policy toward apartheid South Africa, these additional prerequisites for effective policy change were present. As a result, policy changes were accomplished that seemed to defy the economic and geopolitical considerations which had until then held sway. It is thus reasonable to conclude that, when there are strategic conjunctures of circumstances that open decision-making to a wider range of options, the efforts of ethically motivated citizens' organizations can contribute in important ways to the shaping of foreign policy.

However, this judgment must be tempered. The changes that were secured to aid policies in the period 1966-76, and to policy toward South Africa in 1985-87, were weakened in their implementation by those in government unconvinced by them. Moreover, the confluence of circumstances that had made these changes possible was replaced by others, which facilitated a dismantling of the new policies. As discussed above, in each case policies returned once more to the pursuit of commercial and international political objectives.

This is not to suggest that efforts to win more ethically responsive foreign policies are of no avail when the changes being sought are in conflict with Canadian geopolitical interests or with dominant class economic interests. Canadian aid policies and Canadian policy toward apartheid South Africa were, for a time, significantly changed, and the resources being devoted to meeting the basic needs of the poorest were increased. For a longer time, the rearguard action in CIDA was strengthened, allowing the organization to retain its ethically more responsive policies and programs. Similarly, the intensification of anti-apartheid measures by the Mulroney government made a significant contribution to the struggle of South African blacks to overthrow their oppressive system. However, the history of these policy initiatives makes it clear that those promoting more ethically responsive foreign policies must recognize that their victories will be few and insecure, and that on most issues they will be opposed by social and political forces that enjoy a well-entrenched dominance in Canada.

One final point remains to be made. The ability of civil society organizations to win ethically more responsive foreign policies is much influenced by the ethical responsiveness of the political culture that is dominant within the society as a whole. Lumsdaine made an important contribution to our understanding of these issues when he linked the emergence of the international aid regime to the social values that had become prominent in most of the industrialized countries in the years between 1945 and the late 1970s. However, those values have more recently been in marked retreat, providing less and less of a foundation of support for foreign aid within Canadian society.

Canada itself has become a meaner, less compassionate society. Both the federal and the provincial governments have demonstrated a declining concern for the welfare of the very poor in our society. With this erosion of social welfare values, the linkage between these values and foreign aid has weakened, marked by severe cuts to its budget and an erosion of its quality. A generous aid program, which would give primary emphasis to reaching and helping the poorest peoples and countries, can no longer be assumed to express internationally the ethical values that are dominant in Canadian society. Civil society structures that advocate such policies no longer seek to bring public policy into line with what were once widely shared Canadian social values. Rather, they are engaged in the more substantial and daunting task of generating, within Canada itself, a greater moral concern for the welfare of those beyond its borders.

Notes

1 Kim Nossal provides a forceful and influential statist analysis in *The Politics of Canadian Foreign Policy*, 3rd ed. (Scarborough, ON: Prentice Hall, 1997). For an exposition of the dominant class approach, see Cranford Pratt, "Canada: An Eroding and Limited Internationalism," in *Internationalism Under Strain: The North-South Policies of Canada, the Netherlands, Norway and Sweden,* ed. Cranford Pratt (Toronto: University of Toronto Press, 1989), 24-69. The two approaches are authoritatively contrasted in David Morrison, *Aid and Ebb Tide: A History of Canadian Development Assistance* (Waterloo, ON: Wilfrid Laurier University Press, 1998), 430-42; and in David Black and Heather Smith, "Notable Exceptions: New and Arrested Developments in Canadian Foreign Policy Literature," *Canadian Journal of Political Science* 26 (1993): 745-74. See also Cranford Pratt, "Competing Perspectives on Canadian Development Assistance," *International Journal* 51/2 (1996): 235-58.

2 Were dominant class analysis to be left at that, its delineation of the determinants of foreign policy would be too schematic. Room was needed within dominant class theory for the haphazard and unintegrated responses of government to societal pressures and, in particular, given the realities of politics in Canada, to the lobbying of specific business inter-

ests for policies of special interest to them but unlikely to be in the long-term interests of capitalism in Canada.

3 This reconsideration of the role of ethical values in the shaping of Canadian aid policies has been stimulated by the analysis and insights of David Halloran Lumsdaine in his major comparative study of foreign aid, *Moral Vision in International Politics: The Foreign Aid Regime, 1949-1989* (Princeton, NJ: Princeton University Press, 1993). Though richly comparative, it is primarily focused on the evolution of the aid program of the United States. I discuss Lumsdaine's analysis and the extent to which it is transferable to the study of Canadian policies in Cranford Pratt, "Moral Vision and Foreign Policy: The Case of Canadian Development Assistance," in *Ethics and Security in Canadian Foreign Policy,* ed. Rosalind Irwin (Vancouver: University of British Columbia Press, forthcoming). This section of my essay draws on that fuller analysis.

4 This is true, in my view, of Keith Spicer, *The Samaritan State: External Aid in Canadian Foreign Policy* (Toronto: University of Toronto Press, 1966); Leonard Dudley and Claude Monmarquette, *The Supply of Canadian Foreign Aid: Explanation and Evaluation* (Ottawa: Economic Council of Canada, 1978); Robert Carty and Virginia Smith, *Perpetuating Poverty: The Political Economy of Canadian Foreign Aid* (Toronto: Between the Lines, 1981); Monique Dupuis, *Crise mondiale et aide internationale: stratégie et développement Tiers-Monde* (Montreal: Édition Nouvelle optique, 1984); Kim Nossal, "Mixed Motives Revisited: Canadian Interest in Development Assistance," *Canadian Journal of Political Science* 21/2 (1988): 35-36; Patricia Appavoo, "The Small State as Donor: Canadian and Swedish Development Assistance Policies Compared 1960-1976" (Ph.D. diss., University of Toronto, 1989); Pratt, "Canada: An Eroding and Limited Internationalism"; Martin Rudner, "Canada's Official Development Strategy: Process, Goals and Priorities," *Canadian Journal of Development Studies* 12/1 (1991): 1-19; Mark W. Charlton, *The Making of Canadian Food Aid Policy* (Montreal and Kingston: McGill-Queen's University Press, 1992); Cranford Pratt, ed., *Canadian International Development Assistance Policies: An Appraisal* (Montreal and Kingston: McGill-Queen's University Press, 1994, 1996); and Morrison, *Aid and Ebb Tide.*

The major exceptions are: Noël Alain and Jean-Philippe Thérien, "Welfare Institutions and Foreign Aid: Domestic Foundations of Canadian Foreign Policy," *Canadian Journal of Political Science* 27/3 (September 1994): 529-58; and Réal Lavergne, "Determinants of Canadian Aid Policies," in *Global Poverty: The Determinants of the Aid Policies of Canada, Denmark, the Netherlands, Norway and Sweden,* ed. Olav Stokke (Uppsala: Scandinavian Institute of African Studies, 1989), 33-89.

5 The close correlation between socially responsible domestic values and generous foreign aid programs is authoritatively analyzed in Noël Alain

and Jean-Philippe Thérien, "From Domestic to International Justice: The Welfare State and Foreign Aid," *International Organization* 43/2 (Summer, 1995): 523-53.

6 These were: the Parliamentary Task Force on North-South Relations, *Report to the House of Commons on the Relations between Developed and Developing Countries* (Hull, QC: Supply and Services, 1980); *For Whose Benefit?,* Report of the Standing Committee on External Affairs and International Trade on Canada's Official Development Assistance Policies and Programs (Ottawa: Supply and Services, 1987); and the Special Joint Committee Reviewing Canadian Foreign Policy, *Canada's Foreign Policy: Principles and Priorities for the Future* (Ottawa: Parliamentary Publications Directorate, 1994).

7 *Strategy for International Development Cooperation 1975-1980* (Ottawa: CIDA, 1975); and *Sharing Our Future: Canada's International Development Assistance* (Ottawa: Supply and Services, 1987).

8 For a full discussion of Canadian aid in these years, see Morrison, *Aid and Ebb Tide*, 99-142.

9 OECD, *Development Assistance: Efforts and Policies of the Members of the Development Assistance Committee 1978 Review* (Paris: OECD, 1979), 191.

10 CIDA, *Strategy for International Development Cooperation 1975-1980.*

11 For a fuller development of the analysis in these paragraphs, see Cranford Pratt, "Humane Internationalism and Canadian Development Assistance Policies," in *Canadian International Development Assistance Policies,* 334-70.

12 As quoted in Phillip Rawkins, "An Institutional Analysis of CIDA," in *Canadian International Development Assistance Policies*, 162.

13 CIDA, *Strategy for International Development Cooperation 1975-1980*, 34.

14 *For Whose Benefit?*, 12.

15 House of Commons, Special Joint Committee Reviewing Canadian Foreign Policy, *Canada's Foreign Policy: Principles and Priorities for the Future* (Ottawa: Parliamentary Publications Directorate, 1994), 48.

16 *Canada in the World: A Government Statement* (Ottawa: Department of Foreign Affairs and International Trade, 1995), 40.

17 The two most substantial and penetrating studies of the development of Canadian policy toward South Africa are: Linda Freeman, *The Ambiguous Champion: Canada and South Africa in the Trudeau and Mulroney Years* (Toronto: University of Toronto Press, 1997), 139-48; and Renate Pratt, *In Good Faith: Canadian Churches Against Apartheid* (Waterloo, ON: Wilfrid Laurier University Press, 1997).

18 The most authoritative treatment of Canadian policy in these early years is Brian Tennyson, *Canadian Relations with South Africa: A Diplomatic History* (Washington, DC: University Press of America, 1982).

19 Renate Pratt provides an authoritative account of this work of the churches in *In Good Faith*. Linda Freeman surveys the development of a wide range of organized anti-apartheid lobbying in Canada from early in the 1970s; see Freeman, *The Ambiguous Champion*, 139-48.

20 For an early and authoritative analysis of the 1977 policy, see T.A. Keenleyside, "Canada-South Africa Commercial Relations, 1977-82," *Canadian Journal of African Studies* 17/3 (1983): 449-67. It is closely examined as well in Freeman, *The Ambiguous Champion,* 73-102, and in Pratt, *In Good Faith,* 51-56 and 65-93.

21 Quoted in Pratt, *In Good Faith,* 52.

22 This is also the judgment expressed in what are considered to be the four most thorough, scholarly examinations of these policies: Keenleyside, "Canada-South Africa Commercial Relations, 1977-82"; Pratt, *In Good Faith*; Freeman, *The Ambiguous Champion*; and Clarence G. Redekop, "Commerce over Conscience: The Trudeau Government and South Africa, 1968-84," *Journal of Canadian Studies* 19/4 (Winter 1984-85): 82-105.

23 This is the oft-quoted reason officially given for not imposing restrictions on Canadian trade with South Africa in 1970. Secretary of State for External Affairs, *Foreign Policy for Canadians. United Nations* (Ottawa: Queen's Printer, 1970), 36.

24 Authoritative analyses of Mulroney's policy initiatives are to be found in Freeman, *The Ambiguous Champion,* 125-234, passim; and Pratt, *In Good Faith,* 187-336, passim.

25 In asking for these recommendations, Clark specifically advised the task force to send them to his personal assistant rather than to the Department of External Affairs. Pratt, *In Good Faith,* 173-80.

26 This is also the judgment offered by Freeman, *The Ambiguous Champion*, and by Pratt, *In Good Faith.*

27 See Redekop's early and excellent study of Canadian policy entitled, "Commerce Over Conscience," cited above.

28 Pratt, *In Good Faith,* 344.

29 Freeman, *The Ambiguous Champion*, 297.

30 Ibid.

7

ECOLOGICAL ETHICS

Roger Hutchinson's Methodology and Engagement in Canadian Initiatives

DAVID G. HALLMAN

Roger Hutchinson seems to me to be a very pragmatic idealist. He believes that the world can be changed for the better, but recognizes that the journey is slow and contentious and requires a lot of small steps. Applied ecological ethics in Canada is one of the many areas of contemporary social issues where Hutchinson's pragmatic idealism has had an impact.

Over the past twenty-five years, the United Church of Canada and the larger Canadian ecumenical community have broadened and deepened their focus on ecological concerns. Efforts have been made to explore scriptural, theological, ethical and spiritual dimensions of the ecological crisis and to draw on new insights as the faith communities become engaged in education and advocacy on specific issues. The major ecological issues addressed by Canadian churches at a national level are nuclear energy, acid rain, forestry, ozone depletion, climate change and biotechnology.

I have had the opportunity to work with Roger Hutchinson over the years on a number of projects that attempt to apply Christian ethics to difficult ecological and social justice problems. He has brought a skeptical and disciplined eye to these initiatives, insisting on methodologies that facilitate a responsible sharing and hearing of differing perspectives.

Notes to chapter 7 are on pp. 147-48.

This essay will begin with reflections on his book *Prophets, Pastors and Public Choices: Canadian Churches and the Mackenzie Valley Pipeline Debate*[1] and then will look at four case studies of Hutchinson's applied ecological ethics. First, I will focus on his engagement with the Canadian ecumenical Taskforce on the Churches and Corporate Responsibility and its work on forestry issues. Second, I will discuss his involvement in ecumenical and secular debates concerning attempts to prepare an "Earth Charter" before and after the 1992 Rio Earth Summit. The third area I will examine is the work of the Canadian churches and the World Council of Churches on the issue of climate change. Finally, I will take a look at his participation in some denominational and ecumenical reflections on the increasing role of biotechnology in Canadian society.

Hutchinson has consistently pressed the United Church of Canada and the broader ecumenical community to avoid romanticizing or demonizing participants in contentious ecological struggles, to create opportunities and atmospheres in which people holding varying perspectives on an issue can listen to each other with respect, and to analyze issues and engage in advocacy based on the best possible information and the clearest possible appreciation of realizable goals and objectives.

Hutchinson's role as a Christian ethicist in these issues involves a significant degree of complexity in terms of both how he perceives his function and how others experience his involvement:

> As an ethicist, I have a role to play in the conversation through which church activists, other church leaders and members and church-related academics together assess the faithfulness and effectiveness of particular activities. Looking back upon these activities to see how the issues were perceived, how judgements were made and defended, and how different groups within the churches related to one another is an integral part of the action-reflection process of the churches themselves. Just as the surgeon adopts a specialized focus and disciplined detachment to diagnose and remove a tumour, the ethicist applies her or his specialized training to diagnose and cure distorted communication. In neither case does specialization and detachment reflect a lack of commitment to the remedy being sought.[2]

In my experience, discomfort in a conflictual situation has never been a reason for Hutchinson to consider deviating from his principled methodology. In fact, conflict seems to summon further resources of energy from him because of his concern to address conflict based on fundamental differences or on the difficulties the parties may be having in understanding each other as a result of their varying perspectives, world views and methods of communicating.

With the exception of his work related to the Mackenzie Valley Pipeline debate, none of the areas of engagement that I will address have constituted a major focus of his activity. Rather, they give insight into Hutchinson's broad interests and how he brings his skills to bear on a wide range of contemporary social and ecological problems.[3]

The Mackenzie Valley Pipeline Debate

Hutchinson's analysis of the churches' engagement in the pipeline debate is most fully explored in his book *Prophets, Pastors and Public Choices:* 7book serves as a historical account of the public debate on whether or not to build a northern pipeline to bring natural gas to southern markets. That public debate was focused primarily on the work of an inquiry, headed by Justice Thomas Berger, to look into the potential impacts of a pipeline on Native communities and the environment and to recommend the conditions that must be met if the pipeline proposal were to proceed.

But Hutchinson's book has least two other significant purposes. It examines the role of Christian churches as active participants in the public debate, both in terms of pressing for a particular policy option (for example, a moratorium on pipeline development until the just settlement of Native land claims), and in relation to the conflicts within the church communities on the issue. The advocacy position adopted by the Canadian churches and coordinated through the work of the ecumenical coalition, Project North, played an important role in moving the proposal for a pipeline from being an "inevitable next step" in northern development to being the subject of vigorous public debate, with the originally anticipated approval far from assured. That shift received a major boost from the churches' engagement, a role labelled by Hutchinson as the "prophetic function." On the other hand, there were some within the churches who were quite uncomfortable with such a strong advocacy position and who felt that the appropriate role for churches was to be more pastoral toward those who were working on northern industrial development within government and industry and less judgmental about their activities and motives. This distinction provides useful imagery for the analysis, but Hutchinson acknowledges that the prophetic-pastoral juxtaposition was more a continuum than a dichotomy and that it would be an oversimplification to imply that the "prophets" did not have pastoral concerns and that the "pastors" had no justice commitments.

Hutchinson is quite candid in his analysis of the impact of the roles played by the differing segments within the church communities. For instance, he identifies what he sees as the strengths and limitations of the ways in which the prophetic function was executed:

> By pressing the moral and religious aspects of the debate the churches, acting through the inter-church coalition Project North, helped to expand the framework within which the debate took place. However, the way in which Project North drew sharp lines between the converted and the unconverted, and between prisoners of greed and opponents of injustice, reflected a tendency to deal with opponents as stereotypes rather than as moral agents and participants in a serious public debate.[4]

The other major purpose served by *Prophets, Pastors and Public Choices* is its articulation of the methodology promoted by Hutchinson to discern the various sources and levels of communication among parties in conflict in order to facilitate clearer debate on core issues and to increase the potential for more broadly supported public policy decisions. His work has contributed to applied ecological ethics in Canada by helping people to recognize different levels of social discourse. His methodology is informed by the work of other social ethicists, as we see in his utilization of Nicholas Wolterstorff's identification of factors contributing to our individual understandings of reality—for example, "prior conditioning, our location in the social order, the kinds of experiences we have had, what we already believe about the situation in question, our beliefs about the nature and purpose of human life, and so forth."[5] Having helped people recognize that they may be coming at an issue from very different starting points, Hutchinson's methodology moves on to encourage dialogue among participants in order to reach agreement on the focus of attention—i.e., which aspect of the issue is being, or should be, debated at any particular point in time. For Hutchinson, facilitating this discernment among the various parties is one of the roles of the ethicist.

Such a role is not particularly easy or comfortable. In the case of Hutchinson's involvement in the Mackenzie Valley Pipeline debate, he found himself being viewed suspiciously by both the proponents and the opponents of the pipeline proposal. The complexities were related, at least in part, to the perception of the ethicist as being either an activist engaged in the debates or a detached observer, analyzing the developments from a distance:

> This analysis of the pipeline debate moves back and forth along the engaged-detached axis. From the standpoint of whether or not the pipeline ought to be built, I help to rationalize (i.e. to clarify the ethical and theological reasons for) the churches' controversial anti-pipeline stance. Proponents of the pipeline will therefore see me as an engaged and biased critic of the pipeline. On the other hand, my willingness to provide a sympathetic account of the critics of Project North's confrontational style will make me appear at best detached and at worst unsympathetic to the liberationist cause.[6]

Prophets, Pastors and Public Choices provides an early and detailed articulation of Hutchinson's methodological approach to Christian ethics as it is applied to a specific conflict with social and ecological dimensions. The next cases that I will examine relate to other ecological issues to which Hutchinson applied this methodology, and in which he and I had some involvement together.

Case 1: Forestry

The practice of forestry has been a catalyst for major social and ecological conflicts in Canada, particularly over the past two decades. Concerns about the ecological impact of clear-cutting and logging in old-growth forests have led to confrontations, blockades, economic boycotts and demonstrations at industry shareholder meetings. Added to the environmental concerns are the protests over the intrusion of forestry activities into areas where Aboriginal land claims remain unsettled. Differences of perspective, experience and world views have limited the capacity for dialogue among the various parties.

The Taskforce on the Churches and Corporate Responsibility (TCCR), a Canadian ecumenical coalition, was one of the earlier organizations in the country to take some multi-stakeholder initiatives toward the development of a more sustainable approach to forestry. Roger Hutchinson, both personally and through his methodology, played a role in the TCCR's approach.

The TCCR was created in 1975 to facilitate research and advocacy on issues relating to the social responsibility of Canadian corporations in their activities, both in Canada and internationally. Made up of representatives of the mainline Protestant denominations, the Canadian Conference of Catholic Bishops and many Catholic religious orders, the TCCR has brought pressure to bear on corporations through correspondence, dialogue with senior management, shareholder resolutions, participation in the companies' annual general meetings, and lobbying government for appropriate legislative and regulatory measures. Relatively early in the TCCR's existence, issues arose that had not only a major social dimension, but also, an environmental impact: acid rain, nuclear fuel cycle, oil and gas development on land claimed by Aboriginal peoples, and so on.

From the early 1980s, as a result of both social and ecological concerns,[7] the TCCR became involved in a variety of specific forestry issues: mercury poisoning of Native peoples in the English-Wabigoon River system; herbicide spraying in Cape Breton; and Haida land claims in areas being forested in the Queen Charlotte Islands in British Columbia. By 1985, forest land use and forest management conflicts had become significant items on the TCCR agenda. Moving beyond a case-by-case involvement, the TCCR began to work toward a broader frame of reference by writing to fifty-two Canadian forest products companies asking for their policies on forest management. The request generated limited response, and the TCCR discovered that the forestry sector was largely disinterested in or hostile to the idea of such corporate public policies.

The TCCR decided, as a next step, to use a recommendation from the National Round Table on the Environment and the Economy

(NRTEE),[8] encouraging companies to adopt and implement environmental principles and policies. But the TCCR realized that, to pursue its dialogue with companies about the need for such policies, its members would need a clearer idea about what such policies should include and how they should be implemented. To develop this understanding, the TCCR decided to create its own Model Code of Environmental Practice for Forest Land Management. Enter Hutchinson, methodologically and personally.

In February 1989, the TCCR and the Hutchinson-initiated Centre for the Study of Religion in Canada (later renamed the Centre for Research in Religion) at Emmanuel College, University of Toronto held a two-day consultation on forestry codes of practice, bringing together a wide variety of people with different interests in forestry. The event is described in the 1988-89 TCCR annual report:

> On the first day of the consultation, a small working group of foresters and church representatives drafted an initial version of the code. On the second day, thirty people representing various perspectives on forest use and regions of Canada met to offer comments on the initial draft. Participants included professional foresters and environmental specialists from business, universities, governments, unions, non-governmental organisations, and church representatives.[9]

This two-stage process was a design developed by TCCR planners working in conjunction with Roger Hutchinson. It allowed for an initial articulation process to delineate the main principles and the organization of a model code through the collective preparation of a first draft. The fundamental ethical principles of relevance to sustainable forest land management needed to be discerned, phrased in ways that would be accessible to a diverse audience, and then organized in a logical structure with implications for policy and practice. The participants were under considerable pressure to produce a draft for testing on the second day. Members of this initial group represented various disciplines and perspectives, but shared enough of the TCCR's basic orientation to ecological sustainability and social justice that they were able to come to a consensus on what to incorporate in a first draft. The responsibility for preparing a text was then shared among them.

Hutchinson and the consultation planners from the TCCR invited a more diverse group to attend on the second day—a broad cross-section of church members, academics, professional foresters, environmentalists, Aboriginal participants and representatives from various sectors of the forestry industry. Unfortunately, there was a limited response from the industry. A few companies sent their senior environmental or forestry specialists, but most appeared suspicious of this initiative. Even so, the dialogue on the second day was animated, with considerable diversity of perspective being expressed on the first draft of the code. The challenge was for participants to allow the various perspectives to be expressed, to listen with respect and to debate. The consultation was not intended to be a decision-making event, so there was no pressure to reach a final agreement on the text. The consultation met with mixed reaction from the participants. Nevertheless, it did provide a jump-start for the development of a model code.

The draft of the model code then went through considerable rewriting. Comments from consultation participants, as well as material from the environmental policies and codes of practice of forest sector companies, the Canadian Paperworkers Union, industry associations from other sectors, the International Chamber of Commerce, and the International Union for the Conservation of Nature and Natural Resources, were considered. Eventually, the code was adopted by the TCCR as a basis for dialogue. Hutchinson's approach to facilitating dialogue among parties with significantly different perspectives continued to influence the TCCR's use of the model code.

Case 2: Earth Charter

Prior to the Earth Summit, which was held in Rio de Janeiro in June 1992, Maurice Strong, as secretary general of the conference, officially called the United Nations Conference on Environment and Development (UNCED), had a dream that one of the outcomes would be an "Earth Charter." He envisioned it as an identification of the key ethical principles that should govern the relationship between human societies and the rest of the natural order. The role of the Earth Charter in relation to the natural world should be similar to that of the United Nations Declaration of Human Rights in terms of the relationship between individuals and governments.

UNCED organizers approached religious communities, among others, to aid in drafting an Earth Charter. The World Council of Churches took on the task of hosting an inter-religious gathering which would bring together representatives of various faiths to discuss what they felt should be included. Roger Hutchinson agreed to be one of the Canadian participants. The gathering, held in Bossey, Switzerland, on 8-10 August 1991, drafted a statement entitled "One Earth Community: A Declaration and Statement of Principles for an Earth Charter,"[10] and the statement was presented to the third preparatory meeting for UNCED.

However, governments attending the Earth Summit in Rio did not agree to the kind of text that Maurice Strong had envisaged. Rather than adopting a short poetic Earth Charter, the conference supported a "Rio Declaration" of much greater length and specificity. One of the main dynamics that propelled this movement toward a more legalistic document (in terms of international "soft law") was the negative reaction of governments and civil society members from countries of the economic south. They saw the proposed Earth Charter as too general in its outlook. It made undifferentiated statements about the responsibility of humankind to care for the Earth and ignored the political and economic forces that resulted in social and ecological injustice for the poor of the world. One southern diplomat scolded his northern colleagues for wanting a pretty document that their children could hang on their bedroom walls, whereas children in his country had no bedroom walls upon which to hang anything.

Efforts continued after UNCED to develop an Earth Charter, coordinated largely through the Earth Council which Maurice Strong had helped to found. A contribution to these efforts was organized by the Franciscan Centre of Environmental Studies, based in Rome, and again Hutchinson was invited to participate in the consultation and respond to a draft. Hutchinson's sensitivity to the limitations of the then-predominant approaches to the practice of ethical analysis is apparent in this comment: "I remain as sceptical as always about these Western male exercises in Earth Charter creation."[11] He elaborated on this concern in his written feedback to the organizer of the consultation process at the Franciscan Centre: "My overall impression is that you can expect to hear from environmentalist, feminist and Third World perspectives that the document places too much emphasis on human responsibility for the rest of nature and not enough on the human place within nature."[12]

This critique illustrates Hutchinson's role as a Christian ethicist concerned about the voices not being heard—voices of those who would approach the task of Earth Charter creation with very different world views and assumptions. His analysis focused not only on process but on the content of the Franciscan draft text as well. Reflecting back on the southern critique of a predominantly northern Earth Charter draft, Hutchinson commented: "The main difference between the Earth Charter discussed before and at Rio and the Rio Declaration was that the latter insisted on naming the "we" who caused the current mess and the "we" who were the victims of unjust, unsustainable patterns of development." He observed that a social justice perspective would criticize both the impact of the rich industrialized North on the poor countries of the South, and the policies and social structures which victimize poor and powerless classes in northern countries.[13] After some further suggestions on specifics in the Franciscan Centre's draft, he concluded with a characteristically succinct Hutchinson comment, incisive on several levels: "The principles seem harmless with the exception of #6.[14] It is aggressively human-centred."[15]

The Earth Charter drafting process coordinated by the Earth Council and the U.S.-based Center for the Respect for Life and Environment has gone through several stages since Hutchinson's involvement. The hope of the organizers from the Earth Council is that it will be adopted by the United Nation's Rio +10 Conference in 2002, when progress (or lack of it) in implementing the environmental agreements signed at the Earth Summit in 1992 will be reviewed.

Case 3: Climate Change

The issue of climate change has been a priority for both the United Church of Canada and the World Council of Churches for more than a decade. The churches view climate change as an issue with profound ethical dimensions. A significant part of the accelerated warming of the atmosphere is attributed (with increasing scientific consensus) to the polluting emissions that have accumulated in the atmosphere, mainly from wealthier industrialized countries, over the past 150 years. However, the destructive climatic consequences will be suffered disproportionately by poorer developing countries of the economic south and by future generations.

On several occasions, Roger Hutchinson invited me to address the students in one of his classes about the churches' engagement in this issue. He was interested in using this as a case study because it represented an effort by the faith community to inform itself about a complex ecological issue, analyze it from a theological and ethical perspective, and actively work for changes in public policy, industrial practices and personal lifestyles to reduce the emission of the greenhouse gases contributing to climate change.

Hutchinson, professor of church and society at Emmanuel College at the time, would press me, as a representative of the institutional church, to articulate how the church discerns its role and makes decisions on issues where there is active public debate, and where powerful economic and political interests contest the church's analysis. He would then invite his students to consider how ecological issues such as climate change challenge their understanding of the mission of the church as a faith community with local, national and global expressions.

Biotechnology and Genetic Engineering

The final example that I will cite of Hutchinson's involvement in ecological issues is from the area of biotechnology and genetic engineering. There is a detailed essay on the subject in this collection, so I need not consider this issue in depth. I will simply focus on it as another illustration of the way in which Hutchinson brings his methodological interest in ethical clarification to bear on an issue where conflicting perspectives prevail and debate exists within the church and the broader society.

In 1999, the United Church commissioned the TCCR to prepare an analysis of the current issues and concerns related to biotechnology and genetic engineering. The United Church realized that many of its members were becoming increasingly interested in the emergence of biotechnology. Some were farmers who had begun to utilize genetically modified seeds because of their advantages—for example, the diminished need for the use of chemical fertilizers and pesticides. Other members had read of the potential negative environmental and health consequences of genetically modified organisms. They were uncomfortable with the lack of choice and of disclosure of information to consumers in Canada, who had no way of knowing if the food products they were buying contained genetically modified substances.

Before moving to develop policy statements, the United Church's Division of Mission in Canada felt that it would be important for it to help its members and respective policy committees to better understand the issues being raised by the use of biotechnology (specifically in the agricultural sector), to provide opportunities for dialogue and debate among members holding various perspectives, and to draw on the expertise of Christian ethicists to assist people to clarify the ethical dimensions of the issues. Choosing such an approach owes more than a little to the influence of Hutchinson's methodology.

Once the TCCR overview of major issues and concerns in agricultural biotechnology had been prepared, four Christian ethicists were invited to read the material and prepare commentaries—Eric Beresford from the Anglican Church of Canada, Richard Crossman from the Evangelical Lutheran Church in Canada, Heather Eaton from St. Paul University (Roman Catholic) and Roger Hutchinson from the United Church. These four essays and the TCCR overview were then published by the United Church as *Biotechnology and Genetic Engineering: Current Issues, Ethics and Theological Reflections.*[16]

Hutchinson's essay focuses on xenotransplantation—the transplanting of animal organs into humans. He acknowledges the consistency of his approach:

> The method I will describe has been developed in courses I have taught during the past 30 years in the University of Toronto's Department and Centre for the Study of Religion and Faculty of Forestry of the University of Toronto and at Emmanuel College in the Toronto School of Theology.[17]

He goes on to state, "The central feature of this approach is the identification of different levels of clarification characterized by different types of claims and arguments."[18] Hutchinson uses his methodology to examine the gap that often occurs, and is sometimes promoted, between "experts" and the "public"; the competing perceptions as to whether ethics and theology are primarily expressions of intuition, emotion and passion, or whether they can be seen as rational, public discourse; the different approaches of applying principles to cases or starting with concrete cases and applying a practical moral reasoning process to facilitate dialogue among the stakeholders; dimensions of ethical clarification brought to the issue by various participants—principles, consequences, ways of life; and, finally, post-ethical clarification, which he describes as "a return from the rigorous defence of empirical claims and ethical arguments to the story-telling, confessional style of the first level."[19]

His essay thus echoes the creative yet rigorous methodological approach articulated in *Prophets, Pastors and Public Choices: Canadian Churches and the Mackenzie Valley Pipeline Debate.* Though his involvement in the Mackenzie Valley Pipeline debate was almost thirty years earlier than his contribution on xenotransplantation, his consistency is a remarkable testament to the utility of his methodology.

Notes

1 Roger Hutchinson, *Prophets, Pastors and Public Choices: Canadian Churches and the Mackenzie Valley Pipeline Debate* (Waterloo, ON: Wilfrid Laurier University Press, 1992).

2 Ibid., 7.

3 I should acknowledge that my description and analysis of his engagement in these four cases derive from my own notes, recollections and files, and thus suffer from the limitation of not being as comprehensive as they would be if Hutchinson were reporting this history himself.

4 Hutchinson, *Prophets, Pastors and Public Choices*, 8.

5 Ibid., 32.

6 Ibid., 7.

7 A helpful summary of the involvement of the TCCR in forestry issues can be found in Peter Chapman, *Corporate Policies and Corporate Accountability in Forest Land Management* (Toronto: TCCR, 1992), available from 129 St. Clair Ave. W., Toronto, ON M4V 1N5 (Web site: www.web.net/~tccr).

8 The NRTEE had been established by the Canadian federal and provincial governments as a response to the Brundtland Commission (the World Commission on Environment and Development).

9 TCCR, *1988-1989 Annual Report*, 5-6.

10 The United Church of Canada drew upon the draft prepared at the Bossey consultation and developed its own policy statement, which was tested and revised in light of input from partner religious and non-religious organizations in Canada and in developing countries. The United Church draft statement was presented to the 34th General Council of the United Church of Canada in August 1992, further amended and then adopted as a United Church policy statement entitled "One Earth Community: Ethical Principles for Environment and Development."

11 Roger Hutchinson, personal correspondence with David Hallman, 3 August 1994.

12 Roger Hutchinson, Centre for the Study of Religion in Canada, Emmanuel College, Toronto to Rev. Bernard Przewozny, Franciscan Centre of Environmental Studies, Rome, 3 August 1994.

13 Hutchinson to Przewozny. This would amend paragraph 9 in the Franciscan Centre's Earth Charter which read: " We aknowledge that, due to lack of foresight and harmful activities, we have created situations which often require immediate correction of errors. All efforts must be made to improve our knowledge of global environmental change."

14 Principle 6 in the Franciscan Centre's draft read: "The cultural, moral and spiritual environment of persons and communities must be given more emphasis by religious, political and other leaders so that the Earth may be cultivated and administered as humankind's common home."

15 Hutchinson to Przewozny.

16 *Biotechnology and Genetic Engineering: Current Issues, Ethics and Theological Reflections*, (Toronto: Division of Mission in Canada, the United Church of Canada, 2000).

17 Ibid., 88.

18 Ibid.

19 Ibid., 93.

8

GENETICALLY MODIFIED FOOD

Beauty or the Beast?

KAREN KRUG

Introduction to Methodology

Roger Hutchinson has long pursued a methodology for ethical clarification that allows for systematic comparison between differing positions on social issues. He has developed a model to move discussion forward in cases where interested parties with conflicting ideas about appropriate action reach an impasse. The method proposes four stages of analysis that lead toward informed action—storytelling and definition of the problem; factual clarification; ethical clarification; and post-ethical analysis (although as the clarification takes place, each stage may be revisited again and again). The first stage allows for parties to report their feelings and to recount, in their own way, their version of the issues at stake. The two subsequent stages seek to analyze the perspectives into two types of claims—testable, empirical claims and untestable, value claims. In the final stage, observations are made about the identity of the interested parties, their underlying beliefs about the meaning and purpose of life, and their political commitments and affiliations. This apparent *compartmentalization* is not the end of the methodology, but the process by which it leads to greater recognition of the *interconnectedness* of factual and value claims and the significance of this relationship for the kinds of narratives we tell and the identities we adopt.[1]

Notes to chapter 8 are on p. 166.

Hutchinson's model is a fine analytical tool that facilitates clarity in debates over social issues, yet it is founded on the acknowledgment that no analysis in and of itself can dictate right action. The thinking underpinning this approach is optimistic. It fosters the possibility of consensus on action without agreeing about all the details, yet it is realistic in recognizing that implementing a policy is infinitely more difficult than agreeing on it. Developed by one with an engineering background and strong theological interests, it is a model that allows a person to place one foot in the realm of the secular and the scientific and the other in the religious and spiritual realm. The model reflects the commitments of a fine humanitarian, an individual generous in deeds and in thought, and one with a genuine interest in understanding the views of others on a host of socially relevant subjects. The model fosters integrity by supporting action based on reasoned reflection and engagement with the views of those with whom one disagrees. Despite these admirable motives, like all models the methodology is only as good as the analyst who uses it. It is with this humble awareness that I will attempt to illustrate the value of Hutchinson's methodology by using it in the following analysis. With this same modesty, I claim myself as one student among several generations who now view this model as a practical tool for making sense of complexity and for choosing ethically sound action. I am confident this legacy will continue.

Breaking positions down into particular kinds of claims—compartmentalizing—allows one to see exactly how factual and value claims are linked together and integrally related to the ideologies that influence one's self-identity and the kinds of actions one supports. Once components have been identified, it is useful in trying to understand complex positions and identities to compare and contrast them both horizontally and vertically. A horizontal comparison would make observations about relationships between like categories: for instance, comparing and contrasting the factual claims inherent in one position with those from a second position. A vertical comparison would look across categories within a single position to highlight linkages or interdependencies among different claims or standpoints. Both processes are useful when one seeks to understand a position that differs from one's own, or to understand in more detail the logic, passions and assumptions underpinning one's own position on an ethical issue.

Hutchinson's method for ethical clarification is designed with an awareness that the kinds of actions we support emerge not only from particular facts but also from values that we accept, and that these facts and values are intertwined in particular ways with the ideologies to which we all subscribe, either consciously or unconsciously. To illustrate how this methodology can foster greater understanding and support nuanced comparisons between widely or moderately differing positions regarding ethical issues, I have undertaken an analysis of two authors' perspectives on food-related biotechnology. The articles were chosen so that quite different views on the selected issue could be presented and so that direct comparisons between the two positions would be possible.

Images of Biotechnology and Food

Debate over food biotechnology tends to be polarized: one side argues that biotechnology will save us from evils such as global starvation; the other portends disaster should we continue on this high-technology course. In the latter instance, biotechnology is portrayed as "the beast," while in the former it is presented as "beauty." One author, Andrew Kimbrell, refers to Monsanto as "the Frankenstein Corporation," a "monster corporation"[2] because of its involvement with biotechnology, particularly with what has been dubbed "terminator technology" (genetically engineered seeds that cannot reproduce, and hence must be purchased each year). There are references to biotechnology's biological pollution as "malignancy" and to corporations that promote genetic modification as "the *real* terrorists."[3] In contrast, others argue that "biology will be the driving force of the *Golden Age*…[and that soon] biotechnology will enable…people to live a longer and healthier life, and produce local varieties of agricultural plants custom designed to local conditions."[4] Such advocates see biotechnology as part of a utopian future in which specific vitamins can be incorporated into staple crops;[5] diseases will be fully understood, cured or prevented;[6] everyone will have enough to eat; the environment will be cleaner and healthier; and protected natural areas will be increased. In this essay, versions of the beauty and the beast arguments will be examined to uncover the internal logic of each position and to clarify where the factual and ethical differences lie. Position A, the beatific vision of beauty, will be represented by Anthony Trewavas in an article entitled "Much Food, Many Problems."[7] The beastly vision, Position B, will be represented by Andrew Kimbrell in an article entitled "Why Biotechnology and High-Technology Agriculture Cannot Feed the World."[8]

The "Beauty" of Biotechnology

Definition of the Problem

Technophobia and complacency brought about by easy access to cheap and healthy food (a product of modern intensive agriculture) make the general public in well-developed countries *unreasonably* negative about biotechnology and willing to ignore the fact that we need this technology if we are to feed the world.

Factual Clarification

Due to the cheap, plentiful food supplied by modern intensive agriculture, those in the West eat a much healthier diet now than people did at the end of the nineteenth century. The resulting longer lifespans encourage people to be wary of any new approaches to food production and their potential health risks. This resistance has led to uninformed and unreasonable rejection of genetically modified (GM) food. Technophobia has destroyed the possibility of discovering positive uses for GM technology—i.e., a banana tree that would express cholera vaccine and contribute to the survival of many Third World people. In particular, those fanatically opposed to GM food express ignorance about the realities of existing farm practices, ignore important facts about plants, and are oblivious to the reality that many of their criticisms of biotechnology also apply to general agricultural practice.

Misrepresented Dangers

Concern has been expressed about the creation of "superweeds," as plants engineered to be resistant to specific herbicides interact with weedy relatives, transferring this herbicide resistance. However, there are varieties of plants that have been bred conventionally from plants with natural tendencies to resistance. The same concern about the creation of superweeds is not directed at these varieties (for example, Synchrony beans that are "naturally" resistant to sulphonylurea herbicide). A greater threat than GM plants with herbicide resistance is the introduction of alien species, yet anti-GM activists do not advocate strong action to contain these threats.

The concern that, once released, transgenic plants cannot be controlled is misplaced because, like all domesticated plants, they will lack the key characteristics that allow weedy plants to propagate indefinitely in the wild. Seeds distributed by birds, or by natural events, would have low survival rates. In weeds that develop herbicide resistance, alternative herbicides can be used for control, so that the threat is not uncontrollable. (Some herbicides, such as glyphosate, are effective and innocuous.) Alternatively, the concern that pollen from GM plants will travel to contaminate other plants can be addressed by ensuring that adequate buffer zones are created. Such a small percentage passes beyond long-established and internationally adopted buffer zones that crop purity across boundaries is not a problem. However, concern about transfer by pollen could effectively be addressed by transferring genes through chloroplasts, since most plant crops have no chloroplasts in their pollen.

Problems with Conventional Agriculture

Conventional agriculture relies on the use of at least five broad-spectrum pesticides each year. Eventually, pesticides will not work as control mechanisms because plants develop resistance to them. Pesticides also kill pests and non-pests indiscriminately. GM technology would allow pesticide use to drop dramatically, allowing the return of wildlife to croplands. In rejecting GM technology, environmentalists actually contribute to continued decline in wildlife.

The green revolution benefited people in developing countries. Increases in food production due to the green revolution helped offset the rapidly growing population in the undeveloped world. The food requirements of at least one billion extra people were satisfied because approaches were adopted that went beyond traditional agriculture. Unfortunately, conventional breeding is unable to increase cereal yields further. Anticipated increases in population and unpredictable natural disasters will heighten food demands for the future. Current increases in world food production are now unable to keep pace with food demands. Given that ecological disasters such as global climate change are wreaking havoc, we need to be prepared with as many strategies as possible.

Limitations of Organic Agriculture

Organic agriculture cannot provide the solution to world food needs. Average crop yields from organic agriculture are about one-half of those from intensive farming. Relying on manure as fertilizer would increase the land base required for organic food production and, thus, would lead to the destruction of wilderness areas.

The organic agriculture philosophy is founded on the fallacy that food not treated with human-made chemicals is pure until the chemicals are added, but in fact almost all the carcinogens consumed by people are naturally manufactured by plants (including food plants) to restrict predation. There is an inconsistency between organic agriculture advocates' rejection of GM crops and their acceptance of plants such as triticale, which have been "unnaturally" produced using embryo rescue and cell culture. "Natural" techniques would produce similar crops in the end, but at ten times the cost and taking ten times as long to generate.

Furthermore, the various practices of organic agriculture have not been investigated to determine their safety for humans. Using bacillus thuringiensis (Bt) spores as insecticides is one practice shown to have negative consequences for human health. Contamination by mycotoxins and bacterial infection are two additional risks.

Organic agriculture advocates falsely believe that organic approaches eliminate competition and allow humans to work with nature. However, the competition for resources is built into the ecology of our planet. Ultimately, competition leads to evolution, vitality and creativity—to new dynamic equilibria in which the human spirit (a biological characteristic unique to humans) is integrated.

Ethical Clarification

We should not expect to have a risk-free world. Those who object to the development of superweeds through biotechnology should acknowledge that the same types of danger evolve from the careful breeding of naturally resistant plants. We should be more concerned about the introduction of exotic or alien species of plants that interact with indigenous ones, polluting genetic information and resulting in unnatural and uncontrollable gene flow.

Opposition to GM technology is dangerous and short-sighted. Those who live in the Third World are worthy of our concern and deserve the health benefits and the access to nourishing food that GM technology could provide. Thus, genetic manipulation should be publicly funded and should attempt to minimize the destruction of pests and diseases that limit production.

It should not, however, be a priority of biotechnology to develop plants that are resistant to herbicides. Environmental activists (along with others) should care about reducing pesticide use, maintaining biodiversity and limiting human impact on the Earth's ecosystems. It is better to control pests and diseases selectively through GM technology than to use chemicals that wipe out species indiscriminately.

We should not delude ourselves into thinking that organic agriculture is the solution when it is negative and restrictive. Instead, we should diversify our use of technology to keep our options open for the future. It is beneficial to use pesticides in moderation, but we should also foster agriculture that is flexible and diverse in its use of technology, and efficient in land use. Good agriculture will recycle farm resources, retain soil fertility through green manure and crop rotation, use zero tillage and integrated pest management techniques, and use water efficiently. Toward these ends, we should be creative in our use of genetic manipulation.

We should foster the kind of competitive spirit that has led to the development of genetic engineering. Humans should not think of themselves as being at war with or in competition with nature, but, rather, should seek to be guided by the positively competitive human spirit, which leads toward a new dynamic equilibrium within nature.

Post-ethical Clarification

Trewavas is a plant biologist. He notes that very few of the people who object to biotechnology are plant biologists. Although he has a clear leaning toward biotechnology because of his scientific background, he intentionally points out that he does not embrace "big, insensitive agribusiness"; he is not captive to the interests of corporate agribusiness. He is critical of organic agriculture and anti-biotechnology activists for their misguided perspectives, yet he expresses a concern for health and environmental issues, as well as for the people who are suffering and deprived in the Third World.

The ethical perspectives he presents are primarily utilitarian in nature. He expresses concern about the negative consequences of failing to use GM technologies—consequences such as world hunger, environmental pollution and destruction of natural habitat. Yet, his position is underpinned by the teleological-sounding claim that the competitive, challenge-driven human spirit should be fostered since it is exclusively inherent in human nature. This deontological claim is accompanied by the inference that it is the ontology of nature (and therefore right) to seek the dynamic equilibrium in response to the inevitable disruptions of its components, which are necessarily locked into the ongoing competition for limited resources.[9] Although a deontological claim is at the root of Trewavas' moral argument, a series of consequentialist claims are also necessary for his argument. Thus, Trewavas adopts the ethical standpoint of an idealist, placing himself neither solely in the consequentialist nor in the deontological court.

Biotechnology as "the Beast"

Definition of the Problem

Advocates of biotechnology (including high-technology agriculture) claim that it is necessary to feed the hungry world, but using these approaches alone can lead only to further starvation by contributing to food dependence and the "enclosure phenomenon."

Factual Clarification

Hunger and Its Causes

Hunger exists. Current statistics estimate that 786 million people go hungry every day. Hunger is increasing. In fact, the number of people experiencing hunger increased by 11 percent between 1970 and 1990. Hunger is not caused by our inability to produce sufficient food. Per capita food production has increased along with world hunger, suggesting that it is not total food production that is the primary cause of hunger. (In South America, the number of people suffering from hunger rose by 19 percent, while per capita food supplies rose almost eight percent. In South Asia, hunger and food per capita both increased by nine percent.)

The primary cause of hunger today is food dependence. With the emphasis on the production of exports to generate capital for industrial development, peasants have lost their access to land for growing food for personal consumption. In the Third World, more than half a billion people are in this situation. With the loss of their land (enclosure), their communities and their food independence, peasants tend to head to the cities where they hope to find work. There, they must compete with others for an insufficient number of low-paying jobs. The alternative is to remain in rural communities and work on the industrialized farms for meagre wages. Without land on which to grow their own food, or sufficient money to purchase it, such people end up hungry, regardless of production levels.

Best Farm Types

Large, technologically intensive farms are supported by pro-biotechnology advocates as a means to maximize food production and to address world hunger. However, such approaches are likely to accelerate the enclosure trend. As the size of farms and the use of technology increase, the number of farmers decreases, rural communities are destroyed, and rural people move to cities in search of employment. This migration leads to higher unemployment, crime, food dependency and hunger.

Like most technologies, biotechnology primarily benefits those who adopt it initially, by giving them a competitive edge as prices drop. Those who wait to adopt biotechnology tend to have smaller farms with less capital for initial investment. They often suffer from falling product prices in the period before they have access to the new technology. This leads to greater inequality among farmers and to bankruptcy for many small producers.

Despite the claims of pro-biotechnology advocates, medium-sized (not large) farms tend to be the most efficient by conventional standards of efficiency. However, when additional factors such as environmental and social impacts are included, large farms fare even worse. For example, large farms lead to 40 percent more erosion and use more artificial inputs than smaller ones. Larger farms' increased use of pesticides, hormones and other toxins leads to human health costs, which are treated as irrelevant externalities. Also ignored in conventional efficiency analysis is the impact of the dislocation of millions of farmers over the decades. Because of the emphasis on measuring outputs, the increased efficiency of smaller farms is often underestimated, as the savings in terms of inputs are ignored. The nature of smaller farms allows for increased diversification and, thereby, leads to a whole variety of efficiencies (for example, crop rotation, the planting of companion crops). A United States National Research Council study assessing the true efficiency of large industrial farms concluded that the biggest were not necessarily the best. The combination of reduced pesticides, fertilizers and antibiotics per production unit, lower production costs, reduced adverse environmental and health impacts, and comparable or higher yields per unit made smaller farms more efficient than larger ones.

Yet, biotechnology advocates argue that, unlike large-scale, high-technology-based agriculture, organic and other low-technology approaches will require increasing amounts of land for food production, if the world is to be fed. The green revolution, which relied on technology and chemical-intensive agriculture, created only a temporary rise in production. The eventual degradation of the soil, proliferation of pests, chemical contamination, eutrophication and loss of biodiversity were the results of the monoculture approach forced upon the poor in the Third World.

Presenting biotechnology as the solution to the problems identified with the chemical-intensive approach to agriculture is misleading. For one thing, the same companies advocating biotechnology as a way to eliminate chemicals in agriculture have developed and marketed chemical-resistant varieties of seeds that make increased chemical use possible. They have been less successful in creating pest-resistant varieties. Furthermore, these technologies themselves may threaten organic agriculture. For example, a natural pesticide, Bt, which is selectively applied by organic farmers, has been engineered into different varieties of plants to make them pest resistant. When it is used in this way, widespread pest resistance to Bt is likely, reducing the effectiveness of organic approaches.

The Dangers of Biotechnology

Biotechnology will destroy existing options for chemical-free agriculture. However, an even greater danger is its potential for producing biological pollution. There are already many examples in the United States of the dangers of introducing exotic species—the gypsy moth, kudzu vine, and the organisms that cause chestnut blight and

Dutch elm disease. Each genetically altered organism is a potential "exotic" that could harm the environment. The long-term impact of thousands of GM organisms could be much more dangerous than the effects of petrochemicals. Because the organisms can multiply, disseminate and mutate, any problems can spread and possibly become irreversible. Resistance transferred to weeds from cereal crops, for instance, may require massive chemical responses and still be beyond human control.

In addition to environmental problems, social problems will be created as biotechnology extends the enclosure process. The genetic commons are enclosed as transnationals patent the genes, plants and animals necessary for agricultural production—genetically sterilized seeds that cannot be saved—and make all farmers and consumers more dependent upon corporations for their survival.

Ethical Clarification

We have an obligation to feed hungry humans. The best way to do this is to maintain people's food independence. We ought to learn from the green revolution that was foisted on the Third World. We should minimize the control of multinational corporations such as Monsanto, which are guilty of sleight of hand in manipulating people into thinking that they are benefiting from their actions when it is actually the companies that profit.

In addition to addressing starvation, we also have a responsibility to preserve nature and human health by avoiding the application of pesticides, hormones and other poisons in food production. For this reason, we should support organic agriculture. We must take into account external factors in assessing the efficiency of farms, and thereby help to preserve the unique character of small, diversified farms that maximize efficiency.

While chemical pollution should concern us, we must avoid biological pollution, as it can be even more dangerous and malignant. Therefore, we should avoid using biotechnology unless we can be certain it is safe.

Post-ethical Clarification

Kimbrell is described as an "activist attorney." His identification as an activist suggests that his perspectives run against those of the mainstream. He is also the founder and president of the International Centre for Technology Assessment and the Jacques Ellul Society. These commitments demonstrate his concern with ethical issues and his unwillingness to adopt technology uncritically. Furthermore, his involvement in organizations dealing with economics and globalization reveals his interest in corporate activity and its impact on citizens around the world. All these focuses are integrated into his analysis of biotechnology in agriculture.

Kimbrell's article appears in a special edition of *The Ecologist*. The magazine agreed to publish the edition after another journal backed down, fearing a backlash from Monsanto. This fact, in itself, indicates much about the nonconformist commitments of the contributors.

The primary arguments made against biotechnology in Kimbrell's article are consequentialist in nature. It is argued that this technology is linked to the industrial agriculture model, and ultimately will lead to environmental degradation, human health problems and increased starvation. No particular arguments are presented to explain why humans ought to concern themselves with the environment or with human health and nourishment. This lack of explanation suggests that these latter claims are more deontological in nature; that is, they stand on their own, independent of an appeal to non-moral consequences. Insofar as he combines the two approaches, Kimbrell is an idealist.[10]

Horizontal Comparison of Positions A and B

Definition of the Problem

The two authors define the problem in opposite ways. Trewavas argues that we need biotechnology if we are to feed the world, and despairs that the misinformed and inconsistent general public prematurely rejects it. Kimbrell contends that, contrary to the arguments made by the corporations controlling and profiting from biotechnology, the biotechology approach will actually increase global starvation.

Factual Clarification

The most substantial disagreement between the two authors emerges from their differing beliefs about empirical reality. This is positive in the sense that it points to possibilities for resolving disagreements. In the face of clear evidence on one side or the other, the positions may be altered. However, both articles include arguments against existing positions that they believe to be false. In the final analysis, each is seeking to refute the factual claims presented or assumed by those who hold opposing views.

Both authors agree that there is starvation, but they disagree about its cause. The decisive question is whether starvation results from production levels that are insufficient to support growing populations or from a lack of food independence caused by the enclosure phenomenon that results from corporate, technology-intensive agriculture.

Another area of debate concerns the extent of the dangers posed by biotechnology. Both authors recognize that corporations can profit from biotechnology, and they regret that decisions related to biotechnology projects have not been made with public interest as the main consideration. Trewavas believes that this danger can be offset by maintaining public control over biotechnology; however, Kimbrell suggests that other dangers are too grave to surmount. Trewavas states that the danger of GM traits spreading beyond controlled regions and plant types is not serious. He affirms that buffer zones, the natural characteristics of wild and domesticated plants, new chemical treatments and particular biotechnological approaches to gene transfer could address this potential threat. Kimbrell argues that these control mechanisms are insufficient because biotechnology is even more potent than petrochemical technology. Trewavas questions whether the technologies that created canola, Synchrony beans and triticale are any more benign than those of genetic manipulation. Both authors agree that all alien species pose a hazard. (Kimbrell's explicit recognition of this reality calls into question Trewavas' contention that anti-GM activists ignore the parallels between alien species produced through genetic modification and those produced through "conventional" means.) While Trewavas argues that the dangers of biotechnology are exaggerated and that those of petrochemical agriculture are downplayed, Kimbrell rejects petrochemical-intensive agriculture and biotechnology-influenced agriculture, arguing that organic agriculture can address the problems created by both. Citing the example of the natural pesticide, Bt, used by biotechnologists in gene transfer, Kimbrell worries that biotechnology agriculture can threaten organic agriculture practices, and thereby reduce the range of techniques and approaches available to us in the future. In contrast, Trewavas argues that biotechnology is one necessary part of a diversified approach to agriculture.

Different assessments of the strengths and weaknesses of existing forms of agriculture point to the empirical question of whether organic agriculture is a sensible solution or a misguided attempt to go back to an inadequate approach. One major question relevant to this general area of inquiry is whether organic agriculture is less efficient and productive or more efficient and productive than biotechnology- and petrochemical-based agriculture. A related question is whether organic agriculture will use more natural space or less natural space than biotechnology- and petrochemical-based agriculture. Kimbrell and Trewavas disagree about whether the green revolution helped the Third World feed more people or led to increased starvation. Trewavas maintains that the green revolution was the only thing that allowed starvation levels to moderate in the face of population increases, but he also argues that it has contributed as much as it can. Kimbrell counters that the green revolution's monoculture approach led to enclosure and greater food dependency and to by-products such as soil degradation, pestilence, chemical contamination, eutrophication and loss of biodiversity. Kimbrell is critical of the impacts of conventional agriculture, but Trewavas points to some of the impurities of organic agriculture. He asserts that many organic techniques are untested and that some are known to endanger human health; that plants contain natural toxins, including carcinogens; and that organic farmers uncritically use seeds produced through "unnatural" techniques such as embryo rescue and cell culture.

Ultimately, Kimbrell and Trewavas disagree about whether it is possible to develop a form of agriculture that is not based on competition. Trewavas points out that agriculture is a human activity that, by definition, is based on competition among species for limited resources, and that the ecosystem can adapt to the initiatives we take to fulfill our species' self-interests. Implicit in Kimbrell's support for organic agriculture is the perspective that through organic approaches we can create a form of agriculture that involves cooperation, not competition, with nature.

Ethical Clarification

Although there are many disagreements between the two authors about the factual claims, there is a surprising consistency in the ethical commitments expressed by both in all but their conclusions—whether or not biotechnology is an appropriate approach for agriculture. There is consensus that we should address starvation, protect the environment, reduce pesticide use, preserve biodiversity, restrict the spread of alien species and limit human impact on the planetary ecosystem. Their shared commitment to these values is based on their concern for the environment and for humanity.

However, despite their commonly held values, the two authors fundamentally disagree about the consequences of biotechnology. Trewavas supports biotechnology, but argues caution in our approach to it. He believes that we should aim for public funding of biotechnology rather than accept corporate control. He rejects goals such as the production of herbicide-resistant plants, but supports the use of biotechnology to create positive traits such as more nutritious plants, higher yields and increased pest resistance. In contrast, Kimbrell rejects biotechnology in agriculture altogether, seeing it as an extension of the high-technology, petrochemical-intensive, corporate agricultural model.

Each author assesses organic agriculture differently. Trewavas insists that we should not pin our hopes on organic agriculture, but instead should employ a range of techniques. Ideal agriculture would recycle farm resources, integrate green manure, rotate crops, undertake integrated pest management, aim for zero tillage, use water efficiently and find appropriate roles for genetic manipulation. Kimbrell maintains that the best approach is organic, low-technology, diversified agriculture.

Post-ethical Clarification

In significant ways, the identities and world views of the two authors underpin their arguments. As a biologist working out of a university, Trewavas maintains a position consistent with the perspective of most scientists working in biotechnology. As an activist with a legal background and involvement in many organizations doing social analysis, Kimbrell presents an argument most consistent with the views of the engaged public. That Trewavas should align himself with the scientific community and Kimbrell with the social activists is not surprising, given their professional backgrounds; it is consistent with their identities and commitments. For Kimbrell, the core of the problem is social, not scientific; for Trewavas, the issue is predominantly scientific. Kimbrell is concerned with the control and distribution of food;

Trewavas is interested in using science to find new ways to increase food production.

The differences in identities underscore a major factor that separates the two analysts. Trewavas demonstrates strong faith that science can solve most problems. He argues that we can invent new herbicides if plants become resistant to old ones, and expresses confidence that we will be able to control the spread of GM plants. Kimbrell exhibits faith in staying as close as possible to natural systems, hence supporting organic, low-technology, diversified approaches to agriculture. In keeping with these different approaches, we can associate particular moral horizons with each.

The contrasting positions of Trewavas and Kimbrell reflect opposing perspectives on the role of biotechnology in agriculture. The differences that these opposing viewpoints might make in our designs for the future are manifest in the utopian visions for agriculture described in the parallel columns below.

Vision One

Permaculture is a design system for creating sustainable human environments. Permaculture deals with plants, animals, buildings, and infrastructures (water, energy, communications). However, permaculture is not about these elements themselves, but rather about the relationships we can create between them by the way we place them in the landscape.

The aim is to create systems that are ecologically sound and economically viable, which provide for their own needs, do not exploit or pollute, and are therefore sustainable in the long term. Permaculture uses the inherent qualities of plants and animals combined with the natural characteristics of landscapes and structures to produce a life-supporting system for city and country, using the smallest practical area.

Permaculture is based on the observation of natural systems, the

Vision Two

Biotechnology will enable us in the fairly near future to enable people to live a longer and healthier life, and produce local varieties of agricultural plants custom designed to local conditions.

On the agricultural side, a new generation of plants will be designed to produce their own nutrients and their own compounds to protect themselves against pests, thereby radically reducing the need for fertilizers and pesticides, and freeing farmers of their dependence on distant factories....The new plants will contain oils that are healthier for the heart, tastier, more nutritious, and easier to digest. Some will carry high levels of substances that fight cancer and other chronic diseases.

In the Golden Age, different communities will have very different diets, tuned to their own agriwisdom contained in traditional farming systems and modern scientific and technological knowledge. Although based on good ecological models, permaculture creates a cultivated ecology, which is designed to produce more human and animal food than is generally found in nature.[11]

cultural growing conditions and cultural preferences.

Because more can be produced on less land, more territory is available for other species. Land marginal for agriculture has been returned to more natural types of ecosystems.[12]

The first vision is drawn from Bill Mollison's introduction to permaculture, a design system he developed decades ago and that has led to a global permaculture movement. In this vision, imitation of nature is highly prized. This approach relies on observation of nature and of what already occurs naturally to foster good designs that will improve human conditions without disrupting the delicate balance of nature. Scientists are now "rediscovering" these "natural" approaches, such as using mixtures of varieties or species within plots to "naturally" limit fungal disease and other problems.[13] Bioengineering has no place in this first vision.

The second vision is drawn from a futuristic article by Jeffrey McNeely, chief scientist at the World Conservation Union. In this vision, human ingenuity is the key to success. Miraculous discoveries and inventions will enable humans to progress beyond the existing limitations of nature, to create something so vastly superior that these (or subsequent) discoveries will address human needs and solve any problems created along the way. Bioengineering is a prime example of the kind of human inventiveness that drives this second vision. Ultimately, the debate about biotechnology reflects fundamental differences in our visions of the kind of future we imagine for ourselves and for subsequent generations.

General Conclusions

If we are to take at face value the ethical commitments professed by both those who vilify and those who embrace genetic modification of food crops, common commitments emerge—to foster human health, to end starvation and to protect the environment. These shared commitments may be building blocks for achieving agreement concerning social policy actions. However, careful empirical research is required if scientists and social activists are to have the factual information required to come to agreement about suitable policy directions.[14] Analysis of the selected articles suggests that whether one sees biotechnology as beauty or the beast depends more upon one's interpretation of the facts than upon the ethical values one holds. It remains to be seen whether empirical tests can be designed to satisfy those on both sides of the issue.

Notes

1 Roger Hutchinson, *Prophets, Pastors and Public Choices: Canadian Churches and the Mackenzie Valley Pipeline Debate* (Waterloo, ON: Wilfrid Laurier University Press, 1992); and Roger Hutchinson, "Towards a 'Pedagogy for Allies of the Oppressed,'" *Studies in Religion/Sciences religieuses* 13/2 (1984): 145-50.

2 Andrew Kimbrell, "The Frankenstein Corporation: Monsanto's Merger with American Home Products," *The Ecologist* 28/5 (1998): 305.

3 Zac Goldsmith, "Ecowarriors or Vandals? Who are the *Real* Terrorists?" *The Ecologist* 28/5 (1998): 312.

4 Jeffrey McNeely, "A Golden Age," *People and the Planet* 8/4 (1999): 26-27.

5 Gordon Conway and Gary Toenniessen, "Feeding the World in the Twenty-First Century," *Nature* 402 (1999): C55-C58.

6 Yousef Haj-Ahmad, "Biotechnology Will Change the Way We Live," *Surgite!* (Fall 2000): 7.

7 Anthony Trewavas, "Much Food, Many Problems," *Nature* 402 (1999): 231-32.

8 Andrew Kimbrell, "Why Biotechnology and High-Technology Agriculture Cannot Feed the World," *The Ecologist* 28/5 (1998): 294-98.

9 Trewavas, "Much Food, Many Problems," 231-32.

10 Kimbrell, "The Frankenstein Corporation," 306ff.

11 William Mollison and Reny Mia Slay, *Introduction to Permaculture* (Tyalgum, Australia: Tagari Publications, 1991), 1.

12 McNeely, "A Golden Age," 26-27.

13 Martin S. Wolfe, "Crop Strength through Diversity," *Nature* 406 (2000): 681-82.

14 Rosie Hails, "Genetically Modified Plants—The Debate Continues," *TREE* 15/1 (2000): 14-18.

9

BEYOND "SURVIVAL OF THE FITTEST"

Pastoral Resources for Rebuilding Rural Community

CAMERON R. HARDER

As a parish pastor and a theologian, I have struggled to understand and to cope with a painful discrepancy in rural Canada. Roger Hutchinson has helped me find the tools to begin this task.

Here is the incongruity. On the one hand, rural Canadians long for a vibrant future for their communities. A survey of 7,000 rural Canadians undertaken by the federal government in 1997 and a series of eighty-seven rural community round table discussions held in Manitoba in the 1990s yielded a common vision. Participants said they hoped for self-sustaining communities with ample opportunities for employment; public recognition of the value of rural Canada to the identity and well-being of the nation; the opportunity to make informed decisions about their own future; improvements in the quality of life; access to health care and education at a reasonable cost; communities rich in culture and supporting family living; services and employment to retain and attract people; and educational opportunities and community services to sustain steady growth.[1]

On the other hand, this vision of a lively rural community seems far off the path of present demographic trends. Except for urban hinterlands, the rural population has been declining steadily for decades. The absolute number of people living on farms in 1996 was one quarter of

Notes to chapter 9 are on pp. 195-202.

what it had been in 1931. The percentage of Canadians living on farms had dropped during that period from 32 percent to less than 3 percent.[2] This population decline was accompanied by a savage dismantling of the rural institutions that sustain healthy human life. Churches, schools, grain elevators, hospitals, recreational facilities, hotels, agribusinesses, stores, post offices, even coffee shops closed down or were forced to move into larger centres.

What makes it so difficult for most rural communities to implement the vision described above? In *Something's Wrong Somewhere: Globalization, Community and the Moral Economy of the Farm Crisis*, Christopher Lind exposes the process by which globalization of agricultural markets and agribusiness rips decision-making power from the hands of local communities. That loss of self-determination is largely reflected, he says, in the dismantling of the rural institutions that have provided a structure for communal conversation and processes for common action. It takes a *community* to implement a vision. Community, in Lind's eyes, is defined by relationships of trust, interdependence, caring and commitment. However, the agricultural practices and structures that have developed in Canada over the last century have fostered competitiveness, domination and indifference.[3] They reflect an ideology that I will refer to as "survival of the fittest."

The deep fissures it has created are obvious. Growing farms swallow struggling neighbours in order to expand their own operations. Farmers who could profitably cooperate in their operations cannot find the courage to open their books to each other. Small hog farmers and acreage owners protest the development of mammoth hog facilities, while others welcome the promise of jobs.[4] Town businesses struggle under the weight of unpaid farm debts, while farmers resent the rising prices for inputs charged by local dealers. Organic farmers battle neighbours whose chemicals or genetically modified seeds drift onto their fields. Members of the Western Canadian Wheat Growers battle for a freer market with members of the National Farmers Union, who support the Canadian Wheat Board's marketing monopoly. Non-Natives resent Natives who have purchased farmland through the settlement of Aboriginal treaties and then taken the land out of production.

In other words, it is not enough that many individuals share broad values about community revitalization. Rural communities need a *place*, a *process* and a *philosophy*, which will support the rebuilding of trust, clear analysis of rural problems and construction of effective plans for action. As far as *place* is concerned, the church is one of the few institutions remaining in many rural towns that has a mandate for building community. Rural congregations are uniquely positioned to foster the relations of trust and the depth of conversation necessary to help a community grapple effectively with its future.

This essay is an effort to offer some assistance. It leads the reader into an analysis and theological challenge of the survival of the fittest *philosophy* which supports divisiveness; in so doing, it also demonstrates a *process* for community conversation which may result in the adoption of a new world view that can truly sustain rural communities.

I must acknowledge here my debt to Roger Hutchinson. I began a reading and research course with him during my doctoral studies at the Toronto School of Theology. To my delight, I discovered that he had grown up on a farm in Alberta just outside the town where I was a pastor at the time. He was familiar with the parameters of the rural crisis that I was investigating and eventually became my thesis advisor. In addition to sharing his expertise, he was warm and hospitable (underrated qualities in education!). He also pressed me to remain honest, to stay grounded in the data of my interviews, to be open to the input of many voices. Perhaps most importantly, his analysis of the Mackenzie Valley Pipeline debate helped me to recognize a process for fruitful discussion that might work in rural communities.[5]

Hutchinson noted that the pipeline debate often faltered because participants were not communicating on the same level of discourse. Some were sharing personal stories, while others were trying to ascertain publicly accessible facts; some were making ethical judgments, while others were expressing post-ethical beliefs.

Hutchinson recognized that each form of discourse has its own integrity. Personal stories are subjective and in one sense non-debatable. But telling them allows participants in the debate to hear the personal *impact*—practical, relational and emotional—that the present situation has had on others. It helps them to be open to each other, to take each other into account. Discussions of fact help participants to become aware of consequences that their personal position has tended to ignore. Of course, facts are weighted—valued—differently. A consequence regarded as trivial by some can be considered vitally important by others. This is where discussions often break down. In the apparent interest of tolerant multiculturalism, Canadian public debate rarely goes beyond the simple identification of competing values.

As Hutchinson points out, values are not free-floating. They are embedded in world views, in belief systems that broadly inform people's decisions. These are based on fundamental assumptions that are difficult to debate. They are even more difficult to change because they are fortified by cultural relations, histories and rituals. But identifying them at least allows participants to speak each other's language. It reveals a pattern to actions that previously seemed chaotic or confusing to other participants. It also allows conversation partners to bring inconsistencies to light: "If you believe this, then why are you doing that?"

Finally, exposing underlying belief systems opens up new options for the future. The status quo tends to acquire a patina of sacred inevitability: things are the way they are because God (or fate) has designed them to be that way. History, however, tells us that our social and political orders are constructed rather than inevitable. Hearing how others envision human life opens up the possibility of a future that was previously unimaginable because hope had been captive to assumptions now revealed to be historically conditioned and not absolute.

It must be said, on the one hand, that this form of community conversation is not easy in a rural context. As Kathleen Norris points out in *Dakota*, the "myth of independence…makes it difficult to come together and work for the things that might benefit us all."[6] It is also difficult to gather around one table farmers who are insolvent and their neighbours who would like to buy them out, town business people who resent the support given to farmers but not to them, bankers who want to make sure their loan portfolios are in good shape, consumers concerned about the price of food, and so on. Envy and suspicion tend to replace trust. Competition is seen as more life-giving than cooperation. Open conversation is severely restricted.

On the other hand, I believe that the *will* to engage in this sort of conversation exists in our rural communities. In the federal survey of rural Canadians, respondents expressed a strong desire for better cooperation between farm and non-farm interests in local communities. They also were convinced that rural areas have an unusual capacity for such community spirit if there is the leadership to encourage and direct it.[7] Local clergy, and other designated ministers, already carry some of those leadership responsibilities.

The challenge for rural churches today is to take the bit between their teeth and initiate the conversation. I suggest that it might move in four stages: (1) attend to what is happening—listen to each other's stories, pay attention to the facts, do some research; (2) identify the underlying values and beliefs; (3) assess the "truthfulness" of these beliefs—how they fit with the facts, their capacity to carry rural hopes and dreams; and (4) nurture a rebellious imagination. Allow the Bible to reframe what is happening and open up alternatives. Find together a world view that is truly applicable to rural people. I will try to show how I have moved through this process in my own research and how the process might be used in a rural community.

Attend to What Is Happening

We can never get a full picture of what is happening, of course; reality is wonderfully, frustratingly complex. To *sketch* it, then, requires attending to some details and ignoring others. To do that, we use filters controlled by our beliefs about what really matters.[8] In a sense, then, one's goal becomes one's starting point; it is necessary to have some intuition about what is going on in order to know what in all the detail is significant. One hopes, of course, that close attention to the detail will modify, perhaps radically, those initial beliefs.

As a Lutheran pastor and a doctoral student, I began my research by relying on the intuitions of rural people as to what mattered in their context. I asked them to tell me their stories.[9] I heard a great deal of anguish. Henry told me that he was leaving the land he had settled. He said his farming operation was small by today's standards but had generally been debt-free. It had provided a decent living for himself and his family. Why, then, was he leaving? Because he could not shake a deep sense of grief and despair. One farm in his area had expanded to absorb all the others, leaving a once-thriving community with only three families. There was no one to visit, no one for his daughter to date, no curling teams, no health facilities, no churches left. The community that he loved had been swallowed up.

Harold, another farmer, described how he had bought land in the 1980s, rented more and purchased large equipment to farm it. But low grain prices, skyrocketing rentals and interest rates put him into unrepayable debt. Worst of all, he lost his land and his home to a neighbour.

Harold's creditor (a fellow church member) sold the property below market price, just a day or so before Harold raised the money to pay off his debt. A number of relationships were damaged by that experience. Harold and his wife stopped attending church because the creditor's presence enraged him: "I was like a rattlesnake—ready to strike," he said. Even on the street they could not make eye contact. Harold also dropped out of leadership positions in the community, ashamed of his bankruptcy and the image of "one who doesn't pay his debts" that he felt it gave him. His formerly positive relationship with his neighbour was dead: "I pulled his daughter out of the ditch and I took the tractor over and pulled him out, too, one time." "Now you'd just leave him there, wouldn't you?" his wife said. "Yeah, I probably would!" he answered.

The grief, anger and shame I heard in these stories are common. But these feelings are not commonly expressed in public. The suffering in rural communities tends to be hidden because public exposure of one's wounds is shameful. To appear too vulnerable causes a loss of face. And if it exposes the weakness of a community, the whole community is shamed.[10] So the painful stories are rarely brought (voluntarily) to light. As Kathleen Norris notes, a good story in a rural community is one "that doesn't remind us of the bad times, the cardboard patches we used to wear in our shoes, the failed farms, the way people you love just up and die. It tells us instead that hard work and perseverance can overcome all obstacles."[11] Norris says that local histories tend to tell stories of "perseverance made heroic" in a steady march of progress from homesteading to the present. Clergy told me that they encountered this same phenomenon in their rural churches. "It's denial, sheer denial," one lamented. The denial allows dominant belief systems to continue unchallenged because their real effects are obscured.

It is not easy to help a community attend to its suffering. Those who are relatively advantaged by the present arrangements—wealthy farmers, perhaps, or agribusiness managers—have a stake in leaving things as they are. Walter Brueggemann notes that it is not the managers of the status quo who hope for deep and lasting change: "People excessively committed to present power arrangements and present canons of knowledge tend not to wait expectantly for the newness of God."[12] "Who hopes?" he asks. Those who are *articulate sufferers*—"those who enter their grief, suffering and oppression, who bring it to speech, who publicly process it and move through it and beyond. They are the ones who are surprised to find, again and again, that hope and social possibility come in the midst of such grief (cf. Rom. 5:3)."[13]

A first step, then, is identifying inarticulate sufferers and helping them to find their voice. Church leaders have the freedom to visit people's homes when they notice signs of withdrawal or distress. Gentle but firm probing may offer families their first opportunity to speak openly about financial difficulties. Contact can then be made through the pastor with others in similar difficulty (preferably in another parish). Together, in relative safety, farmers are able to speak about their distress and feel the shame diminish as they find that other respectable people are struggling too.

Church leaders also have an important role in revealing suffering as something that belongs not outside of God, forsaken by God, but (since the Forsaken One *is* God) at God's heart. Worship is key. Too often it has tended to soothe the grief and anger of those hurt by the current economic arrangements and to assuage the guilt of those who benefit from or contribute to the injustice in them. In so doing, worship serves only to draw off energies for change. However, it is not soothing that sufferers need, but lament. Strangely, there are very few laments in, for example, Lutheran hymnals, although the Psalms have many. Clergy might invite their poets to write some pointed words to a good hymn tune—words that capture the particular anguish and grief that sit so heavily at the heart of shrinking communities. And their preaching must be contextual. Preachers are effective when they carefully explore the real world of their community—its fading hopes, its fractured relationships, its economic ironies—and speak a word that is truly *good* news, not just old, or nice, or irrelevant news, to the particular darkness that their community faces. When pain is publicly acknowledged, respectfully shared, it loses some of its power to shame. There is freedom in telling one's story.

An effective way to bring a community's pain to expression is through a public forum. In analyzing the way in which public consensus develops around certain issues, Michael Walzer notes that, initially, people are willing to gather on the basis of very broad (what he calls "thin") principles—like some of those expressed earlier in the vision statements: "improvements in the quality of life" and so on. Human society, however, does not live and is not changed at the level of such principles. As he notes, societies are particular. They are made of particular members, each with unique memories of personal and communal life. Humanity in general, however, has no such memories, no rituals, no shared understandings about what is good. Social critique, therefore, according to Walzer, naturally begins not with discussion of universal principles, but with particular stories. It is "home grown." Each one's distinctive reality is "thickly" described in its colourful concreteness.[14]

In those stories, it becomes apparent that different definitions of the problem are, as Hutchinson puts it, "rooted in different experiences, different responsibilities and different loyalties."[15] It may happen, however, that the participants discover an area in which their perspectives converge—an "overlapping consensus" out of which common action may later take shape.

In a couple of the communities in which I conducted interviews, clergy worked together to prepare a public telling of stories from various perspectives in the community. A farmer who had gone bankrupt (and was now living outside the community or perhaps in town), a farmer who was expanding, a lender, a pastor, a health-care worker, a town business person and a parent were invited to tell their stories. They described the effect that the current agricultural climate was having on themselves, their families and their clients. Their stories encouraged others to speak. Divided communities became more clearly aware that they shared a common future—that the loss of farm families closes down town businesses too, and that schools, hospitals and curling rinks do not last long as a result either. It became clearer that, if only the "successful" have a right to stay in a community, then the reward for success will be a lonely life without neighbours or human services.

Identify Underlying Values and Beliefs

Woven through the stories that were shared with me were two very different accounts of what it means to be fully human. On the one hand, I heard rural folk talking about the importance of community in terms like those of the vision articulated at the beginning of this essay. They said that neighbours help each other when there is a fire or an illness. They said that, when a farmer expanded his or her own operation by buying up a bankrupt neighbour's land and equipment, they viewed it as "cannibalism." They told me how much they valued the respect of their community and how ashamed they felt when they thought that respect had been lost. They spoke of the pain of seeing their common life dismantled by the loss of schools, churches, stores and other local institutions. They worked hard to help their children take over the farm, or at least stay in the community, even mortgaging their own futures to make that possible. And when they were forced to leave, by insolvency or for some other reason, they said it felt as though they were "cutting off an arm"—leaving part of themselves behind.

On the other hand, many justified the loss of smaller farms and general depopulation as an inevitable transition to a modern agricultural economy. They said, "You have to keep growing, or you'll start dying." "Farming is a business," they insisted, "and it's a business in which size matters." Growth was regarded as a personal affair, however. They spoke of farming as highly competitive. They said they enjoyed the independence and personal freedom it offered. They insisted that their children manage without substantial help from parents. There was a tendency to treat farm losses phlegmatically—"It's a winnowing; only the strong survive in this business." If aggressive expansion turned out to be ill-timed, and they lost the farm, they were not completely devastated, believing that there were other opportunities in the city.

A number of researchers have noticed these two clusters of values. Most attribute them to the influence of ethnicity. Sonya Salamon's field studies have been particularly important in this regard.[16] She found that farmers of German or Western European peasant background seemed to place a high value on community, and on farming as a way of life. They were more concerned with continuity and traditions than with rapid "progress." They valued hard work as a more reliable means to success than innovation and technology. Farmers of British background, a large number of whom emigrated as a result of the rapid urban population growth brought on by industrialization in the 1800s and early 1900s, saw farming as a chance to grasp true independence. They were looking for freedom from urban bureaucracy, deadening class restrictions and government interference. They saw the "frontier" as a place where people's strength, intelligence and virtue would determine their fate.[17]

Salamon is able to identify particular North Dakota communities in which one or other of these two clusters of values—often referred to in the literature as "yeoman" and "entrepreneur" (or "yankee"), respectively—is dominant. Something similar appears to have developed on the Canadian Prairies. Settlement tended to take place either in a somewhat individualistic, haphazard fashion, predominantly by pioneers of British descent, or in tightly connected ethnic communities, particularly by settlers of German (especially Mennonite), Ukrainian and French descent. The continuing impact of the two groups is suggested by the fact that, in Saskatchewan, for example, 53.7 percent of the population, according to the 1996 census, claimed one of these latter three as their ethnic origin, while 45 percent claimed English or Scottish. However, they are no longer as neatly divided into communities as they once were. Yeomen and entrepreneurs are found sitting together in church pews, as neighbours in the fields, as brothers and sisters in the same family. In fact, I discovered that both sets of values (even though conflicting) were often held by the same individual in regard to different elements of his or her life.

Overall, it is entrepreneurial values and perspectives (more urban than rural in both origin and character) that seem to have shaped Canada's agricultural economy in the last thirty years. Mechanization has made it possible for farmers to milk, feed, plant, weed and harvest without help from neighbours. The co-ops of the 1920s and 1930s have been replaced by large agribusinesses owned by uninvolved shareholders and often even larger umbrella corporations. In many places, competition has taken on a savage face.

However, yeoman values persist and interact with the others—although not always in ways that are helpful. Elsewhere, I talk about the shame that many farmers experience when their farm becomes insolvent.[18] The shame is a yeoman trait—present in most cohesive agrarian societies around the world—in which one's "self" is experienced as a construct of community opinion. Those who lose the community's respect—that is, their personal "honour"—experience it as a diminishment of self; they are shamed. They tend to withdraw from and be isolated by the community. For the most part, their perspective on the community's strengths and weaknesses, and their voice in any conversation about its future, are lost.

The criteria for losing honour in modern Canada, however, are increasingly tied to the entrepreneurial values of land accumulation, profit and visible prosperity, rather than responsible community participation or careful stewardship of one's land and heritage.[19] Dorothy said, "Driving around the country you notice that some people have machinery too big for their operations. It's because status is determined by who can boast about the biggest machinery."

The interaction of these values seems to be establishing a kind of Nietzschean capitalism in rural Canada. Progress, growth, expansion are seen as the keys to successful farming. But the pursuit of them is highly individualized; each individual competes to be the über-farmer. Cooperative enterprise has become increasingly difficult, not only because entrepreneurial values (with their urban roots) tend to make it less acceptable, but also because the yeoman values that should support it interfere through the imposition of shame. Farmers struggling to make a profit in a highly competitive market are unable to open their books to each other (a prerequisite for cooperative work) because they are afraid that they will lose face—that their bottom line will not equal that of their neighbour.

The belief system in which these values are embedded might be called "survival of the fittest." The underlying entrepreneurial perspective insists that only the fittest *can* survive; its yeoman overlay adds that only the fittest *should* (deserve to) survive.

I heard this philosophy expressed by farmers—solvent and insolvent—lenders, input dealers, even pastors. In various ways, they said or implied that, no matter how bad the weather, the markets, government agricultural policy, credit lending instruments or other extra-personal influences, a farm's success is due to the fitness, especially the character and skills, of its operator. For example, at the beginning of the 1998 crash in commodity prices, the Royal Bank sent this assurance:

> By all indications today is a time of tremendous opportunity for *business-minded* farmers who can position themselves in a dynamic, global marketplace....For some it can be an intimidating time. But for farmers who are *on top of their game*, the next 10 to 20 years will be exciting, challenging and potentially very rewarding.[20] [emphasis mine]

Marvin observed that, in his community, it was assumed that farmers who went bankrupt were *not* on top of their game, personally or professionally: "One group says he deserved it or whatever. He bought too many lottery tickets or he drinks too much, or he had too many cigarettes." Bill added, "Some people in the farm community want to stand back and say, 'He must have been a bad manager; he made his mistakes. The sooner he's out of the business, the quicker I'll be able to sell what I sell for more money and more profit.'"

The character of "fit" farmers was described to me in language reminiscent of that used by the writers of British imperial adventure fiction in the late nineteenth century to describe "frontiersmen." Authors such as Connor, Henty and Butler wrote stirring accounts of life on the "margins of the empire," in a vast unspoiled land where independent, free thinkers could shape their own destinies. The Canadian frontier, according to popular writer Robert Ballantyne, a Hudson's Bay fur trade clerk, offered unparalleled conditions for the pursuit of one's fortune. Courage, skill, independence and hard work were all that were required for success.[21]

Clifford Sifton, Wilfrid Laurier's minister of the Interior and Canada's agricultural architect at the turn of the century, built on the image by selling Canada as a place where one could fail only if one were unfit. It was his job to promote the Canadian West to potential immigrants. He plastered Europe with posters that showed new farmers expanding their holdings rapidly to become owners of large plantations within a few years. Others displayed trees growing on the Prairies sporting fruit the size of watermelons.[22] The West, he convinced them, was a fertile utopia where only the foolish and feeble could fail to make a fortune.

The reality, of course, was somewhat different. The immigrants discovered that early frosts and long Canadian winters made farming here a tough and uncertain business. Thousands went south to warmer climes.[23] According to James Woodsworth, one of our church leaders, this simply made the winnowing process more stringent. The hardships, he claimed, were "relieving Canada of the Negro problem and keeping out the lazy and improvident white."[24]

My interviewees told me that success on a farm requires not only the right kind of character, but also enough capital to achieve "economies of scale." Larger farms are thought to be more efficient and therefore more profitable. This assumption, too, appears to have deep roots. Gerald Friesen notes that, when the West was being opened to settlement, the government gave a free quarter section to settlers who could "prove up," but made sure it was adjacent to sale land that they could buy when they completed their residency. This made it unlikely that a large number of small farms would develop in an area, and gave the edge to farmers with capital. The government also gave huge tracts of land to the railway, which then resold it to settlers. Normally, it was those with capital wanting to amass larger holdings who could take advantage of such sales.[25]

Canada's commitment to increasing the size and productivity of its farms was given a boost by the starvation that followed the two world wars. Farmers felt called to feed the world. A "breadbasket" motif not only appeared in my interviews, but also showed up again and again in government policy documents ("the prairies are the world's breadbasket") and lenders' promotional material ("it's Canada's job to feed the world").[26] The answer to greater food production was found in the adoption of new technologies. The tractor, the truck and the combine gained wide acceptance in the 1920s. But they significantly altered the farm economy. By increasing the farmers' need for capital, they gave a distinct advantage to farmers who brought significant wealth into the enterprise.[27] The machinery also gave farmers the independence that the frontier images had promised them. By multiplying the acreage that could be handled by a farm household, it allowed them to manage at seedtime and harvest without their neighbours and undercut the need for hired hands. Thus, subsistence farmers who depended on wage labour to supplement their income (up to 75 percent of the agricultural labour force in Alberta as late as 1936) were deprived of an essential source of income and had to leave their farms.

After World War II, the federal government provided large loans for "mechanization" and "modernization." The effect was a tripling of the number of tractors per farm between 1961 and 1996, a doubling of the number of trucks, and similar growth in the numbers of swathers and combines.[28] Again, these initiatives clearly benefited larger farms and farmers with extra capital. The net effect has been a rapid shrinking of rural communities.

It was not necessary that this be so. Presumably, technologies could have been developed to make farming more intensive rather than extensive—more efficient on small plots of land rather than on huge plantations. But that did not fit with the vision held by Canada's political architects.

The 1969 Federal Task Force on Agriculture report gave rather blunt expression to the conviction that the farming community would be healthier if the chaff were winnowed out and the remaining farms increased in size. The report was prepared for the purpose of informing government policy for the following decades. In the course their research, the members of the task force met with a variety of politicians, agricultural experts and farmers. From those interviews they concluded that two-thirds of Canadian farms were essentially "non-viable" because their operators had not "kept up"; they had exercised poor management. The report referred to them as a "social problem," although it added, "It would be improper to criticize such people as perverse." It went on to say that these farmers had been made "marginal" and "sub-marginal" by technological developments that "changed the requirements to be a successful farmer." They "could not change as fast in their attitudes and capacities as did the economic and technological environment surrounding (and partially submerging) them." According to the report, these unfit farmers could be distinguished from the "farming elite of large-scale, business-oriented, technically-experienced operators" by their lower levels of education and experience. They showed evidence of "lack of ability, lack of initiative or an uncooperative spirit."[29] (In other words, they were stupid, lazy or stubborn.)

These farmers lived in or close to poverty, the report said, because overpopulation had divided the agricultural pie into too many slices. In the end, it concluded, "The most attractive answer to the problem of low incomes in agriculture is that labour move to employment in other industries"—in other words, these farmers should get out of farming. The results would be better for all: "Increased mobility out of farming helps to achieve a higher per capita net farm income for those left in farming while at the same time obtaining better paid employment for those who leave agriculture." Too often, it cautioned, solutions to this "small farm problem" had been hampered by agricultural leaders who were "loathe to recognize the need for a widespread exodus from farming." The only real solution, it insisted, was to develop "much more effective policies to take men out of farming."[30]

Federal government support for farms that are larger and/or better managed (usually assumed to be synonymous) is reflected in the government's subsidy programs. The federal Standing Committee on Agriculture notes that the government's subsidy programs have often been "untargeted"—meaning that they have distributed cash payments to farmers according to acreage or gross income, rather than need.[31]

This means that the lion's share of government support has tended to go to a few large or wealthy farms, helping them to become larger or wealthier. Money from the Special Canadian Grains Program, for example, was paid out at a fixed price per acre for each crop. The result was that, in 1985, of the money spent by the Canadian government, $1.1 billion went to high-income farmers (an average of $15,429 per farmer), $386 million to middle-income farmers (average $5,311) and only $150 million to low-income farmers (average $1,029), who in many cases may have needed it the most.

More recently, federal programs have become "targeted." However, they do not target farmers who need the most support. Rather, there is a tendency to try to reward "good managers" and withdraw support from the "bad." For example, this appears to have been what motivated the Saskatchewan government to cancel GRIP 91, a revenue insurance plan to which farmers and government contributed. Farmers took the government to court for breaking the contract.[32] In its defence, the government told the court that it cancelled the contract because it was concerned about "moral hazard": it felt that the program would not adequately distinguish between good and bad farmers. The government was worried that many would use the program as a form of welfare and lapse into poor farming practices—using cheaper fertilizers, putting marginal lands into production, even lying about their historic yields. This would run up the cost of payouts, putting the government's budget in the red.

In fact, when all the figures came in, it turned out that, in spite of the temptation, farmers had done nothing of the sort. They had continued to farm as responsibly as before. In his decision, Judge Laing noted that there had not been actual evidence of mismanagement, that any costs from misuse of the plan had already been built into the premium structure, and that there were monitoring provisions in the program to protect against misuse. Nonetheless, the concern that some of the "unfit" might be supported by the program was enough for the government to act precipitously to break the contract.

The present Agricultural Income Disaster Assistance (AIDA) program shows evidence of having been formed out of the same "survival of the fittest" philosophy. In its 1999 formulation, those farmers eligible for the most money were those who had done well for three years in a row and had suffered only in the most recent year. Those who needed the support the most—those who had had several difficult years (often because of drought or floods)—received the least because they were viewed as liabilities. Radio advertisements for AIDA encouraged farmers to apply, but only if they were experiencing serious financial problems "for which they are not responsible."[33] The difficulty in distinguishing uncontrollable factors from management skills led to the development of an application form that was so complicated that, on average, it cost $600-$700 in accountants' fees to complete it.[34]

Federal agriculture minister Lyle Vanclief made the situation plain in an interview with the *Winnipeg Free Press* in November 1999. Responding to criticism of the government's refusal to reinstate historic grain sector supports (removed in 1995), he said that the government's position was a form of "tough love." A larger aid program would send the wrong signal to profitable operations. "I've had [successful] farmers say to me very clearly, and these are not my words, 'Don't you dare bail those bastards out.'"[35] In other words, the loss of support helps to force out of farming people who really do not belong there because they cannot adapt.

This belief that only the fittest can survive is reinforced by the moral conviction that only the fittest *should* survive. Christian churches seem to play a key role here. The farmers whom I interviewed seemed to believe (or perceived their congregation to believe) that prosperity is a sign of God's favour—that is, of their *spiritual* fitness. One might call it "the survival of the righteous." Dorothy said that, in her community, the buying of bigger and better machinery was "a competition to show who has been most blessed by God." Farmers modestly say, when people comment on the success of their business, "Well, we've been blessed." For those who lose their farms, however, the implication is that the blessing has been withdrawn. For some reason, usually assumed to be a defect of character or skill, they have been cursed. During her bankruptcy, Nora said, "I feel like I've been cut adrift from God."

Randy's experience of the church as he lost his farm was ambivalent. On the one hand, the minister preached about God's love, and sometimes he really needed to hear that. On the other hand, he heard a great deal of judgment in churchgoers' comments about farmers in difficulty. In the end, he decided, "There are some fine people in the churches," but "if you're having financial difficulties, stay the hell out of them, 'cause you're not going to get a second's worth of sympathy or a pinch of help from them." Interviewees often told of insolvent farmers dropping out of church, and of getting little or no support from pastors or other church members.

Rural sociologists William and Judith Heffernan reported the same from their study of American farm families in the mid-1980s.[36] United Methodist leaders in the United States found that efforts to train rural pastors in dealing with the farm crisis met with a good deal of apathy and resistance. They reported that pastors lacked understanding about the crisis, denied the existence of the crisis, responded inappropriately, withdrew from families in financial trouble or expected that families in trouble would come to them, and often never showed up when farmers were being sold out.[37]

Although there are numerous reasons for the inability of many rural churches to respond to farmers in distress,[38] there is an unavoidable element of judgment. If others are managing under the same weather and market conditions, then this one who has failed must be foolish, lazy or a spendthrift. By failing to pay their debts, such farmers put local businesses at risk. They are the "prodigal sons" or daughters who have squandered the family inheritance through "loose living" and no longer deserve to be called children. They are the "unrighteous leaven" contaminating the lump, the goats that must be separated from the sheep.

Assess "Truthfulness"

The third stage is to begin to examine the veracity of this belief system—is it true that only the fittest *do* and *should* survive? Exploration of these questions can take place in a variety of rural contexts—in private conversations, at coffee shops, in community workshops, in congregational discussion groups, in special interest groups. In such contexts, clergy might want to raise several questions that probe the assumptions behind "survival of the fittest" thinking in agriculture. The first set of questions (a-c) has to do with concrete truthfulness—congruence with the facts. The second set of questions (d-e) that must be raised to determine the veracity of a "survival of the fittest" philosophy addresses the capacity of this belief system to carry the hopes and values of a people.

Who Are the "Fit"?

What are the definitions of farming fitness used to judge "farmers of the year" in this particular area? Are there respected farmers using very different approaches to farming—that is, is there more than one way of being fit?

How Does Size Relate to Fitness?

Is size necessary for survival? Look, for example, at the structure of the food system. What would one conclude from the facts presented by the National Farmers Union (NFU) to the Senate Standing Committee on Agriculture and Forestry, 17 February 2000? In that presentation, the NFU noted that modern food production takes place in a chain. On the input side are oil, fertilizer, seed, chemical and machinery companies. On the output side are grain companies, railways, packers, processors, retailers and restaurants. On both sides, every link in the chain, nearly every sector, is dominated by a small number (between two and ten) of multi-billion dollar multinational corporations.[39] In the middle of the chain are Canada's 270,000 comparatively small farms. Of all the links in that food chain, they are the least profitable. Gross revenues from one company alone—Cargill—were $75 billion in 1998, compared to *total* Canadian gross farm revenues of $29 billion. Perhaps the best measure of profitability is the return one gets on what one has invested—that is, net income (or profit) divided by one's equity (i.e., one's assets minus one's debts). Farmers earned just 0.3 percent return on their equity in 1998, while agribusinesses earned 5 percent to over 200 percent returns on theirs. A return of even 3 percent would make farming viable, according to the NFU. It suggested that there is no shortage of money in the agri-food system; it is simply that the large and powerful players are able to grab and keep more than their proportionate share. The NFU's conclusion was that "one would immediately have doubts that extremely numerous and relatively tiny family farms could extract fair and adequate revenues and profits from a chain dominated by firms a thousand to a million times larger." Is it possible for farmers acting cooperatively to exercise enough power to maintain a profitable place in the food chain? If so, how is that cooperation to be achieved?

How Does Efficiency Relate to Fitness?

There have been dramatic changes in farm efficiency over the last century. According to the United States Department of Agriculture, in 1890 forty to fifty labour-hours were required to produce 100 bushels of wheat on five acres with gangplow, seeder, harrow, binder, thresher, wagons and horses. By the 1980s, only three labour-hours were required to produce 100 bushels of wheat on three acres with tractor, thirty-five-foot sweep disk, thirty-foot drill, twenty-five-foot self-propelled combine and trucks. This huge increase in labour-cost efficiency has been almost offset, however, by greatly increased capital costs for machinery. With prices for wheat at the beginning of the twenty-first century close to what they were one hundred years earlier, a highly mechanized wheat farm must be extremely productive if it is to generate enough profit to support a family.[40] Are farmers on these farms more "fit" than those who choose to reduce the costs of their input by using smaller or older machinery, by sharing machinery and investing a greater amount of their own labour on a smaller piece of land, or by investing with others in the processing of their raw product so that they receive retail, not just commodity, prices? Which is most sustainable in the long run?

How Do Size and Efficiency Relate to Each Other?

In view of the above, does "economy of scale" really mean that all larger entities are more efficient and more effective, or does it mean, as Ursula Franklin has suggested, that there is an economy (a set of technologies and trade patterns) that is appropriate to the size of a particular enterprise?[41] Marty Strange, in his survey of U.S. farm efficiency studies, found that peak efficiency (lowest cost of production per unit) is possible on most types of farms when one or two people are kept fully employed making full use of the best technology. He concluded that

> half of [American] food comes from farms that are larger than they need to be to be fully efficient. From the point of view of the public, then, American agriculture must be considered big enough. There is really little public purpose in encouraging further farm-size expansion.[42]

How Does Fitness Relate to Sustainability?

Is a farmer regarded as fit if he or she maintains efficiency by off-loading costs onto others? If the land can only support his or her practices for forty or fifty years before becoming exhausted, then the land and the next generation bear the costs. Are there costs for large confined-animal operations that are not borne by the owners? Who, for example, bears the costs of air and groundwater polluted by manure? Are some farmers surviving because they are able to evade their share of social and economic responsibilities? Ursula Franklin suggested that a community needs to keep three sets of books: the customary dollars-and-cents ledger (with a column for money *saved*); a catalogue of social impacts—human and community gains and losses; and an accounting of gains and losses in both the natural and the artificial environments.[43]

Who Is Actually Surviving and Why?

Even if one assumes that a good number of those who lose their farms are not the best managers, how does one account for the bankruptcy of those who are regarded as very "fit" by their community? I interviewed several who had received "farmer of the year" awards from their community (sometimes more than once), and yet had gone bankrupt. Were the community's standards of "fit" inappropriate? Had the community misevaluated a farmer's adherence to those standards, or had that farmer been overwhelmed by external forces that he or she could not fully control?

Is the Playing Field Level?

Do the fittest actually have a chance to survive, or is the likelihood of survival tilted toward certain players regardless of their managerial or productive ability? In this regard, one might want to ask about differential subsidies. How do the tariffs and price controls applied to protect dairy products and eggs, and the removal of the transportation subsidies for grains, affect the survivability of farmers in those sectors? How do heavy European and American subsidies affect the ability of Canadian farmers in those sectors to survive? Lending patterns are also significant. During the 1980s, lenders required that debtors sign secrecy agreements when they settled an unrepayable debt. Were those who were unable to get their debt reduced disadvantaged? During that period, some large lenders illegally charged escalating interest on fixed-rate loans.[44] If a farm was pushed into insolvency as a result, was that a sign of poor management on the farmer's part?

What Kind of "Survival" Are We Striving for?

To begin, one might ask participants how rural life has changed, especially for those who have been in the community for a long time. What aspects of their lives have been enhanced? What has been lost? How do they measure their standard of living? In monetary terms? What about good access to schools, churches, health care, recreation? If the latter are included, can survival really be regarded as an individual achievement, or does it require a community? Participants may find this obvious, but it might be noted that studies in Canada, the United States, Australia and New Zealand document a strong correlation between increased farm size and decline in the quality of community life—a decreased sense of a shared interest in farming and an increase in competitive factions among farmers,[45] a withdrawal by both men and women from community participation into farm work or private consumption,[46] a loss of local leadership,[47] and a loss of educational, health and social services, together with a decline in community self-determination.[48] Are such effects being felt in this particular community? If so, how much do they matter? What kind of future for rural Canada can honestly be imagined if survival is seen only in terms of individual farm growth? The research suggests that we could be left with a few lonely "wheat kings" dominating rural Canada. A handful of massive, muscled survivors of an agrarian wrestling tournament, having thrown their neighbours out of the ring, will rule an empty landscape. This is not the future that rural Canadians hope for, if the federal survey and community round-table discussions mentioned earlier are representative. Nonetheless, if nothing changes, the embrace of these values in agricultural practice and social habit seems likely to be the future. Recognizing this may help to bring a divided rural community to the point of really committed conversation.

Who Should Survive?

One might ask: Remember some who have left the community. What did we lose when they left? What gifts—other than economic—did they bring to us? Is our community better off now that they are gone? As a philosophy, the "survival of the fittest" seems to take aim directly at the heart of the concept that every human being deserves respect. It assumes that treating people as if all were of equal value has a destructive effect on society and culture. It inhibits the rise of superior human beings to their proper status in society and exalts those with very little to contribute. To treat all with respect may doom humanity at best to mediocrity, at worst to extinction.[49] The questions for the community are then: Do you believe that the survival of rural Canada is dependent on culling those who are not successful farmers? Are those who have less economic power worth less than the powerful? Perhaps the most basic question (and one that leads into the next section) is theological: Is our future in the hands of the brightest and best human beings, or is it in the hands of God—are we on our own, or is there one who holds our future?

Nurture a Rebellious Imagination

This brings us to the fourth stage in helping a community deal with the belief system that supports its economic structures. Once the stories of suffering have been told, and the "truth-telling" strengths of the belief structure have been tested, the final task is to develop a "habitable" world view for this community.

This can be the most difficult of the four stages, for several reasons. First, according to the 1998 National Rural Dialogue, rural dwellers feel that their "'close-knit' community can also be a 'closed-in' community." Because there is shame attached to failure, new ideas with the potential for disaster are not always welcomed.

Second, and also because of the shame, those who are most aware of the inadequacy of the present world view—those who have invested heavily in it and failed—are isolated, their voices muted in the community's conversation.

Third, discourse about alternative belief systems may be difficult, because many community members are not part of organizations such as churches, which teach their members how to assess and articulate the beliefs that inform their behaviour and values. Others who *are* adherents to such groups may be tempted to use their convictions in a way that shuts down debate. In fact, church members and leaders have often done just that.

On the one hand, that dark side of the church's history cannot simply be set aside. It takes skilful leadership to keep conversations from moving to close off alternatives. On the other hand, the Bible does offer a potent resource for re-imagining reality. In *Prophets, Pastors and Public Choices*, Hutchinson suggested that our Christian tradition serves us most effectively when we use it as "scaffolding" within which to construct creative new options for human life.[50] In my experience, the Bible can be used in this way even with groups that include non-believers. Participants are invited, for the space of the conversation, to enter a story that differs from the one that our society tells—one in which humans are not on their own. They have the opportunity to view their lives from inside its framework (or, as Lindbeck would say, to inscribe their own world into the biblical world[51]). The intent is not to develop a biblical ethic of farm economics that is good for all times. The Bible does not offer simple "answers" for social issues. Rather, it provides a broad vision of human life under God, which reorients us and suggests that the status quo may not be adequate. That vision challenges us to find new ways of organizing our common life. Hutchinson observed the effect of biblical "scaffolding" in the context of Project North:

> [T]he use of the Bible evoked a common memory that God cares for the oppressed and for the resources of the earth. Project North was tapping the disclosive power of biblical stories and symbols to generate an openness to new possibilities and to call into question existing assumptions and priorities. These appeals created a moral ethos in which only barbarians would refuse to care about justice for natives and stewardship of non-renewable resources.[52]

This process of biblical re-framing has two elements. People who represent very different perspectives are willing to gather for conversation about the biblical world because they agree on certain "thin" biblical principles—i.e., "love your neighbour," "care for the suffering." (We earlier noted the same thing regarding conversations about the modern, rural economy.) These principles provide a level of comfort and help to bind the group to a sense of common purpose and conviction. However, they operate at a very general level. The actual *entry* into the biblical world (as into the modern context) takes place through its "facts," its concrete details. The exploration moves inductively from detail to larger picture. Participants immerse themselves in the *thickly* woven colours and movements of the Bible, including its social context. In the process, they begin to discern its heart, its plot and the intentions of its principal player. At the same time, connections between the two worlds (the ancient and one's own) become apparent. Participants are invited to ask themselves, "If this is what God is up to, then how does our behaviour in the farm crisis and how do our 'survival of the fittest' values fit in? Do they further God's story or take us on a detour? Are they in tune with the basic character and intentions of the one who is moving the narrative forward?" In the process, some assumptions about what is "good" or "inevitable" may be challenged.

Used in this way, the Bible opens up alternatives. It nurtures a rebellious imagination, revealing the present economic and social arrangements not as unavoidable or God-given, but as a human construct—one that can be reconstructed. Allow me to close with an example of how one might explore "survival of the fittest" thinking within a biblical scaffold.

Religious leaders can help their congregations access the biblical imagination by showing them that Israel's prophets spoke within an agrarian context that, while obviously different in many ways, has important similarities to their own. For example, biblical scholars have noted that, as in other agrarian societies, honour and shame were core features of social interaction.[53] Land had become a focus for social power and destructive competition,[54] the accumulation of debt had become a major factor in the destruction of Israel's rural life,[55] and, to encourage lending, legislation had been enacted that circumvented borrowers' rights.[56]

The concentration of land was of particular concern to the biblical writers. The last of the Ten Commandments tells us not to covet our neighbour's house. According to scholar Marvin Chaney, the Hebrew word translated "house" here refers to a family's primary unit of production, and includes its fields, cattle and residence.[57] In 1 Kings 21, the prophet Elijah calls down God's wrath on King Ahab's desire to gather the best land for himself. Although already a very large landowner, Ahab covets the choice little vineyard that belongs to Naboth. He schemes to get it, killing Naboth in the process. Elijah pronounces judgment on the powerful who destroy their neighbours.

Similarly, Micah condemns those who "covet fields, and seize them; houses, and take them away; they oppress householder and house, people and their inheritance" (Mic. 2:2). He warns that the land will be redivided, with the coveters excluded, not even able to attend the meeting in which it is parcelled out again (Mic. 2:4).

The prophet Isaiah perhaps says it most plainly, in words that are eerily modern. He pronounces judgment on the vision of a depopulated, and corporately run, rural community: "Alas, you who join house to house, who add field to field, until there is room for no one but you, and you are left to live alone in the midst of the land!" (Isa. 5:8).

Yahweh's vision for human community is much different. Israel clearly recognized that land is our lifeline—it is the source of our food and sustenance. Israel's story begins with humankind (*adam*) being formed out of soil (*adamah*). That connection persists in modern English in terms such as "human" and "humus," "earth" and "earthling." In the biblical view, being connected to the land is an essential part of being human.

As such, the land is given to *all*, not just to the wealthiest, the smartest, the greediest or the most powerful. God recognizes our need for a place to grow food and to grow families, to grow communities and to put down roots—a place to call *home*. God graciously provides the land—not as our right, however, but as a gift of love. It is not given because of one's noble birth, good management skills or moral uprightness. In the biblical view, one does not have to earn land or deserve it; one does not have to be wise or strong enough to defend it. This gift of social security is rooted, according to the Torah, not in intrinsic human worth, but in the sovereign ownership of God: "The land shall not be sold in perpetuity, for the land is mine; with me you are but aliens and tenants" (Lev. 25:23).

God owns the land and graciously chooses to let us use it—to bring about *God's* vision for human life. The Bible gives no indication that it includes lonely corporate farms, exhausted families working on the farm and off, demoralized churches and vacant schools. Rather, it imagines healthy, vibrant communities. That is why the Bible talks about jubilee. According to Leviticus 25, every fifty years debts on the land were to be forgiven and the land redistributed so that the dispossessed would have a place, a piece of turf, in the community. There does not seem to be evidence that Israel was successful in carrying out jubilee, at least not on a regular basis, perhaps for obvious reasons. Nonetheless, it makes clear God's intention: the land is to be populated and shared, not concentrated into the hands of a few.

Discussion about these matters could take several directions. One might ask about our relationship to the land. Is it important for Canada to have significant numbers of people on the land, to remind us that we are made of dust and shall return to dust? Is there a danger that, if this is forgotten, we may believe that we are gods, free to loot the earth as if it belonged to us? If only large corporations farm the land, who will be responsible for its care? On a family farm, those who own the land work it, and they know that they alone are responsible for its care. But, with corporations, the buck never stops. It gets passed from the workers to the managers, to the chief executive officer, to the board of directors and, finally, to the shareholders who are such a diverse, unconcerned group that they cannot exercise any real responsibility. Is it possible that significant portions of Canada's rich land will be "farmed out" under that kind of corporate management? How does personal ownership relate to responsible stewardship, particularly in view of the fact that God ultimately owns the land? How does ownership relate to justice? On the one hand, land titles and other legal instruments protect the modern Naboths from expropriation. On the other hand, such titles become security for debts and are easily lost to creditors.

It is worth asking whether there are benefits to landlessness. Can one be over-dependent on the land? Israel's prophets insist that even land is not Israel's ultimate security—Yahweh is. So, Israel's training as a nation included forty years of landlessness. As the prophet reminds them,

> He humbled you by letting you hunger, then by feeding you with manna, with which neither you nor your ancestors were acquainted, in order to make you understand that one does not live by bread alone, but by every word that comes from the mouth of the LORD. (Deut. 8:3)

Gathering food each morning that they had not grown, food that perished in a day and could not be accumulated or traded, the people of Israel learned that, for both low- and high-born, it is ultimately Yahweh who is the source of life, not the land. Several centuries later, when trust in Yahweh hit an all-time low in Israel, the land was taken away again. The purpose of that loss, according to the prophets, was that the people of Israel might get back in touch with God, their landowner.

What does this mean for modern farmers? When they lose their land, is it an opportunity to depend more heavily on God? Or is it God's judgment on farmers who have become over-dependent on the land?

There is a significant difference between the two, and who is qualified to decide which it might be (if either)?

In my interviews, some of the farmers who had left their land reported that the experience, though deeply painful, had some liberating qualities to it as well. They realized that they could live without being on their land, that God was in the city too. Many who were still on their farms, however, and in danger of losing them, expressed deep fears about life off the farm. Discussion leaders could explore some of these fears. They might ask about the effect that these fears have on farm management practices, on decisions regarding how to deal with farm debt, on a family's emotional and spiritual well-being and so on.

Recognizing the land's *penultimate* (not ultimate) value to human community, the facilitator might also ask how a community protects opportunities for many to remain on the land while helping those who leave the land to do so with dignity.

The question of debt and jubilee could be explored. From whom is the land to be taken if it is going to be given to the landless? Who loses money when debts are not paid? Is credit dehumanizing or is it a means by which the community temporarily shares its resources with people so that they can get underway in business? One might suggest that, in a sense, jubilees are inevitable. When land and power are concentrated in too few hands, economies become locked, frozen. When debt accumulates in an economy beyond the debtors' ability to repay, some form of jubilee becomes essential. In the 1980s, billions of dollars in farm debt were written off because the farms were no longer worth what was owed on them. However, that remission of debt was done in a way that was bitter and shame-ridden. Farmers were forced to sign secrecy agreements, preventing them from helping each other in their dealings with powerful lenders. They were left feeling that the entire responsibility for the debt rested on their shoulders alone. One could ask how debt remission (and avoidance of debt in the first place) might be incorporated more effectively into the structure of agriculture. Assuming that sinful humans will tend to mess up the economic structures they create, how does one effectively institutionalize jubilee so that communities can be repopulated and so that families can begin again?

Another option would be to explore ways in which land in rural communities has become a focus for competition and the exercise of power. To what extent are such practices due to the valuing of land as a "right" and a "personal possession" rather than as a gift? Some farmers spoke to me of being "cannibalized" by their neighbours. Is this a common image? What does the use of that term say about those who use it, in terms of their relationship to the land? When one feels pressure constantly to expand one's operation, what attitude toward the land does that reflect? What role do corporate farms and lenders play in the concentration of land in the hands of a few? Is this ultimately healthy for the community (keeping the industry viable), or unhealthy (dispossessing many of land)?

Israel's prophets lay the foundation of the biblical framework for a discussion of the survival of the fittest. Jesus builds on it as he introduces the theme of his ministry in Luke 4 as that of jubilee—freeing the imprisoned (who were mostly debtors in his day).[58] Is he renewing the vision of the prophets before him that no family should be without land, and the honour and security in the community that come with it? Or is he stretching the understanding of jubilee to include the honouring now of a growing population of the landless (of which he is a member!)?

Jesus refuses to assign worth on the basis of economic accomplishment or social status. Instead (shamelessly in the view of his society), he invites everyone to his table indiscriminately.[59] He does this, as his parable of the Pharisee and the tax collector indicates, because he believes that our worth is not determined by us or by our accomplishments. That prerogative is God's alone. God assigns us all worth not because we deserve it, but because God is gracious. So, at the pool of Bethzatha (John 5), Jesus heals a man who is too weak to be first into the water when its healing power is stirred up (first in would be healed). The fittest of the sick survive by making it into the water before the others, but Jesus makes sure that the weakest survive also.

Paul follows in Jesus' footsteps, writing in 1 Corinthians 12 that even the weaker members of the body have an essential place. None is to be discarded. In fact, Paul regards weakness (including his own "thorn in the flesh" [2 Cor. 12]) as an essential reminder that we are not gods. It keeps us in mind of our limits, of our need for one another and of our dependence on God. Most astonishingly, Paul dares to say that, if we focus our hopes on those who are most successful, we may miss out on God: for "we proclaim Christ crucified, a stumbling block to Jews and foolishness to Gentiles, but to those who are the called, both Jews and Greeks, Christ the power of God and the wisdom of God....God chose what is weak in the world to shame the strong; God chose what is low and despised in the world, things that are not, to reduce to nothing things that are, so that no one might boast in the presence of God" (1 Cor. 1:23, 27b-28). The glory of God and the glory of humanity come together, Christians believe, in the one who, according to conventional standards, is the "loser" of Nazareth—the crucified and risen Jesus.

In this sort of biblical framework, submerged rural values of interdependence and mutual support are allowed to surface. A good example is the vision that Baldur, Manitoba has produced for its community; it is strong, broad and humane. Baldur's residents imagine it as a place where "historical, cultural, agricultural, natural and human resources are promoted as valued assets and *all* facets of the population are encouraged to exercise their ownership of the community through positive, active involvement as they are able [emphasis mine]."[60] Is there hope that such visions can be realized in the face of overwhelming global, national and local pressures working to "weed out" and reduce our rural population? I see signs of hope in communities that, like Baldur, have successfully reversed the trend.[61] Often, broad changes in consciousness occur as a result of local experiments—minor resistance—which open a community to new ideas that spread to others.[62] Whatever the future holds for rural Canada, I would like to help it find confidence for its vitality not in a winnowing of the weak, but in the gracious sustaining power of God.

Notes

1 Government of Canada, *Canadian Rural Partnership: Responding to Rural Canadians—Federal Framework for Action in Rural Canada* (http://www.rural.gc.ca/framework_e.phtml); Government of Manitoba, *Manitoba's Community Round Tables: Strong People Building a Stronger Tomorrow* (Selkirk, MB: Manitoba Rural Development, 1998).

2 Government of Canada, *1996 Census of Agriculture* (http://library.usask.ca/data/agriculture/agcensus96/ag96t.htm); in 1931, there were 3,289,140 people living on farms out of a total Canadian population of 10,363,240. By 1996, the farm population had shrunk to 851,410 out of a total population of 28,751,593. This decline was much more pronounced in some provinces—for example, Saskatchewan and the Atlantic provinces—than others.

3 Christopher Lind, *Something's Wrong Somewhere: Globalization, Community and the Moral Economy of the Farm Crisis* (Halifax, NS: Fernwood, 1995).

4 For example, Hardisty, Alberta is currently in the middle of an intense battle over the introduction of an 80,000-hog facility into its community by the Taiwan Sugar Corporation. Local clergy report people in their congregations being strongly "for" or "against" the facility.

5 Roger Hutchinson, *Prophets, Pastors and Public Choices: Canadian Churches and the Mackenzie Valley Pipeline Debate* (Waterloo, ON: Wilfrid Laurier University Press, 1992). See also Roger Hutchinson, "Study and Action in Politically Diverse Churches," in *Christian Faith and Economic Justice: Toward a Canadian Perspective*, ed. Cranford Pratt and Roger Hutchinson (Burlington, ON: Trinity Press, 1988), 178-92.

6 Kathleen Norris, *Dakota: A Spiritual Geography* (Boston, MA: Houghton Mifflin, 1993), 32.

7 They said, for example, that they wanted to "foster strategic partnerships, within communities, between communities and among governments to facilitate rural community development" and "strengthen rural community capacity building, leadership and skills development." Government of Canada, *Canadian Rural Partnership*.

8 Ludwik Fleck's work in the 1930s on the way in which values influenced the "facts" in syphilis research offers several excellent illustrations, and was an important contribution to the new discipline of the sociology of knowledge. See the new translation of *Genesis and Development of a Scientific Fact*, ed. Thaddeus J. Trenn; trans. Fred Bradley and Thaddeus J. Trenn (Chicago: University of Chicago Press, 1979). Phyllis Beck Kritek, *Negotiating at an Uneven Table: A Practical Approach to Working with Difference and Diversity* (San Francisco: Jossey-Bass, 1994), 62-63, offers some helpful applications to the context of communal debate.

9 From 1995 to 1999, under Roger Hutchinson's guidance, I completed formal interviews with twenty-nine farmers who were or had been in the process of bankruptcy or foreclosure. Another thirty-five interviews were with solvent farmers, lenders, input dealers, politicians and others involved in the changes occurring in agriculture. Most interviewees were from the Prairie provinces. Names and place identifiers have been changed to protect anonymity.

10 For more on this, see Cameron Harder, "Overcoming Cultural/Spiritual Obstacles to Rural Revitalization," in *The Future of Rural Communities in an Era of Globalization*, ed. Roger Epp and David Whitson (Edmonton, AB: University of Alberta Press, 2001).

11 Norris, *Dakota*, 81, 85-86.

12 Ben was one of these managers. He expressed his position to me in this way: "Well, I think that in any part of our world, there are people or organizations that can be unjust, but…I can't see that the whole system can be unjust, itself."

13 Walter Brueggemann, *Hope Within History* (Atlanta, GA: John Knox Press, 1987), 85-86.

14 Michael Walzer, *Thick and Thin: Moral Argument at Home and Abroad* (Notre Dame, IN: University of Notre Dame Press, 1994), 8.

15 Hutchinson, *Prophets, Pastors and Public Choices*, 117.

16 See Richard T. Ely and George S. Wehrwein, *Land Economics* (New York: Macmillan, 1940); John W. Bennett, *Northern Plainsmen* (Chicago: Aldine, 1969); more recently, Kathleen N. Conzen, "Historical Approaches to the Study of Rural Ethnic Communities," in *Ethnicity on the Great Plains*, ed. F.C. Luebke (Lincoln, NE: University of Nebraska Press, 1980), 1-18; S.C. Rogers, "Mixing Paradigms on Mixed Farming: Anthropological and Economic Views of Specialization in Illinois Agriculture," in *Farm Work and Fieldwork: American Agriculture in Anthropological Perspective*, ed. M. Chibnik (Ithaca, NY: Cornell University Press, 1987). Salamon's work appears in several places: Sonya Salamon, "Ethnic Communities and the Structure of Agriculture," *Rural Sociology* 50 (Fall 1985): 323-40; "Family Farming and Farm Community Character," in Chibnik, *Farm Work and Fieldwork*; "Culture and Land Tenure" (paper presented at the Rural Sociological Society, 1992); and, especially, *Prairie Patrimony: Family, Farming and Community in the Midwest* (Chapel Hill, NC: University of North Carolina Press, 1992). Note that P. Mooney, *My Own Boss?: Class, Rationality, and the Family Farm* (Boulder, CO: Westview 1988), subdivides the two types of values into "model" and "marginal" versions (based on the relative degree of success in keeping the operation viable).

17 See Gerald Friesen, *The Canadian Prairies: A History* (Toronto: University of Toronto Press, 1987), 104ff.

18 Cameron Harder, "The Shame of Farm Bankruptcy" (Ph.D. diss., University of St. Michael's College, Toronto, 1999), 48; "Justification and the Farm Crisis in Canada," in *Justification in the World's Contexts*, ed. Wolfgang Grieve (Geneva: Lutheran World Federation, Department for Theology and Studies, 2000); "The Shaming of Canadian Farmers: A Christian Response" *Consensus* 21/2 (1995): 59-75.

19 Vanclay and Lawrence describe a similar shift in Australian farming from (using Weber's terminology) "substantive" to "formal" rationality—from seeing profit as a means to a substantive end (community well-being) to seeing it as an end in itself. F. Vanclay and G. Lawrence, "Farmer Rationality and the Adoption of Environmentally Sound Practices: A Critique of the Assumptions of Traditional Agricultural Extension," *Journal of Agricultural Education and Extension* 1 (April 1994) (http://www.bib.wau.nl/ejae/v1n1-5.html).

20 Royal Bank, *Expand, Sell, Diversify: What's Your Next Move?* (http://www.royalbank.com/agriculture/yearly_expand.html).

21 For example, see R.M. Ballantyne, *The Young Fur Traders* (London, n.d.) or William F. Butler, *The Great Lone Land: A Narrative of Travel and Adventure in the North-West of America* (London: S. Low, Marston, Low & Searle, 1872). For a description of similar writings, see Irene Spry,

"Early Visitors to the Canadian Prairies," in *Images of the Plains: The Role of Human Nature in Settlement*, ed. Brian W. Blouet and Merlin P. Lawson (Lincoln, NE: University of Nebraska Press, 1975), 165-180.

22 The posters appear in David Goa, "Secularization among Ethnic Communities in Western Canada," in *Religion and Ethnicity*, ed. Harold Coward and Leslie Kawamura (Waterloo, ON: Wilfrid Laurier University Press, 1977), 13-17.

23 See, for example, the story of the "Sons of Freedom," in Pierre Berton, *The Promised Land: Settling the West, 1896-1914* (Toronto: McClelland and Stewart, 1984), 79.

24 James Woodsworth, "Thirty Years in the Canadian North West." Unpublished document of the Methodist Church in Canada, Young People's Forward Movement, 1909, 124-125. Quoted in Ben Smillie and Norman Threinen, "Protestants—Prairie Visionaries of the New Jerusalem: The United and Lutheran Churches in Western Canada," in *Beyond the Social Gospel: Church Protest on the Prairies*, ed. Ben Smillie (Saskatoon: Fifth House, 1991), 75. In the same article, Smillie quotes Robert Haliburton, a member of the "Canada First" movement, as saying, "May not our snow and frost give us what is more value than gold or silver, a healthy, hardy, dominant race" (76). The quote is taken from Carl Berger, "The True North Strong and Free," in *Nationalism in Canada*, ed. Peter Russell (Toronto: McGraw-Hill, 1966), 3, 6. Smillie adds, "Ironically, Haliburton's lecture had to be given in the summer because ill health forced him to spend his winters in warmer climates!"

25 Friesen, *The Canadian Prairies*, 312, 319.

26 See, for example, *Challenge for Growth* (Ottawa: Canada Department of Agriculture, 1981); Royal Bank, *Look at Your Farm from a World Perspective* (http://www.royalbank.com/agriculture/yearly_look.html).

27 A survey conducted in Saskatchewan in the early 1930s showed that those who started farming with about $7,000 possessed almost exactly that amount thirty years later; those who started with $17,000-$18,000 had doubled their net worth in that time. William Allen, W.C. Hope and F.C. Hitchcock, "Studies of Farm Indebtedness and Financial Progress of Saskatchewan Farmers Report No. 3: Surveys Made at Indian Head and Balcarres, Grenfell and Wolseley, and Neudorf and Lemberg," *University of Saskatchewan College of Agriculture Extension Bulletin* 65 (1935), cited in Friesen, *The Canadian Prairies*, 317.

28 Government of Canada, *1996 Census of Agriculture*.

29 *Canadian Agriculture in the Seventies*. Report of the Federal Task Force on Agriculture (Ottawa: House of Commons, Canada, 1969), 20-23.

30 Ibid., 31, 32, 411. It is interesting that, in the mid-1980s, Canada introduced the $46 million Canadian Rural Transition Program, designed to help 9,000 farmers find other work. Although the program was apparently designed to alleviate stress for farmers already committed to leaving the

land, it also had the (apparently intentional) side effect of encouraging those who were wavering to leave. See Marvin Anderson, "Going, Going, Gone: Selling the Family Farm," *Our Times* (March 1986): 26-27.

31 Government of Canada, Standing Committee on Agriculture, "The $22 Billion Problem: Options for the Financial Restructuring of Farm Debt," *Report to the House of Commons* (Ottawa: House of Commons, Canada, July 1988), 84ff.

32 See Judge Laing, *Bacon and Svenkeson v. Saskatchewan Crop Insurance Corporation and the Government of Saskatchewan*, judgment rendered for Saskatchewan Court of Queen's Bench, Case no. 1420, 11 July 1997, 5.

33 One such advertisement, for example, was aired on C95 FM, Saskatoon, throughout July 1999.

34 "AIDA: What It Does, Why Farmers are Complaining," *Western Producer*. (http://www.producer.com/standing_editorial/farm_crisis/non_farmers/aida.html).

35 Brian Bergman, "Winter of Discontent," *Maclean's*, 28 February 2000, 18.

36 Referred to in Dennis Thompson, "A Flourishing of Faith and Service," *Christian Social Action* (June 1989): 19. It should be noted that Thompson expresses the observation that churches in the United States had become more sensitive to this issue by the end of the decade. My research indicates that, in Canada at least, there is still a long way to go.

37 Gladys L. Campbell, "Building Bridges of Understanding: National Program Division Responds to the Rural Crisis," *Christian Social Action* (March 1988): 28-29.

38 Sara E. Wright and Paul C. Rosenblatt discuss some of these reasons in "Isolation and Farm Loss: Why Neighbours May Not Be Supportive," *Family Relations* 36 (1987): 391-95. See also Harder, "The Shame of Farm Bankruptcy," 43.

39 The presentation stated, for example, that on the input side three companies retail and distribute the bulk of Canadian gasoline and diesel fuel; three produce most of the nitrogen fertilizer; nine companies make the pesticides; four companies are gaining control of the Canadian seed market; three produce most of our major farm machinery. On the output side, the situation is the same: nine grain companies collect Canadian grain; two railways haul it; two companies dominate the beef-packing sector, and a handful dominate pork packing; three large firms manufacture 87 percent of the pasta in Canada; four corporations mill 80 percent of Canadian flour; three companies manufacture the bulk of the soft drinks sold; four companies produce most of the cereal; five companies control food retailing in Canada; a handful of restaurant chains control an increasing portion of the restaurant business. The presentation included detailed figures on incomes, return to equity and other statistics related to the profitability of these companies. See "The Farm Crisis, EU Subsidies, and

Agribusiness Market Power." Presentation by the National Farmers Union to the Senate Standing Committee on Agriculture and Forestry (http://www.nfu.ca/feb17-brief.htm).

40 United States Department of Agriculture, *A History of American Agriculture 1776-1990: Farm Machinery and Technology*. Report prepared by Economic Research Service (http://www.usda.gov/history2/text4.htm).

41 As Ursula Franklin pointed out in *The Real World of Technology*, CBC Massey Lectures (Toronto: CBC Enterprises, 1990), 26, "scale" initially referred to the size appropriate to a thing, not to reduced costs to owners that come from increased size. What is best is not necessarily what is biggest, but rather what conforms to the needs of all—including the environment, the human community and future generations—and makes wise use of available resources and technologies.

42 Marty Strange, *Family Farming: A New Economic Vision* (San Francisco: Institute for Food and Development Policy, 1988), 83; see also 80-81. John Kenneth Galbraith, a world-renowned economist, noted that, even before the dissolution of the USSR, the Russians were considering moving away from large state-run farms because the smaller, family-run operations were so much more efficient. See the video Borrowed Time (Toronto: 49 North Productions, 1990).

43 Franklin, *The Real World of Technology*, 129.

44 For an example of one of the infamous cases that came to court, see Judge Galligan, *Royal Bank of Canada (Plaintiff) v. John Allen Wilford and Wendy Jennifer Wilford (Defendants)*, judgment rendered for the Supreme Court of Ontario, O.J. No. 626 Action No. 1502/83, 11 June 1986. See also Larry Whaley, "Recovering Interest Overcharges," in *Fighting the Farm Crisis*, ed. Terry Pugh (Saskatoon: Fifth House, 1987), 75.

45 Bob Stirling and J.S. Conway, "Factions Among Prairie Farmers," in *The Political Economy of Agriculture in Western Canada*, ed. G.S. Baran and David Hay (Toronto: Garamond, 1988), 73-86.

46 Janet Fitchen, *Endangered Species, Enduring Places: Change, Identity and Survival in Rural America* (Boulder, CO: Westview Press, 1991), 28-41.

47 A.D. McLeod, "You Have to Be Tough to Farm in Saskatchewan," in *Political Economy of Agriculture*, 34.

48 Geoffrey Lawrence, "Agricultural Restructuring and Rural Social Change in Australia," in *Rural Restructuring: Global Processes and Their Responses*, ed. Terry Marsden, Philip Lowe and Sarah Whitmore (London: David Fulton, 1990), 117. The concentration of land is further advanced in Australia and New Zealand and the social effects even more dramatic.

49 Glen Tinder sees Nietzsche as the one who has taken this philosophy to its logical outcomes. See Glen Tinder, "Can We Be Good Without God?" *The Atlantic Monthly*, December 1989, 69-85.

50 Hutchinson credited the term "scaffolding" to Linell E. Cady, "Foundation vs. Scaffolding: The Possibility of Justification in an

Historical Approach to Ethics," *Union Seminary Quarterly Review* 41/2 (1987): 45-62.

51 George Lindbeck, *The Nature of Doctrine* (Philadelphia: Westminster Press, 1984), 118.

52 Hutchinson, *Prophets, Pastors and Public Choices*, 128; see also 118ff.

53 See, for example, Bruce Malina, *The New Testament World: Insights from Cultural Anthropology*, rev. ed. (Louisville, KY: Westminster/John Knox Press, 1993); Bruce Malina and Richard Rohrbaugh, *Social Science Commentary on the Synoptic Gospels* (Minneapolis, MN: Fortress Press, 1992); John Pilch and Bruce Malina, eds., *Biblical Social Values and Their Meanings: A Handbook* (Peabody, MA: Hendrickson, 1993).

54 See Marvin Chaney, "You Shall Not Covet Your Neighbour's House," *Pacific Theological Review* 15 (Winter 1982): 2-13.

55 See Douglas Oakman, "Jesus and Agrarian Palestine: The Factor of Debt," *Society for Biblical Literature: Seminar Papers* 24 (1985): 57-73.

56 See Martin Goodman, "The First Jewish Revolt: Social Conflict and the Problem of Debt," *Journal of Jewish Studies* 33 (Spring-Autumn 1982): 417-27.

57 Chaney, "You Shall Not Covet," 5-6.

58 Jesus says that he is inaugurating the "year of the Lord's favour." This phrase from Isaiah has often been interpreted as a reference to return from exile. However, Ringe makes a strong case that it represents the reinstallation of the jubilee laws. See Sharon Ringe, *Jesus, Liberation and the Biblical Jubilee* (Philadelphia: Fortress Press, 1985).

59 For more, see Jerome Neyrey, "Meals, Food and Table Fellowship" in *The Social Sciences and New Testament Interpretation*, ed. Richard Rohrbaugh (Peabody, MA: Hendrickson, 1996), 159-82; "Ceremonies in Luke-Acts: The Case of Meals and Table Fellowship," in *The Social World of Luke-Acts: Models for Interpretation*, ed. Jerome Neyrey (Peabody, MA: Hendrickson, 1991), 361-87. See also Kathleen Corley, *Private Women, Public Meals: Social Conflict in the Synoptic Tradition* (Peabody, MA: Hendrickson, 1989).

60 *Manitoba's Community Round Tables*, 40. For more information on community round tables and how they function, see *Local Round Tables: Realizing Their Full Potential* (Ottawa: National Round Table on the Environment and the Economy, 1994); and *Building Consensus for a Sustainable Future: Guiding Principles* (Ottawa: National Round Table on the Environment and the Economy, 1993).

61 For example, see the study of two communities—the smaller of which managed to retain its services and quality of life because it developed integrated, cooperative institutions, and the larger of which lost its services because of the absence of those institutions—by Sonya Salamon and Karen Davis-Brown, "Social Capital Generation and Community Cohesion" (paper presented at the Rural Sociological Society, 1991). For

other examples of community revitalization, see Al Scholz, *Don't Turn Out the Lights: Entrepreneurship in Rural Saskatchewan* (Saskatoon: University of Saskatchewan Extension Division, 2000), and Jerome Martin, ed., *Alternative Futures for Prairie Agricultural Communities* (Edmonton: University of Alberta Faculty of Extension, 1991).

62 See, for example, Danny Yee's discussion of this in his review of James Scott's *Weapons of the Weak: Everyday Forms of Peasant Resistance* (New Haven, CT: Yale University Press, 1985). The review can be found on-line at http://dannyreviews.com/h/Weapons_of_the_Weak.html.

10

FETAL ASSESSMENT

A Feminist Approach to a Bioethical Case Study Using Hutchinson's Method of Ethical Clarification

TRACY J. TROTHEN

Science, technology and medicine present complex issues and challenges. In this essay, I will identify the myriad of ethicial issues involved in a dilemma faced by one family, and show how a feminist theological perspective can help to clarify those issues. I present the family's story from my perspective, as the chaplain involved. To do so, I use Roger Hutchinson's method for ethical clarification to pose the questions and to identify a number of relevant issues.

I had the privilege of having Roger Hutchinson as thesis director for my doctoral studies in ethics at Emmanuel College. Through him, I learned that ethics are grounded in matters of everyday life. Although the heart condition addressed in this essay is very unusual, the people involved are not. Their case generates numerous questions, many of which will be familiar. Its particularity is, in many ways, its strength, but it is also its limitation. I will focus on certain ethical issues relevant to this particular ethical perplexity. My analysis will demonstrate some of the ways in which a feminist theological perspective can enlarge the moral landscape by challenging commonly accepted assumptions.

To begin to understand what is happening in any morally confusing, perplexing or otherwise conflicted situation, Hutchinson directs us to a first level of clarification: the "initial response and definition of

Notes to chapter 10 are on pp. 218-22.

[the] problem."[1] At this level, stories are told and initial understandings of the issue(s) are articulated. The second level of clarification involves the identification of the facts as they are understood by each of the involved parties. Feminist ethicists point out that social location, interpretative framework and world view shape and/or distort the perceptions of any participant, observer or analyst. A hermeneutic of suspicion identifies ethical assumptions that are buried in factual statements. The third level concerns the clarification of ethical claims either directly or implicitly stated: the "focus...[is] on the value judgements being made and on the kinds of reasons given to justify judgements."[2] Hutchinson's fourth level attends to the underlying world views and general faith orientations of the relevant parties. Although all levels will be addressed in this essay, it is the third level on which I will focus, and from which I will raise questions from a feminist perspective.

The Case History

First, the story must be told. The following case is a true story. It happened in 1996. I tell it from my particular and partial perspective as the chaplain.

> Anna is a twenty-nine-year-old, white, middle-class woman from a rural location, who is twenty-two weeks pregnant. She and her husband, Paul (same background), had their first baby, Alicia, two years before this story begins. I, as chaplain, became involved with the family after Alicia was admitted to hospital. Alicia was born with Hypoplastic Left Heart Syndrome (HLHS). HLHS is a congenital condition of the heart in which the left ventricle is malformed and very small. The heart is unable to pump sufficiently to provide an adequate oxygen supply to the tissues of the body. Unfortunately, Alicia was not properly diagnosed until almost a month into her life. Most HLHS infants die, if untreated, by this time.
>
> After Alicia was admitted to hospital for the first time, Anna requested that a hospital chaplain visit her. Anna confided in me and, over the next five months, I heard much of Anna's, Paul's and Alicia's hospital story. Initially, some health-care providers had expressed frustration with Anna. In her search for answers, Anna had become very angry. She was questioning them and made their work

harder. They did not have time, especially with the recent provincial cutbacks, to continue to respond to her. Why could she not trust them? I soon realized that trust was certainly the issue. When Alicia was a newborn, Anna had taken her repeatedly to her physician, concerned that "something was not right." The physician had told Anna to calm down—she was overreacting, as many new mothers are prone to do. Finally, when Alicia was one month old, Anna went one more time to her doctor. She insisted that he refer them to a specialist and refused to leave until he did. Exasperated, he complied. Later that day, Alicia was rushed to the children's hospital for emergency treatment for HLHS. If it had been diagnosed sooner, Alicia's chances of surviving the staged repair would have been greater. Anna was angry and felt responsible. As time went on and the care providers came to understand Anna through learning more of her story, mutual trust slowly developed.

After a five-month hospital stay and surgical interventions, Alicia died. During their time at the hospital, Anna, in particular, learned much about her daughter's condition and about the costs to herself, Paul, their extended family and friends. Shortly after Alicia's death, Anna and Paul separated, but reunited within the year. Approximately six months later, after much thought, they decided to try to have another baby.

Statistics indicate that the probability of HLHS increases, albeit minimally, if a previous sibling was born with HLHS. However, Anna was assured by the cardiac surgeon and her attending physician that, if she were to become pregnant again, she and her fetus would receive supportive care at the hospital. Anna subsequently became pregnant.

Anna and Paul schedule a fetal ultrasound and echocardiogram of the fetus at the twenty-two-week period (it is usually possible at this point to detect any signs of HLHS). The fetal echocardiogram indicates that the fetus may have HLHS. Anna and Paul are devastated. That day, they consult various experts—a cardiologist, social worker, cardiac surgeon, transplant physician and bioethicist—who explain to them the possible sequence of events once the baby is born. First, the baby would be given prostaglandin, which expands the heart duct to allow for further assessment. Should the initial diagnosis be confirmed, the baby would then have surgery to insert a Norwood shunt to improve the blood supply to the heart (a 35 percent mortality rate).

At three to four months, a second shunt, called a Glenn bidirectional shunt, would be inserted (a 4 percent mortality rate). At two and a half to three years, a procedure called a Fontan would be performed (a 10 percent mortality rate). The family is advised that, between the first and third surgeries, 15 to 20 percent of HLHS babies die. Overall, only 20 to 30 percent of these children survive the process. Long-term survival statistics are not available, but it is thought that most, if not all, will require a heart transplant at some point in their teens. Concern has also been expressed regarding neurological complications, although clear statistics have not yet been compiled.[3]

Anna and Paul, after much thought, prayer and consultation with others, and with the support of the chaplain, their family physician, friends and family, decide that they want to continue Anna's pregnancy. Further, after their baby is born they want the baby to receive the initial prostaglandin in order to allow for further assessment. Depending on the outcome, they will decide whether to go ahead with the Norwood procedure. Their decision is based not only on what they believe to be in the best interests of their child, but also on the expected impact on them and the rest of their family.

Anna and Paul return to the hospital. After informing the cardiologist of their decision, they are told that, if they choose to have the baby, whether or not to have treatment is not an option. The treatment protocol as he has outlined it is standard practice. The projected quality of life for the child is uncertain to good, and he believes that he is supported in his conviction by the ethical principle of "best interests" and by the law. He understands why Anna and Paul have reached their decision, but he feels that he (and society) has an obligation to protect the child, regardless of the final assessment.

Sitting with Anna and Paul while they agonized over their decision was difficult. It was clear that they already loved this unborn child. If the child had special needs on a cognitive or a physical level, they would learn how to meet those needs. But if the child would almost certainly die despite treatment, they did not want the child to suffer unnecessarily. Fear and hope intermingled as they confronted the unknown.

The issues changed for Anna and Paul as their story developed. Initially, the issue was the delay in Alicia's diagnosis and care. After Alicia died, the issue became one of faith. Why did God allow this to happen? How do two people stay together when they both grieve so differently? Later, when they had reunited and decided to have another child, the issue became what they would do if their second child also had HLHS. When they discovered that the ultrasound indicated the possibility of HLHS, Anna and Paul struggled with their resolution of this issue only to find that, in terms of hospital policy, they had little choice. This discovery re-framed the ethical issue: What gave the hospital the right to dictate what Anna and Paul, as parents, should do? How could they best protect what they understood to be the best interests of their child? There were several courses of action open to Anna and Paul: to follow the cardiologist's instructions and hospital policy; to opt for an abortion; or to seek treatment for the baby at a different hospital that did not consider the Norwood procedure standard treatment for HLHS. Which option should they choose?

Ethical Issues

The primary ethical issues relevant to this case study will be examined below.

Appropriate Decision-Makers

Possible decision-makers or decision-making bodies include Anna and Paul, hospital professionals, legal bodies, family and friends. Few would argue that, except in unusual cases in which a family member or friend is functioning as the primary caregiver, one or more of these groups are the appropriate decision-makers.

The Bioethics Committee of the Canadian Paediatric Society understands hospital professional team members to be responsible for ensuring the best interests of the child, particularly in cases where the legal guardian(s) or parent(s) fail, from the committee's perspective, to do so:

> The primary concern of physicians caring for children must be the best interests of the child. All infants and children have intrinsic value and deserve our respect and protection. This is true regardless of whether they are handicapped or have the potential to be handicapped and of whether the handicap is physical or mental. This means that all children have a justified claim to life and therefore to such treatment as is necessary to either improve or prolong life.[4]

Because children have "intrinsic value," they "deserve our respect and protection." Furthermore, the Bioethics Committee reasoned, because of this right, "children have a justified claim to life and therefore to such treatment as is necessary to either improve or prolong life." The value judgment that all children have a right to needed treatment that will "improve or prolong life" is connected to another value judgment that is not stated overtly: The best way that a sick child's life can be respected and protected is through the improvement or extension of that life.

However, as Anna and Paul point out, they are the ones who will raise, love and be responsible for their child. The well-being of the child depends first on those who will be the primary caregivers. Similarly, feminist theological ethicist Margaret Farley argues that "those who will bear the responsibility for child-rearing should have primary agency in decisions about childbearing…because this is required for the well-being of offspring."[5] However, scientific facts and reason often tend to be credited above personal experience in our predominant Western world view. As ethicist Karen Lebacqz notes, "While personal experiences are not totally ignored, they tend to be discredited: 'feelings' are not an adequate basis for ethical decision making; only logical analysis of 'facts' will do. This tends to take the decision away from those most intimately involved for they are often not in possession of all of the data and are also inclined to be emotional in their responses."[6] Adding another layer to this picture is the fact that Anna, as a woman in our patriarchal culture, is more readily associated with irrational and emotional reactions and is, therefore, more easily discounted. Both Anna and Paul have clearly indicated that they want this child and desire nothing but the best for him or her. The Canadian Paediatric Society's Bioethics Committee shares with Anna and Paul a commitment to the value of their future child. However, the meaning of this commitment in terms of action may be different for each. The medical response desired by Anna and Paul depends upon the nature of their future child's possible HLHS, whereas the hospital is committed to following standard treatment regardless.[7]

In our North American society, autonomy has often become conflated with extreme individualism, to the exclusion of communal interests and rights. Further, autonomy has tended to be regarded as the preeminent bioethical principle. Individual rights have assumed a priority, often at the expense of the well-being of others in the community whose rights are not valued as highly within the dominant paradigm.[8] An extreme principlist approach runs the risk of ignoring context and relationality. Many feminist theological ethicists have argued implicitly for a moderate postmodern approach that retains certain overarching values and principles, but that does not absolutize them. For instance, both Elizabeth Johnson[9] and Margaret Farley[10] argue for a reconceptualization of autonomy that recognizes the need for the principle of relationality in conjunction with individual rights. The values of community and mutuality in the relationship on which this reconceptualization is predicated are derived from both experience—particularly the experiences of the marginalized—and biblical sources in Christian tradition. These sources of authority inform the concept of relational autonomy that makes clear the need to understand moral agency in a communal context; one's subjectivity and rights exist and need to be understood within this context.

Fetal Diagnosis and Consent Issues

Perhaps the most significant expression of respect for the principle of autonomy, in the health-care context, is informed consent for treatment. In the case of fetal ultrasounds, for instance, informed consent does not often occur. The 1995 study by Sandelowski and Jones[11] of fifteen women and twelve of their partners found that the pregnant women and their partners were rarely asked to give informed consent to prenatal testing. Rather, most often, they followed the advice of their physician and did what the physician considered the "best" and "most responsible" thing to safeguard their fetus. Ignorance regarding the nature of the tests was not uncommon. Some women consented "by default": the woman or couple could not think of an adequate reason *not* to have the tests. Other factors included a perceived "routineness" and "simplicity" to the tests. A number of women said that they wanted to know the "sex of the baby"—after all, "everyone" did this. When one agrees to an ultrasound, to what is one agreeing? It is not just the first picture of one's child.

Prenatal testing has become the norm in contemporary North American medical practice. As Press and Browner note,[12] the last fifteen years have brought dramatic technological advancements in the area of prenatal testing. Previously, such testing was reserved for those women determined to be at high risk of "having a child with a birth anomaly."[13] Now there are non-invasive, simple and inexpensive tests that can be extended to all pregnant women. In their study, Press and Browner interviewed 150 pregnant women regarding their experiences with prenatal testing. The researchers found that informed consent was rarely requested—although provided with little information on the procedure, most of the women accepted the testing. They perceived it as routine and as a way to receive further reassurance regarding their future baby's health. Further, "a majority of women are not dissatisfied with the meagre amount of information they are given regarding…screening."[14]

A further ethical question concerns the effect that prenatal screening may have on the mother's relationship with her fetus: "What effect, if any, do stories of choices lost, told by couples continuing pregnancies with fetuses diagnosed as impaired, have on their relationship with their babies?…[I]s there any association between expressed regret over choices made or denied and parental-infant attachment?"[15] In Anna's and Paul's case, choice is clearly an important factor for them; they believe that they should be the ones making the bottom-line decisions for their future child. Having that choice removed may affect their relationship with their future child.

On a more pragmatic and social, systemic level, there are other questions: How will such diagnoses affect insurance, now and in the future, for the affected individuals? How do such diagnoses and economic concerns, in a *kyriarchal*[16] context, limit a woman's moral agency regarding pregnancy? As feminist ethicist Rosemarie Tong points out, "because at least half of society will not be eager to subsidize health-care for genetically defective or diseased children, such tests are likely to pressure pregnant women not only to determine their fetus' condition but also to do the 'right' thing (by which is presumably meant the scheduling of an abortion) in the event that the news is 'bad.'"[17] Justice requires that these questions be considered and that they be remembered when social policy questions arise. Just communities must seek to redress the injustices experienced by the marginalized.

The issues of consent underline the importance of interpreting bioethical principles of justice and beneficence. If autonomy is defined as relational, it must be linked to a communal understanding of justice. From a feminist theological perspective, the important outcome is not simply what benefits *me*, but is that which takes into account the less advantaged while valuing collective well-being.

The practice of expanding the field of conversation in concrete cases such as Anna's and Paul's emerges again. The decision cannot be made in isolation. Community and mutuality as values that uphold and contextualize individual rights provide correctives to an extreme individualism. In order to conform to principles of informed consent, the hospital needs to be clear with Anna and Paul about the range of possible results of a fetal ultrasound, the implication of each possible result, and the limits to their decision-making freedom placed upon them by hospital policy. Communicating all the relevant information to Anna and Paul is a primary obligation for the hospital and its medical team if they want to attain informed consent. It is possible, however, to deliver the information as "facts" in a tone that merely meets the ethical duty of non-maleficence, that is, of doing no harm. Medical staff could, without much regard for the family's feelings or values, convey the basic information necessary for Anna and Paul to make decisions about their fetus. On the other hand, health-care providers could choose to follow the principle of beneficence, that is, the obligation to do good, a principle often considered to be supererogatory—good and laudatory, but not mandatory. For instance, one is not expected to risk one's own life by pulling a person out of a burning car, but it is praiseworthy if one decides to do so. Feminist liberation theology directs attention to the assumptions behind this constructed meaning of beneficence, and invites ethicists and medical providers to follow its tenets. If community—as the divine call to relationship with self, neighbour, creation and God—is recognized to be of central importance, the duty of beneficence is strengthened, not with the intent of loss of self, but with the intent of the mutual strengthening of identity and being. Beneficence becomes understood in the context of mutuality and communal justice. When the interconnectedness, the profound communal nature, of all life is recognized and highly valued, then mutual beneficence is a necessary outcome.

Without a commitment to community and just relationships, beneficence can become distorted into benevolence and paternalism, and the underlying power imbalances becomes uncritically accepted. In both cases, the helper assists without an awareness or acceptance of the other's power and agency. The intent of the intervention is the patient's benefit but, within the traditional model, benefit tends to be defined by the helper, that is, the one with the power. In Anna's and Paul's case, the hospital, as benevolent caregiver, has assigned itself the right to define, unilaterally, what is most beneficent. The intention may be good, but the result is dangerous and serves to reinforce dominant, systemic power imbalances.

The predominant corrective to paternalism has been an emphasis on autonomy. However, as has been discussed, when autonomy is combined with extreme individualism, the result can be harmful. In the case of prenatal testing, if beneficence is understood in a framework of mutuality (a deliberative model in terms of the health-care provider-patient relationship),[18] then it is necessary that the meaning of prenatal testing be discussed much more directly with women than currently seems to be the case. As a final reflection about the communal context for medical decision-making, ought we not also be considering whether it is just and right that resources are allocated to develop these technologies, much less apply them, when so many in the world do not have access to basic health-care and medical interventions?

The Well-being of Prospective Parents

As Anna and Paul consider the future of their unborn child, their well-being is a concern. Both are very distraught. They desire to do what is best for their future child. Both have indicated that they want to be active decision-makers, and they expect to be kept informed regarding both Anna's and the fetus's medical conditions.

If the biblically based principle of standing with and for the vulnerable is central, as it is to the feminist ethic that informs this essay, then justice requires attention to power imbalances and ways to redress them. As Lebacqz points out, being a patient involves "a change in one's structural and sociological status."[19] Not only patients experience a physical problem for which they are "treated," but they also experience a loss of status and power. The patient's opinion usually takes second place to that of the physician.

Further, if patients have other systemic strokes against them, including gender, culture and language, to name a few, the disempowerment is compounded.[20] In Anna's case, gender can function as a barrier to being heard and respected as a moral agent actively involved in the care of her body and her future baby. If Anna were not white, able-bodied, married and of a socially acceptable age at which to be pregnant, in all probability she would experience further disempowerment. The stereotypes of pregnant women being particularly irrational, given to hysteria and, in general, incapable of sound judgment must be named and deconstructed. Having been dismissed during her first pregnancy as an emotional or hysterical first-time mother, Anna is determined to have her voice heard this time.

The physicians and other health caregivers are also in a difficult situation, although it must be noted that they hold the balance of power. There is no reason to believe that they do not value Anna's and Paul's well-being. It is, however, safe to assume that there are several value systems influencing the decisions about the content and amount of information necessary for Anna and Paul to make informed decisions about their fetus. No doubt there are also differences within the medical team about the means, methods and tone of the delivery of that information. There could have been, although it is now impossible to know for certain, some who believed it best to withhold from Anna and Paul some information upon which they would be powerless to act in order to protect them. The ethical and moral texture in all such situations is ordinarily thick and complex.

The Best Interests of the Child

If the future child has HLHS, the question of the value and quality of this shortened life raises important ethical concerns. Substantive issues relative to the best interests of the child are unclear due to a lack of data regarding long-term survival and quality of life. Some cardiac caregivers are more optimistic than others.

Complicating, or at least adding another layer to, this discussion is the reality that oftentimes death is perceived as the greatest evil, especially the death of a child. It must be avoided at all costs. The question is: When, if ever, is it morally permissible to allow impaired newborns to die? Perhaps it is the point at which the duties of beneficence, non-maleficence and justice indicate that to sustain that life is no longer ethically defensible.

A difficulty with the principles of beneficence and non-maleficence is the often hidden assumption of what is meant by "good" and "harm." Both meanings are socially constructed. For instance, in the dominant Western medical paradigm, death tends to be perceived as the greatest harm. Also, the value of the sanctity of life can be understood in very different ways. It may indicate a reluctance to use all heroic medical interventions regardless of possible harm, or the same value may signal a requirement to "go the distance." Therefore, a medical intervention, such as the HLHS staged repair, is identified as good by many cardiac surgeons, but may or may not be perceived as good by the child's family, weighed against such morally relevant factors as value systems, past experience and faith traditions. This demonstrates the importance of a model for ethical clarification such as Hutchinson's model. His method directs us to identify "factual claims" (that is, claims that are neither necessarily empirically proven nor agreed upon, but that may well be understood by some as factual), and to seek greater clarity regarding their veracity as discerned from different perspectives.

For Anna and Paul, their child's potential suffering must be weighed against the risk of death. They do not see death as the worst possible outcome. Rather, the worst outcome is a life prolonged by painful surgeries, in the face of almost certain death. Clearly, the sanctity of their child's life is valued above compromised cognitive or motor functioning.

"What If" Issues

Anna and Paul, in consultation with their various support groups, need to make "what if" decisions before their child is even born, in anticipation of the possibility that the child will be born with HLHS. Eventually, if each of the three surgeries is successful, their child (probably as a teen) will need a heart transplant. Are they willing to consider this? They must also be prepared to give a "do not resuscitate" order. The decision-makers need to decide to what degree they will pursue heroic medical interventions and at what point, if any, the cost to the child, parents and society may become too high. In other words, possible future consequences of a decision to implement the staged repair ought to be considered.

Standard Treatment[21]

The Norwood procedure and staged repair, at the time of Anna's and Paul's case (1996), were considered medically required and ethically obligatory at their hospital. From the hospital's perspective, the staged repair was the best possible treatment since it provided the only chance of life: no harm can outweigh the harm of death. However, from another perspective, since the medical burdens could outweigh the benefits to the patient, one could argue that the staged repair was an extraordinary measure and, therefore, ought not be ethically obligatory. Proponents of both views claim the best interests of the child to be the most important value. Both are also concerned with consequences, but each is undergirded by different world views and beliefs regarding who is able to make the "best" decision, and what "best" means.

Words can give normative content to ethical claims; medical language can serve to "camouflage" the ethical.[22] The term "standard treatment" seems to indicate that the treatment in question is common and predictable as well as safe, similar to a fetal ultrasound. However, in the case of the staged repair, the "standard" treatment is risky and fraught with ethical difficulties.[23]

A related issue regarding the identification and definition of what constitutes "standard" treatment in a children's hospital is the frequent classification of palliative care as non-treatment; non-treatment is often seen as giving up. As long as there are other options, one does not give up. Palliative care ought to be considered a positive, good treatment option for a child facing almost certain death. When such conditions prevail, pain reduction and other bodily comforts are the greatest good that can be offered when compared to further tests and treatments that will increase pain and suffering and will only delay death. Against this background, perhaps we need to rethink the standard classification in hospitals that palliative care is non-treatment for child patients.

Economics and Resource Allocation

The interests of society also need to be taken into account in making an ethical decision. There is a crisis in health-care. Historically, Canadians have had equal access to health care, but this privilege is threatened in today's medical marketplace. Insufficient resources are now being allocated to health care and, as a result, expensive procedures, such as the staged repair for HLHS and transplants,[24] can have political implications. They must be examined with the principle of distributive justice in mind. Further, the cost of prenatal tests and the assumptions of their relevance, meaning and availability must be examined in a contextual light. Such considerations may increase the resources allocated to health care, may cause a more serious questioning of the appropriateness of the staged repair as standard treatment in all cases, or may lead to an overall reorganization of health-care. Or, of course, the decision may be to preserve the status quo. Clearly, political choices regarding resource allocation must be questioned and rejected when equal access to quality care is not universally available.

"Ableism"

Attitudes toward those in Western society who are defined as "disabled" may well influence decisions about the termination of pregnancies or the non-treatment of newborns whose medical complications will likely make them utterly dependent upon a wide net of support. In our dominant North American culture, autonomy is highly prized, and those whose ability to function as autonomous subjects is in any way compromised can be undervalued. This cultural devaluing may be given increased credibility or reinforcement through selective terminations of pregnancies in which it is suspected or known that the fetus is in some way different from the norm.

Anna and Paul want to have their child and make decisions based on medical knowledge as it becomes available. However, there are many reasons why parents may choose to have prenatal diagnosis with the possibility of selective termination—for example, the desire to have a so-called "normal" child, or to improve their abilities to treat and care for the newborn. Prenatal diagnosis may help them in their decision: Could they, would they, care for a disabled child? Can they bear the stress and suffering that may be involved? Alternatively, parents may choose prenatal testing because it is presented as normative.

Some people argue that the fetus has the right "not to come into existence,"[25] while others believe that the rights of the unborn child should be taken into account in making life-and-death decisions. Both Tong and Farley stress that selective termination can be a form of discrimination and that all forms of discrimination are interconnected. "Feminists should be as concerned about 'ableism' as they are about 'sexism.' Discrimination is discrimination regardless of its object."[26] Others, such as Lynn Gillam, stress the ethical claim that selective termination based on an evaluation of the best interests of the future child does not constitute discrimination.[27] Motivation is difficult to clarify. This question of the meaning of selective abortion is complex. Ethical analysis must seek to clarify motivation, systemic and interpersonal power dynamics, factual claims, and values.

Abortion

Clearly, a related issue is abortion. Abortion may or may not be an option for Anna and Paul; it depends upon such things as the medical test results, advice from the care providers, their own values, formed by their life experiences, and their faith.[28] All these factors need to be clarified and understood in tension with each other.

The Right to Procreate

In Canada, the right to procreate is usually assumed. However, in this world many children are unwanted and neglected. The duties of justice and beneficence require that this right be examined. Further, as Lebacqz queries, "Why do [many women] want [to conceive] so desperately—i.e. what in the system creates this need?"[29] Societal attitudes have an influence on individual expectations and desires. In cultures where women are valued for their perceived capacity to attract men, bear children and nurture them, pressure not just to conceive but to desire to conceive is immense.

Concluding Remarks

The rapid rise in biotechnological advancements has created ethical dilemmas in such areas as prenatal and genetic testing. The decision-making process in the health-care system will better serve Anna, Paul and their fetus when that process is deconstructed and reconstructed in light of the feminist insights I have brought to the conversation in this essay. A feminist liberationist theological perspective can broaden the dominant Western bioethical approach through attention to systems, structures, faith and an alternative vision of relational well-being. Further, such analysis uncovers and challenges certain ethical assumptions, particularly those involving the medical care of women. This case study provides one context for such an analysis. I have chosen to demonstrate one way in which a feminist liberationist analysis can be applied to ethical issues. My purpose was not to arrive at any one decision but, rather, to enlarge the moral landscape through the application of a feminist liberationist theological perspective to one particular case. As such, clearly it is limited in scope. There are many wider-reaching ethical questions to be identified and explored in depth: the lack of justice that is seemingly inherent in a capitalist economic model; the relevance of racism, classism and many other systemic oppressions that are inextricably intertwined; the fact that even the question of how to allocate health-care resources must be raised; the purposes and motivations on which medical research is predicated; and so forth. Indeed, these questions must be explored as part of any commitment to the work of justice. This case is simply one scene within a much broader picture. Hopefully, it will provoke and evoke further questions.

The Hutchinson method for ethical clarification has provided an overarching framework for the clarification of this case study. It is a method particularly well suited to a feminist liberationist theological approach in that it allows, in fact requires, a variety of perspectives (with attention to those that are not often heard), contexts and experiences to be given voice and brought into an ongoing dialogue in which systemic power imbalances and dynamics are identified and clarified. Consensus or arrival at one "right" decision is not the goal; rather, the goal is enhanced understanding and communication, in order that the moral landscape may be enlarged and biases, assumptions, conflicts and misunderstandings illuminated, with the knowledge (and, indeed, the hope) that one's eventual response could be revisited and possibly changed.[30]

Much to the delight and relief of Anna and Paul, Anna gave birth to a healthy little girl. Tests showed that Carrie did not have HLHS. Unfortunately, the ethical questions remain to be faced by the next family in a similar crisis.

Notes

1 Roger Hutchinson, "Towards a 'Pedagogy for Allies of the Oppressed,'" Studies in Religion/Sciences religieuses 13/2 (1984): 147.
2 Ibid., 148.
3 Hypoplastic Left Heart Syndrome is sometimes called "the worst heart disease." It is "the fourth most common critical congenital heart defect." See L.T. Swanson, "Treatment Options for Hypoplastic Left Heart Syndrome: A Mother's Perspective," *Critical Care Nurse* 15/3 (1995): 70-72, 76-79. Some medical centres require that the parents/primary caregiver(s) agree to surgical interventions that have been identified as standard treatment at that particular centre. Other centres have options available, including non-treatment, a heart transplant or the Norwood surgical procedure. If parents/primary caregiver(s) request a transfer to another

hospital because they want a treatment other than that which their current hospital defines as standard, physicians can call in the Children's Aid Society in order to determine whether the hospital is acting in the child's best interests. Hospital cardiac departments regularly review their policies to consider whether or not non-treatment is an ethically acceptable policy. When this case occurred in 1996, staged repair, beginning with the Norwood, was standard procedure at this particular hospital.

Until 1983, when the first successful Norwood procedure was performed, there was no "treatment" for HLHS apart from palliative care, which is usually not defined as an active treatment option. Infants are usually diagnosed in utero (late in the pregnancy) or in the first week of life (but sometimes even then the condition is not detected). Infants are born looking healthy and are usually a good weight. HLHS is almost always fatal by one month of age.

4 *Treatment Decisions for Infants and Children*, Position Statement approved by the CPS Board of Directors (Bioethics Committee, Canadian Paediatric Society, 1986; reaffirmed 02/00, Reference No. B86-01), 1.

5 Margaret Farley, "Feminist Theology and Bioethics," in *Feminist Theological Ethics*, ed. Lois K. Daly (Louisville, KY: Westminster John Knox Press, 1994), 207.

6 Karen Lebacqz, "Bioethics: The Prevailing Approach," in *On Moral Medicine: Theological Perspectives in Medical Ethics*, ed. Stephen E. Lammers and Allen Verhey, 2nd ed. (Grand Rapids, MI: William B. Eerdmans, 1998), 85.

7 Interestingly, the report of a University of Copenhagen study by M. Norup–"Limits of Neonatal Treatment: A Survey of Attitudes in the Danish Population," *Journal of Medical Ethics* 24 (June 1988): 200-06–noted that, although physicians had been surveyed, "there do not seem to be any systematic studies of attitudes amongst the general population to these questions…about the limits of neonatal treatment" (200). The study found that there was "general acceptance [i.e., more than 75 percent of respondents]…that life-prolonging treatment ought to be provided even in relatively severe cases *if this was in accordance with parental wishes*" [emphasis mine], (200, 205). Would there be similar findings in Canada? Since values vary with cultures (see Hutchinson, "Towards a 'Pedagogy for Allies of the Oppressed,'" 149, for his fourth level of post-ethical clarification), we cannot know for certain. What we do know is that, in North America, ultimately the legal system can decide what is best in a particular instance, if one or the other party appeals to the law. Our legal system, it seems, has become our most powerful societal authority. Individual rights are often valued above communal justice and well-being.

8 Consider, for example, recent legal pleas that argue for the right of some men to possess child pornography, with little, if any, concern for the rights of children and those who are concerned about children's well-being.

9 Elizabeth Johnson, *She Who Is: The Mystery of God in Feminist Theological Discourse* (New York: Crossroad, 1992), 126.
10 Farley, "Feminist Theology and Bioethics," 203.
11 M. Sandelowski and L.C. Jones, "'Healing Fictions': Stories of Choosing in the Aftermath of the Detection of Fetal Anomalies," *Social Science and Medicine* 42/3 (1996): 353-61.
12 N. Press and C.H. Browner, "Risk, Autonomy and Responsibility: Informed Consent for Prenatal Testing," *The Hastings Center Report* 25 (1995): S9-S12.
13 Ibid., S9.
14 Ibid., S11.
15 Sandelowski and Jones, "Healing Fictions," 359.
16 I borrow this term from Elisabeth Schüssler Fiorenza, *Jesus: Miriam's Child, Sophia's Prophet* (New York: Continuum, 1995), 14. Schüssler Fiorenza coined this term to mean "the rule of the emperor/master/lord/father/husband over his subordinates." These subordinates can be both disadvantaged females and disadvantaged males, but she sees them particularly as "women who live at the bottom of the *kyriarchal* pyramid and who struggle against multiplicative forms of oppression."
17 Rosemarie Tong, *Feminist Approaches to Bioethics: Theoretical Reflections and Practical Applications* (Boulder, CO: Westview Press, 1997), 232.
18 Tong (137-38) cites the four models of physician-patient relationship described by Drs. Ezekiel Emanuel and Linda Emanuel: (1) paternalistic—in which physicians "use their skills to determine which procedures they think patients ought to undergo, and then they guide their patients to assent to these procedures"; (2) informative-in which "free rein" is given to the patient's autonomy; (3) interpretative—in which the physician gives the patient all pertinent information (as in the informative model) and also helps the patient to clarify values regarding his or her health care; and (4) deliberative—in which both physician and patient engage in discussion and both present their values and preferences with the understanding that difference in opinion is acceptable; the physician will not abandon the patient if the patient has a divergent view. This last model allows both to sort through their ideas. The danger of the informative model and, to a lesser degree, the interpretative model is that patients are left without support or validation; they can feel isolated. The deliberative model is favoured by feminist liberation theologians with the proviso that justice, including empowerment of the patient, be part of this model.
19 Lebacqz, "Empowerment in the Clinical Setting," 806.
20 Ibid., 812. Lebacqz refers to a 1990 study by S.H. Miles and A. August that demonstrates the compounded disempowerment that women experience in both the clinical context and the courts: "In a [United States] study of court cases…when the patient was a man, the court constructed his

preferences for treatment in a large percentage of cases, and allowed those preferences to be determining. But, when the patient was a woman, the court constructed her preferences in only 14% of cases, and her preferences were not determinative of treatment decisions."

21 Standard treatment is treatment identified by a hospital as that proved safe and effective and therefore ethically obligatory—widely accepted in hospital care. Innovative treatment, on the other hand, is treatment in which outcomes and side effects are unknown, but it can be an option in dire circumstances. Experimental treatment lies somewhere between the two—more information is available, but long-term outcomes are still unknown. Ethically, experimental treatment should be offered in the absence of standard treatment, but it might be refused. There are two different types of standard treatment. In the first instance, the treatment is medically required and ethically obligatory due to clear evidence of benefit and insignificant harms. In the second case, the treatment has been proven to have clear benefits but significant drawbacks. As a result, this treatment is medically recommended and ethically optional. Further, treatment is defined as "extraordinary" and not ethically obligatory if it offers no reasonable hope of benefit to a particular patient or if the benefits are outweighed by the burdens that it will impose on that patient.

22 Pat Murphy and George Webster, "Camouflaging the 'Ethical' in Health Care Decision Making." Unpublished paper, St. Boniface Hospital, Winnipeg, 2000.

23 As Roger Hutchinson points out, it is important to "find out who gets to say what the facts are, how they are known, and how they will be used." Cranford Pratt and Roger Hutchinson, eds., *Christian Faith and Economic Justice: Toward a Canadian Perspective* (Burlington, ON: Trinity Press, 1988), 183. This analysis of power dynamics, consistent with the whole of the Hutchinson method, allows a deeper clarification of what is really happening.

24 Thomas G. Storch, "Passive Euthanasia for Hypoplastic Left Heart Syndrome," *AJDC* 146 (December 1992): 1426.

25 See D. Heyd, "Prenatal Diagnosis: Whose Right?" *Journal of Medical Ethics* 21 (1995): 294; Press and Browner, "Risk, Autonomy and Responsibility," S9-S12.

26 Tong, *Feminist Approaches to Bioethics*, 235; Farley, "Feminist Theology and Bioethics," 192-97.

27 Lynn Gillam, "Prenatal Diagnosis and Discrimination against the Disabled," *Journal of Medical Ethics* 25 (1999): 163-71, esp. 169.

28 Beverly Wildung Harrison's book, *Our Right to Choose: Toward a New Ethic of Abortion* (Boston, MA: Beacon Press, 1983), offers a thorough feminist theological analysis of this issue that takes into account systems and structures.

29 Lebacqz, "Bio-ethics," 88.

30 See Roger Hutchinson, "Making Connections and Clarifying Options: A Social Ethic for Allies of the Oppressed." Unpublished paper, Donald Mathers Lecture, Queen's Theological College, 20 March 1991.

11

ARE CLERGY ETHICS A MATTER OF COMMON SENSE?[1]

CHRISTOPHER LIND

Preface

When I began my life as a graduate student, it was my privilege to serve for five years as teaching assistant to Roger Hutchinson. The class, at the University of Toronto, was "Introduction to Religious Ethics," and it was there that I was schooled in what we all came to call "The Method." The genealogy of the method is elaborated elsewhere in this festschrift, in particular Hutchinson's own debt to Gibson Winter. However, there are certain sensibilities associated with his manner of clarifying the roots of moral conflict that may not be apparent to the casual reader.

Like many contemporary ethicists, Hutchinson thinks of Christian social ethics as an inherently interdisciplinary field of inquiry. Every social question requires dialogue with other social sciences in order for all aspects of the problem to be understood. Hutchinson's own training was first in engineering and then in sociology, and it has been that latter discipline with which he has been more frequently in conversation. However, the sensibility characteristic of his use of "The Method" is one I associate with the discipline of cultural anthropology. His analysis of opposing moral arguments requires an understanding from the inside. Sometimes, Hutchinson would invite a controversial speaker to

Notes to chapter 11 are on pp. 236-37.

class, knowing that many students would be outraged by the position being articulated. After the speaker's presentation, the assignment would be to analyze and reconstruct the argument so that the speaker could recognize the argument as his or her own. The speaker was treated as if from another culture. We were asked to suspend our judgment of the position until we could understand the world view within which this argument made sense. The anthropologist whom Hutchinson was most fond of quoting was Clifford Geertz. It was Hutchinson who introduced me to Geertz's work, and my use of Geertz in the essay that follows is a kind of homage to Hutchinson. In addition, while I do not use Hutchinson's method in a formal way in what follows, my attempt to clarify the assumptions within which debates are framed, rather than advocate for a position within the debate proper, is a direct result of being instructed in this style of ethical analysis.

In this essay, I pursue the question of whether ministerial ethics[2] can be thought of as a matter of common sense. I use Geertz to explore the concept of common sense and test my database against his criteria. When it becomes clear that my data meet all of his criteria, I conclude that the widespread assumption that clergy ethics are a matter of common sense neatly summarizes the problem. Common sense is a matter of form, not of content. What is missing is a common culture to supply the content held in common. In a globalized world where cultural content is increasingly fragmented into a pattern we call postmodern, the creation of a common culture within institutions (like denominations) will have to be an intentional act. This deliberate exposure of differences that are either new or kept hidden will be a painful but necessary exercise for the churches.

The database for this essay is drawn from a larger qualitative research study on ethics in ministry that I undertook with Maureen Muldoon, an associate professor at the University of Windsor. The study involved approximately eighty interviews with lay people and members of the order of ministry, in both the Anglican Church of Canada and the United Church of Canada, in the provinces of Ontario and Saskatchewan. The purpose of the study was to determine what the actual ethics of ministers are. This study contrasts with most prior research, which has attempted to determine what the ethics of ministers ought to be.

Clergy Ethics and Common Sense

It is something of a truism in qualitative research to say that all conversations about one's topic become part of the research data. So, when the mother of one of the researchers responded to a discussion about clergy codes of conduct with the comment "What do they need a code of conduct for? They've got the Bible, don't they?" this began a serious, though unexpected, line of inquiry. The response seemed so obvious as to be a matter of common sense.

This led, in turn, to a search for the use of the term "common sense" in our research database. The search showed that the term was used on sixteen occasions by eleven subjects. It also showed that the term was used in a positive sense by women as well as by men, by members of both denominations, by laity as well as by those who were ordained or commissioned, and by people in urban Ontario as well as in rural Saskatchewan. However, it was clearly used more often by lay people than by the ordained (nine to two); it was not used by any of the Saskatchewan clergy.

This was not where our research began. Elsewhere in our study, we concerned ourselves with the question of "professionalism" in ministry. To what extent are ministers professionals, and is the model of professional ethics the right one for thinking about the ethical challenges in ministry? The text from which we drew our list of discussion starters is subtitled "Professional Responsibilities of the Clergy." The author, Gaylord Noyce, identified the problem in pastoral ministry as one of "blurred pastoral identity." He advocated a model of professional ethics as one that would clarify pastoral identity.[3]

However, since our original task was to describe what clergy ethics are in practice, the category of common sense could not now be avoided. The interview subjects invoked this term in relation to a broad variety of issues. For example, Darren, an Anglican layman in Saskatchewan, thought that, when it comes to deciding topics for sermons, "It's common sense knowing what's appropriate and not appropriate." Beverly, an Anglican laywoman in Ontario, ruminated on the question of time boundaries and how strict a minister should be about taking days off and sticking to them. Her conclusion was that "It all comes down to common sense." In discussing how to respond to suspicions of sexual abuse, an Anglican priest identified the key issue as responsibility. "We need to do what responsible people do," Peter said. "We need to obey the law and use our common sense."

For some, common sense is what one uses in the absence of other rules or guidelines. Rick, an Ontario United Church minister, put it this way: "There are limits...but the guiding principle in most issues in life, be they ethical or otherwise, is common sense...[T]here are no rules that are immutable and eternal for human beings, as far as I know." A similar sentiment was expressed by Nancy, another United Church pastor in Ontario: "I don't think there are any guidelines....It's never been an issue up to now....I think that clergy have basically done whatever they felt was appropriate and was okay."

As often as common sense is mentioned, it seems to raise more questions than it answers. If so many ethical questions come down to a matter of common sense, why are the issues so conflicted? Why are the answers not held in common? In response to a question about a minister's management style concerning church finances, Dennis, a lay Anglican in Saskatchewan, said it was just a matter of common sense to ask a layperson with financial expertise to handle the bills. Yet, this "common" sense of things was not held by the minister he was describing.

What is common sense? The American anthropologist Clifford Geertz asked the same question in an essay entitled "Common Sense as a Cultural System."[4] He wanted to come to some systematic understanding of this concept, and one of his first conclusions was "[t]hat it is an inherent characteristic of common-sense thought precisely to deny this [possibility] and to affirm that its tenets are immediate deliverances of experience, not deliberated reflections upon it. Knowing that rain wets and that one ought to come in out of it, or that fire burns and one ought not to play with it...are conflated into comprising one large realm of the given and undeniable, a catalogue of in-the-grain-of-nature realities so peremptory as to force themselves upon any mind sufficiently unclouded to receive them....Common sense rests its [case] on the assertion that it is not a case at all, just life in a nutshell. The world is its authority."[5]

So, common sense by its nature is not something on which we normally reflect. This sets up a natural tension with an approach that treats the ethical questions in ministry as something requiring specialized attention. Even though philosophers over the years have referred frequently to common sense or other ideas considered to be self-evident, the notion of common sense has tended to remain what anyone with common sense knows.[6]

Although common sense carries with it the assumption that this sense has always existed, Geertz argues that we can actually observe common sense changing:

> The development of modern science has had a profound effect—though perhaps not as profound as sometimes imagined—upon Western common-sense views. Whether, as I rather doubt, the plain man has become a genuine Copernican or not (to me, the sun still rises and shines upon the earth), he has surely been brought round, and quite recently, to a version of the germ theory of disease. The merest television commercial demonstrates that. But, as the merest television commercial also demonstrates, it is as a bit of common sense, not as an articulated scientific theory, that he believes it. He may have moved beyond "feed a cold and starve a fever," but only to "brush your teeth twice a day and see your dentist twice a year."[7]

This is a good example of one way in which common sense can change. However, this common sense is still not completely "common." It is not shared by people who favour naturopathic healers. For some, it is a matter of common sense to have children vaccinated against childhood diseases. For others, it is a crime inflicted on an innocent population. For many, it is common sense to have a blood transfusion if you have lost a lot of blood in childbirth—but not if you are a Jehovah's Witness. After sixty years of experience, ordaining women as ministers may now be viewed as just "common sense" for members of the United Church of Canada. However, for members of the Anglican Church of Canada, with only twenty-five years of the same experience, one cannot make this assertion with the same degree of confidence. Here, we come to Geertz's central claim: "Common sense is not what the mind cleared of cant spontaneously apprehends; it is what the mind filled with presuppositions concludes."[8] Common sense does not represent a fixed body of beliefs except, perhaps, in a culture with a sufficiently common base of experience, belief, attitude and history.

Can we say that common sense has anything in common with itself? Geertz claims we can, and, wherever common sense is found as a cultural form, he identifies five common characteristics: naturalness, practicalness, thinness, "immethodicalness" and accessibleness.[9]

By "naturalness," Geertz means those matters considered to be simply "the nature of the case." These are the kinds of items to which we might respond "of course!" or "it figures." "Practicalness" he explains in terms of its opposite. What do we mean when we say something is impractical? We mean this action is likely to be self-defeating. It will not work. To be practical is to be prudent and level-headed, to be wise in a common-sense sort of way. "Thinness" refers to that sense that things really are as they seem to be. Truth is literal, sober and plain. It lies on the surface for everyone to see. There is nothing "deep" about it. The ungainly word "immethodical" means that common-sense thought is inconsistent and proud of it. It is ad hoc and expressed in the kinds of proverbs and epigrams one finds on T-shirts: "A foolish consistency is the hobgoblin of little minds"; or, "If you think you understand the situation, that only proves you are misinformed."[10] Finally, "accessibleness" refers to the assumption that any person who is mentally healthy will be able not only to grasp common sense, but also to embrace it. Common sense is not the province of specialists, but of the average person.

So, do the research subjects in the clergy ethics study use the term "common sense" in the way Geertz describes? I think they do.

For example, Geertz's quality of "naturalness" includes a sense of obviousness. Dennis, the lay Anglican in Saskatchewan, was speaking about conflict in the diocese between the bishop and the ministers and about how decisions are made. He responded with an expectation that a common-sense decision would be obvious:

> I think that the bishop would be certainly open enough to listen to suggestions and would make his decisions, first of all on his own, through his own experience and talents, and explain the "yes's" and the "no's" of a particular situation, so that there wouldn't be the terrible conflict that might arise if they didn't talk amongst each other....I've got a lot of faith in these people putting their heads together and maybe having a bit of a swinging session when they're arguing things out, but they come to a relatively decent and common-sense decision in the end. Obviously the bishop has to be the leader in the diocese....There's always the renegade who has to go his own way to a certain extent, but if he's got

> a good point it's followed by others. If it's a bad point he soon drops it himself.

Alan, another lay Anglican in Saskatchewan, thought that respect for people is so obviously important that it is a matter of common sense. At the same time, he thought that respect is crucial for successful leadership and he saw leadership as a gift:

> I think that everyone has certain talents, whatever, and leadership is a talent and a gift, and it's how they are perceived to get people to follow this. It's utilizing their talents. And...well there again, it's common sense...knowing what's appropriate and what isn't appropriate and how you treat people. And you're going to get people to do things with you if you treat them in a respectful manner, but if you are pounding on the pulpit, saying that this thing has to be done, kind of thing, then you're not going to get people. So it's how you present yourself.

For Geertz, "practicalness" means that common sense solutions work. Sometimes, it is just a matter of common sense or logic that proposed solutions will fail. Susan, a United Church minister in Ontario, put it this way: "I think they have to be logical, you know. Like, if you want your marriage to last, you can't be on forty-five Conference committees. You know what I'm saying? And, okay, if you go to the Presbytery meeting the first Tuesday of every month, or something like that, and occasionally the U.C.W. or the Men's Group, or somebody has a meeting that they want you at, then I think, okay, you have to miss the Presbytery meeting, you know? You have to use your common sense. Probably common sense, as much as morals, enters into it."

It does not matter whether the "practicalness" of the common-sense attitude is supported or contradicted by empirical evidence. Common sense is logical and does not require verification. For Robert, a lay Anglican in Ontario, the issue that demonstrated this was Sunday shopping. "I don't particularly care for Sunday shopping, more from a common-sense point of view than anything else. Just because [the grocery store] A&P is now open seven days a week doesn't mean I spend more money there. It merely means that the amount of money I spend on groceries is spread out and they have to pay more to their help to stay open more. So from the economic and common-sense point of view, I think most of the stores wish they weren't open on Sundays now."

Geertz identifies "thinness" as a quality of something being obvious on the surface—not requiring one to go too deep. This next quotation from Deborah, a United Church laywoman in Saskatchewan, reveals two examples of common sense as "thinness"—the common sense of the speaker and the common sense of the man being described:

> Well, you know, the homosexuality debate was unlike anything the church had gone through before because, you see, everyone that expressed an opinion felt that they were expressing the church's opinion, but they were miles, poles apart, ...[they used] quotations from the Hebrew Scriptures in which they could justify their attitude and stick with that. Then, even when common sense sort of said well, you know, to think beyond that, to really look at that,...like, people would say,...and I heard that over and over again, well it's in the Scriptures. It's wrong because it's in the Scriptures. Well where in the Scriptures? Well nobody knew where it was until somebody had raised, you know, that you could find it in a certain portion of Leviticus and that's good enough....It was at Conference, Saskatchewan Conference, there was an elderly gentleman, I don't think he was clergy, who had said, made the statement—we were standing in line for lunch—and who said that, "If it says in the Bible that it's wrong that's good enough for me." And I'm standing right behind him, these two men, and of course they were...about seventy years old I think, and so the idea was they knew that it was somewhere in Scripture, nobody knew where it was, or exactly what it said, or in what context, and then so somebody would try to counter that and say that, you know, the New Testament makes no reference to homosexuals. Well, never mind.

For Deborah, it is a matter of common sense that Scripture requires interpretation. For the person being described, the Bible is a kind of common-sense book that can be read and understood at a surface level. Obviously, the issues of biblical interpretation and sexual orientation are a good deal more complicated than that, but common sense can appear as divisive as the debates about sexuality. Everyone thinks he or she is speaking plain, old common sense and everyone is taking very different positions.

Frequently, common sense is invoked in situations requiring judgment. It may not be a situation requiring deep wisdom, but just a situation where there are too many variables to have a hard-and-fast rule. Henry, an Ontario Anglican layman, invoked common sense when describing responses to marital strain among clergy:

> I would expect that if they were in an extramarital [affair]...if that happened, that [the clergy] would have enough stamina on a common-sense level, on a personal level and on a spiritual level to be able to go to someone and get some help as to how to handle that. And inside the Anglican Church there are all kinds of people that are designated on a clergy level and on a lay level to deal with that. We have what we call pastoral Archdeacons inside the church where they can go and they can get help. Even now in our diocese he's engaged a counselling service for the clergy and for their staff so that...you know...just like in any organization there are stresses. There are times when priests get burned out. There are times when priests enter into a relationship, be it female or male, outside of their marriage and they've got to be able to go somewhere and get some help to resolve it because, you know, I don't think they're in a position to resolve their own.

The quality of "immethodicalness" Geertz identifies as a quality of common sense that seems to declare "don't even try and make systematic sense of this." The wisdom is practical, situation-specific and learned from experience. Rick, the Ontario United Church minister, who declared that there are no immutable rules, that the guiding principle in life is common sense, was expressing this position. Deborah, the United Church laywoman in Saskatchewan, expressed it this way:

> I don't expect any different kind of awareness of a different kind of ethics for people in that profession than I do for myself. And that's kind of a gut feeling, but I guess if a clergy person does something dumb, then I guess my tendency would be to think, where's your head? Like, why aren't you thinking? Because I think when you're in a leadership position you need to keep that in mind, and I guess it's easy for me to say, 'cause I'm not, you know. And that doesn't mean that I wouldn't do some dumb things too, but I think, yeah, maybe when you're up..., you've had like the benefit of some training, and I guess, the really, the encouraging thing that I'm experiencing 'cause

> I've supervised a few interns, is that...students are, through internship especially, given the opportunity to learn about the importance of common sense. And it's really the bottom line, you know. You can't learn all that in the college. It's just plain common sense in a lot of cases....I see evidence of that when [the students] come, at least they have an idea,...these are possibilities. Whereas, I think twenty-five years ago they didn't. If they didn't have the common sense it was a disaster, that's really what it was. But I guess, yeah, common sense is important in every situation.

The last characteristic of common sense that Geertz identifies is "accessibleness." By this quality he means common sense is not the privilege of an elite group of specialists. Common sense is available to each ordinary person—anyone whose cognitive functioning is not impaired. Alan, the Anglican layman in Saskatchewan, was expressing his frustration with one minister who seemed to lack this quality, and he was perplexed by it:

> I know there are times when you have to get in touch with someone, but sometimes some of them...will put themselves first and expect that, you know, if they call, you immediately have to respond. They interrupt you at a meeting, or I guess it's part of them having respect for the other person, as we mentioned before. I think this, on a regular basis, it makes people shy, and instead of getting people to say "yes" to things, they're more apt to say "no," or more apt to avoid the person, and that type of thing. I know,...you might be in the middle of a meeting, and the priest might insist that they have to speak to you, and it's not an emergency, it's just a matter of a bit of common sense and good manners. But I know it is aggravating at times, and I think the situation that I'm thinking of—it's not just me, it's not just my wife, it's a number of people, and I keep hearing from other members of the congregation.

So, the qualities that Geertz has identified in his analysis of common sense from the anthropological literature are also present in our research sample. One theme that seems significant is the emphasis on common sense as something learned by experience but not taught in schools. Of course, if common sense resists efforts to systematize it, naturally theological schools will find it a difficult subject to teach—but not impossible. At least one interview subject identified common sense as an item learned during internship, and most theological schools have some sort of internship or field education component in their programs. I also note that the concept of common sense seemed more significant for the lay people interviewed than for those in ordered ministry. This would make sense (common sense?) for people without detailed knowledge of the curriculum of theological schools. It is also significant that common sense was frequently invoked as a resource in a situation of complex variables requiring judgment.

In one interview, Rick, the Ontario United Church minister, asked a provocative question. The topic being discussed was gossip. The general direction of his thoughts was that ministers should not participate in gossip by passing it along, but they should pay close attention to it because of its pastoral usefulness. "Is common sense an ethic?" he asked. "And, if so, is that applicable? Sometimes, if somebody's marriage is breaking up, sometimes gossip can be real helpful to know that and then you can do something."

The data suggest that people expect ethics (clergy ethics, professional ethics, Christian ethics) to include common sense, but to include other dimensions as well. As the discussion of the Bible and sexual orientation illustrated so well, common sense has certain common qualities but not a common content.

One set of images, described by the philosopher Ludwig Wittgenstein and used to good effect by other Christian ethicists (see Jeffrey Stout), might help us understand the challenge we face with this concept. He contrasts the road map of an ancient city with the road map of a modern suburb:

> If you want to say that [my invented languages] are incomplete, ask yourself whether our language is complete—whether it was before the symbolism of chemistry and the notation of the infinitesimal calculus were annexed to it, for these are, so to speak, the suburbs of our language. (And how many houses or streets does it take before a town begins to be a town?) Our language can be seen to be an old city: a maze of little streets and squares, of old and new houses, and of houses with additions from various periods; and this surrounded by a multitude of modern sections with straight regular streets and uniform houses.[11]

The modern suburb has streets laid out in a regular pattern. The system is clear and thought out. Even where the streets are not straight, their curves are deliberate. We would say that the modern suburb is planned and rational, regardless of whether we find this an attractive feature or not. Because of this planned and rational character, suburbs tend to look the same regardless of their locality. By contrast, the streets of the ancient city follow routes made familiar by centuries of habit. They twist and turn for reasons no longer obvious. Knowledge of the design of one ancient city may be of absolutely no use when one is lost in another. While many people find their particular ancient city comforting and familiar, we do not duplicate these cities when designing new living spaces. The streets are too narrow for automobiles. Their pattern creates bottlenecks and traffic jams. Emergency vehicles cannot reach their destination quickly enough.

So, too, with expectations of ethical conduct. We carry with us the moral memory and cultural patterns of ancient cities—our ancient cities. The paths are so well trodden that we assume they need no explanation of where they lead and how to follow them. However, in the context of ambulances and mass transit, sexual abuse and pension plans, we discover a need for more deliberate planning and more rigorous attention to potential conflicts.

Since not everyone is living in the same ancient city, what is common sense for one group of people is not necessarily common sense for another group. Is it possible for all of us to live in the same city? Yes, possibly. We have established that common sense is relied on by both clergy and laity, and especially so by laity. Following Geertz, we have affirmed his analysis that common sense has a common form but not necessarily a common content, for it does not spontaneously apprehend a fixed reality but affirms suppositions arrived at on earlier occasions. Where disagreement is fuelled by competing claims to common sense (as in the United Church debate on ministry and sexual orientation), there is no alternative but to unearth the presuppositions and expose them to a critical analysis. By this, one may hope to arrive at some truly common understanding.

This is analogous to what is known in religious ethics as moving from a second-hand conviction to a first-hand conviction. A second-hand conviction is a moral rule ("Thou shalt not steal") that one has learned from others—from church, from parents, from school and so on. A first-hand conviction is a second-hand conviction that has been tested on a first-hand basis and affirmed or modified as required. So, the second-hand prohibition of stealing might have been modified as a result of extreme poverty, and now one holds that it is wrong to steal except in situations where not to steal would lead to starvation. (This was the conclusion at which St. Thomas Aquinas arrived.) Where common sense seems to suggest diametrically opposed positions, as in the debate on sexual orientation and ministry, a first-hand examination of what we really mean by sexuality and what we really mean by biblical interpretation may lead to a revision of what we take for granted as "common sense."

Common sense is cultural. It is specific to specific cultures, and it changes as the culture changes. If we want to increase the common element in common sense, we are talking about creating a more common culture. This is possible within a religion if there are common institutions through which to bring it about. A denominational culture provides such possibilities.

The English cultural critic Raymond Williams urged this approach when dealing with the nation-state: "The inequalities of many kinds which still divide our community make effective communication difficult or impossible. We lack a genuinely common experience, save in certain rare and dangerous moments of crisis. What we are paying for this lack, in every kind of currency, is now sufficiently evident. We need a common culture, not for the sake of an abstraction, but because we shall not survive without it."[12]

However, this task is not easy. Economic globalization is creating a worldwide privilege for the commercial culture characteristic of market society. Cultural forms are fragmented and conflicting in a manner we have come to call postmodern. Simultaneously, market-oriented institutions (e.g., transnational corporations) are being strengthened while non-market institutions (e.g., churches and families) are being weakened, rendering them less able to respond effectively to cultural shifts. It is often said that culture is to humans as water is to fish—it is essential, but taken for granted. In our new degraded environment, the creation of a common cultural content requires a level of intentionality that will be uncomfortably new for many people. We have to create the water in which to swim. This means we will have to expose deliberately the extent to which our common sensibilities are not held in common. It will be painful, but it will also be essential to institutional and community survival. The survival of communities is directly related to the survival of the institutions they inhabit.[13]

In the larger research study, Maureen Muldoon and I are trying to make explicit the contradictions that exist between the different understandings of clergy ethics and the different sensibilities that people claim in common. It is our hope that this critically appropriated understanding of difference will liberate new energy for change. It remains for the churches, whether on their own initiative or on account of initiatives from the societies of which they are a part, to engage in the specific tasks of educational, organizational and cultural reform. "The human crisis is always a crisis of understanding: what we genuinely understand we can do."[14]

Notes

1 The principal researchers acknowledge the financial support of the Social Sciences and Humanities Research Council of Canada and the cooperation of both the Anglican Church of Canada and the United Church of Canada for making this research possible. Publication of the larger study, *Ethical Challenges in Ministry*, is forthcoming.

2 Not everyone is comfortable with the use of the term "clergy ethics." Some people, especially in the United Church, do not use the term "clergy" to describe themselves. Others think the term "clergy ethics" necessarily means that the ethics of those in ordered ministry are different from those of Christians who are not. In this essay, I use the terms "minister" and "pastor" interchangeably for ordained or commissioned members of the United Church. I also use the terms "minister" and "priest" interchangeably for ordained members of the Anglican Church. I use the term "clergy" as a generic category for ordered members of both denominations. I also use the terms "clergy ethics" and "ministerial ethics" interchangeably to refer to the ethical norms of those persons in designated roles of pastoral leadership.

3 Gaylord Noyce, *Pastoral Ethics: Professional Responsibilities of the Clergy* (Nashville, TN: Abingdon, 1988), 11.

4 Clifford Geertz, "Common Sense as a Cultural System," in *Local Knowledge: Further Essays in Interpretive Anthropology* (New York: Basic Books, 1983), 73-93.

5 Ibid., 75.

6 Ibid., 77.

7 Ibid., 87.

8 Ibid., 84.

9 Ibid., 85.
10 Ibid., 90.
11 Ludwig Wittgenstein, "Philosophical Investigations," quoted in Jeffrey Stout, *The Flight from Authority: Religion, Morality and the Quest for Autonomy* (Notre Dame, IN: University of Notre Dame Press, 1981), 1.
12 Raymond Williams, *Culture and Society*, 1780-1950 (London: Penguin, 1963), 304.
13 For more on the creation of community as a deliberate strategy of resistance to economic globalization, see Christopher Lind, *Something's Wrong Somewhere: Globalization, Community and the Moral Economy of the Farm Crisis* (Halifax, NS: Fernwood, 1995).
14 Williams, *Culture and Society*, 323.

12

SPIRITUALITY AND JUSTICE-MAKING IN A CITY CONTEXT

JOE MIHEVC

This essay seeks to make connections between the search for a deeper spirituality and the quest for social justice in an urban context. First, I want to articulate the basis for being inclusive of social justice when speaking about spirituality. Second, given that my context is the city of Toronto, I want to address social justice issues related to the state of this particular city. Lastly, I want to describe the urban spirituality that is arising within social movements addressing justice issues in the city of Toronto.

The Basis for Social Justice within Spirituality

The movie *The Hurricane,* about Rubin "Hurricane" Carter's imprisonment and struggle for freedom, reflects the three stages of the classic understanding of spirituality. The first of these can be described as "waiting and going inward." There are several periods of Hurricane's prison confinement during which he focuses on his interior self and a search for meaning. During these periods, he works at night and sleeps during the day. While he is in the "hole," in solitary confinement, Hurricane has no choice but to go inward in trying to keep his spirit together. When the hope for freedom is distant, he speaks of trying to

Notes to chapter 12 are on pp. 249-50.

find that place within himself which lies beyond the hurt that others can cause him. This is Hurricane's inward search for spirituality.

Hurricane's spirituality is also nurtured through healing relationships—with the Canadians, and with the young boy, Lesra Martin. Through these relationships, he begins again to love and trust others. Developing trusting relationships helps Hurricane overcome the debilitating spirit that prison life affords. He learns to hope again. This second approach to spirituality is a healing one, and derives from trusting and loving relationships.

Lastly, there is the work for change. Hurricane cannot be spiritually whole until he is physically free, until he is out of prison. To free him from prison is a spiritual task in and of itself. Along with grace, it requires truth, conviction, focus and persistence on the part of the prisoner, and a similar spiritual drive from outside the prison by a willing community. It requires an action plan with a detailed strategy.

These three stages—going inward, nurturing trusting relationships and actively working for justice—all need to be held in balance. It is important to be holistic in the development of spirituality. There is reason to caution against a hyperactivism that lacks a calm centre and an inner spirituality. At the same time, however, an equal and opposite danger is present in the tendency to journey inward without any regard for the communal. We cannot create islands of happiness in oceans of despair as we develop our spirituality. As Gregory Baum asserts, "Contemporary religious experience will not allow that people create for themselves, through gifts of consolation, islands of happiness from which the memory of the afflicted has been banned."[1] Spiritual integrity demands that the other, particularly the suffering other, never be excluded from the path of spiritual development. There is justice to be sought within the urban environment of the city of Toronto, and this work must never be separated from the spiritual task.

Being holistic in spirituality means different things to different people. Not everyone is suited to direct social justice work; not everyone is suited to be a monk. It is interesting and revelatory that Thomas Merton, a monk, was the spiritual guide and correspondent of some of the continent's greatest social activists: Dorothy Day, the founder of the Catholic Worker Movement; Daniel Berrigan, the peace activist; Ernesto Cardinal of Nicaragua, one of the practitioners of liberation theology; and Rosemary Ruether, the pioneer feminist theologian.[2] It bespeaks the holistic approach that weaves together a spirituality of the interior life, that of trusting relationships and that of being present to the justice issues in our world.

Social justice and spirituality are rooted in a particular context. A holistic, socially engaged spirituality has as its first reference point the concrete historical-social-political situation in which people are living. This reference point is always changing, always in process, just as our historical context is always shifting. When we talk or write about spirituality, then we are seeking to put into words the experience that we have already had. The first moment is intensely existential; it is how we live out our primary commitments. This is what Gustavo Gutierrez suggests in the title of his book on the spirituality of liberation theology—*We Drink from Our Own Wells*.[3]

The Urban Context of Toronto

There are Christians, along with many people of goodwill and social commitment, who see life in the city as the locus for the development of their spirituality. They do leave the city from time to time to avail themselves of the calm and beauty of the countryside to reinvigorate their spirits, but the primary locus of their life, including their spiritual life, is the building and nurturing of family, neighbourhood and community within the large city.

What is the context for the development of this emergent urban, socially committed spirituality? Toronto. Is Toronto a city that needs a restoration of social justice? Many a Torontonian would say "no," and note that Toronto is often cited as among the most livable cities in the world. Using quality-of-life indicators, it is argued, Toronto scores high in terms of social and cultural standards, medical and health considerations, public services and transportation, housing, economic health and political environment. Taken altogether, for several years now Toronto has enjoyed recognition as the top, or close to the top, city in which to live.

But from a different perspective, from the *underside*, we get a different picture of Toronto. For an increasing number of people, "Toronto the Good" has become "Hogtown," the city that marginalizes its poor. This shift in perspective is necessary if we want to talk about a spirituality of social justice in an urban environment. There are some terrifying trends in this new Toronto that desperately need to be addressed. Three examples suffice to make the point: housing, homelessness and hunger; race relations, access and equity; and the environment.

Housing, Homelessness and Hunger

Recently, a new record was set: a home sold for $10 million in the Bridal Path area at the north end of the city. At the same time, another record was broken. According to Toronto's *Report Card on Homelessness*,[4] the city has more than 30,000 people seeking emergency shelter in Toronto. By 2002, this number will likely increase to 36,000. This number includes 6,200 children (one-third of whom are under four years old), 6,000 youth and 2,070 two-parent families. Street patrols are reporting a growing number of "new" street people that includes families, especially single mothers with children, people with addictions and people with mental-health problems. The Street Helpline, a social service organization trying to place people in shelters, had 6,300 inquiries for emergency shelter in 1997; in 1999, the number skyrocketed to 41,000; the figure for the year 2001 is estimated to exceed 80,000.

On the issue of hunger, in the last quarter of the year 2000 140,000 people (approximately the population of a city the size of Stratford) used food banks every month in the Greater Toronto Area, about 75 percent in Toronto proper. This was an increase of 12 percent over 1999 figures. Almost one-half of all food bank users were children, while 24,000 were people with disabilities.[5] This is clearly a disaster in the making. With the Canadian economy growing at a high rate, it begs the question: Why are the benefits of the economic boom being shared so poorly?

Four major reasons (and several minor ones) can be cited for this increase in homelessness and hunger: the sizable 1995 reduction of welfare payments by the provincial government; the so-called *Tenant Protection Act, 1997*, which gutted rent control and has caused rents to skyrocket over the last few years; the deinstitutionalization of mental-health facilities; and employment insurance cutbacks, which have restricted eligibility and the amount of unemployment benefits available to unemployed people.

Toronto's good image has been tarnished by Third-World conditions in a "land of plenty." The horror of our time is the widening gap between rich and poor. In fact, enormous wealth lies in private hands.

But the wealthier refuse to pay their share. An unfair tax system favouring the rich over the poor, a minimum wage that has not increased in years, corporate salaries and profits that have skyrocketed, all exacerbate the problem.

Race Relations, Access and Equity

A second justice issue is related to the new multiracial, multireligious, multilingual, and multicultural reality of Toronto. As Torontonians look toward the future, the white majority will increasingly become the minority. The city also has the largest urban Aboriginal community and the largest gay and lesbian community in Canada (the third largest in North America). The United Nations, in fact, has stated that Toronto is the most racially diverse city in the world, boasting immigrants from virtually every region.

This is remarkable when one considers that this level of diversity in a metropolitan environment is unique in the history of humanity. This diversity could be something that will truly make Toronto "a light to the world," but it could also become a nightmare, especially when the economy turns downward.

From an equity perspective, there are some trends that are cause for alarm. Michael Ornstein, in a report based on 1996 statistics on ethno-racial inequalities in Toronto, documents that urban family poverty rates for non-European urban families were twice the rates for European families. Unemployment in the African, black and Caribbean communities in 1996 stood at 38 percent for youth and 17.6 percent for adults, respectively, while the comparable rates for those of European background were 15.7 percent and 6.9 percent, respectively. In terms of family income, Torontonians of European origin averaged $68,900 per year, and South Asians averaged $44,300, while blacks, Africans and those from the Caribbean averaged a meagre $31,000.

Ornstein concludes that, "in education, employment and income, the Census data reveal pervasive inequality among ethno-racial groups in Metropolitan Toronto….The characterization of socio-economic polarization in Toronto as a division between a European majority and a visible minority is correct."[6] The tensions are easier to mask during a period of strong economic growth; they will certainly be exacerbated during periods of economic downturn.

The Environment

A third justice issue for Toronto is the environment. People's love affair with the automobile is choking the planet. Air quality in Toronto has never been worse. Toronto's Medical Officer of Health, in her annual *Report on the State of the City's Health,*[7] states that about 1,000 premature deaths and 5,500 hospital admissions are attributable to air pollution. Air pollution is responsible for about the same number of deaths as lung cancer, and for more deaths than breast cancer and AIDS.[8] It is true that more than half of this pollution derives from coal-fired energy plants in the Ohio Valley; however, 80 percent of the remaining pollution is generated by automobiles and trucks.

Virtually every analysis by city planners, futurists and economists concludes that large cities must rethink future transportation needs and urban planning, and build more compactly. Urban sprawl must be replaced by higher density and efficient public transit.

In the area of municipal waste, Toronto residents produce 1.8 million tonnes of garbage per year. Alternative waste diversion strategies have not been implemented in years. The disposal technology of dumping garbage into landfills is not much different from the methods used by people thousands of years ago. The raucous debate at City Council in the fall of 2000 over whether to ship Toronto's garbage to Kirkland Lake showed that Torontonians desire more environmentally sensitive solutions in dealing with their waste. A consumer culture that produces mountains of garbage is neither sustainable nor acceptable.

These social justice issues—housing, homelessness and hunger; race relations, access and equity; and the environment—are key threads in the social fabric of Toronto. Looking at Toronto from the underside uncovers a very different picture of Canada's wealthiest community.

An Emergent Urban Spirituality in Toronto

The issues described above can be overwhelming for social justice advocates who simply remain focused on "Toronto the Bad." Insightfully, Ursula Franklin asked her audience in a recent talk: "What do you do after you take the dim view? What do you do after the 'awfulizing'?" Advocates desperately need a spirituality, a way of being that, though aware of the underside, can take the picture in and flip it into a vision and action plan of social and ecological justice for the city.

Are there grounds for hope as Torontonians face the twenty-first century? Is there an urban spirituality that can nurture this social justice work? I believe there is. It is based on the multitude of groups and individuals working in Toronto for progressive urban social change. This is the well from which hope for the city springs. A unique spirituality is arising. It brings people together. It is evident within tenant groups, social service organizations, unions, service clubs and neighbourhood organizations. We see it in groups organized by women, churches and other communities of faith, environmentalists, gays, lesbians and Aboriginals, and among those who support anti-racism, human rights and the disabled.

Toronto has traditionally been called "Toronto the Good." Today, that takes on new meaning because of the many individuals and groups focused on the task of struggling to be healed, struggling to be whole in the city, struggling to find the justice that has eluded the city so far. These individuals and groups strengthen the social fabric of Toronto in their search for justice and an urban spirituality. When we speak of a spirituality of social justice in Toronto, we are seeking to articulate the spirituality of these people; we are seeking to discover how their work for justice is linked to a search for the God of life.

Certainly, one of the theological tasks is to articulate and gather stories that represent this spirituality. The spirituality of urban social engagement is one of the most theologically underdeveloped. A quick scan of the shelves of a theological bookstore will reveal a large section on spirituality, but only a very small part is related to spirituality for social justice, and most of those books would be from Latin America.

> How do we define this emergent urban spirituality? What are its characteristics?

First, for many Christians the work of social justice involves living out a spirituality rooted in the *imitation of Christ*. This is a classic Christian expression of spirituality. It can also be said that social justice work comes from faith in Jesus Christ. Jesus' life was about journeying and being in solidarity with those suffering injustice and marginalization. Jesus' solidarity was real and tangible, and it cost him his life. Jesus as the Christ reveals that God is present to those who suffer and to those who do justice. The work of social justice in overcoming human suffering is redemptive as Jesus' life was redemptive. Thus, the Good News is that love and justice are stronger than hate, neglect and oppression. Humans connect with the spirit of Jesus as they participate in their own and society's redemption, as they enter the human struggle for justice. That is how people discover the God of Life within and among them, and how they live in the spirit of Jesus Christ.

Second, while Christians speak about spirituality, the terrain of spirituality is not exclusively the domain of Christians. It is part of everyday human existence. One can speak of a non-Christian spirituality or a non-religious feminist spirituality, a creation-centred spirituality, even a secular spirituality.

The spirituality of social justice in Toronto is ecumenical and interfaith, and includes secular humanism. An ecumenism of works rather than an ecumenism of faith is at the root of the spirituality of social justice in Toronto. Muslim leaders were involved in the debate on the "squeegee kids." They spoke publicly, and to City Council, of Allah as being the Compassionate One and, as such, how the city is called to be compassionate. At the opening of a not-for-profit housing unit built for women escaping abusive relationships, the president of Micah Homes commented on how his Jewish faith inspires his involvement. Groups and individuals working on issues of justice in the city come from a host of religious backgrounds that underpin their work and are sustained by varieties of spirituality in their struggles.

Third, this urban spirituality is action-oriented, rooted in the belief that people co-create history with God. There is no dichotomy between the religious and secular spheres. God and grace are present to people as they renew their society. This is not the spirituality reflected in T.S. Eliot's "I said to my soul, be still."[9] It is instead the spirit that shouts out, "I cannot be still" as long as there are oppression and suffering in the world! It is not the spirituality of the self turned inward, but of the self turned outward, toward the world, feeling its pain, rejoicing in its beauty, exercising human agency and finding God's grace—these feed the soul of the social activist.

Fourth, this spirituality of social justice practises the politics of compassion and solidarity. The tragedy of our times is that the dominant politics of the day actually make lack of compassion socially and politically permissible. The "squeegee kid" laws, Premier Mike Harris's biting comments about welfare recipients, the drive for competition running roughshod over everything, reflect a spirit that runs counter to compassion. Having compassion in this social and political environment can be an occupational hazard. One can be accused of, horror of horrors, political naïveté. In many places in Toronto, however, there are people stepping forward and resisting the competition battle cry in order to express their compassion, to show that their humanity and spirituality are intrinsically linked to the humanity of those who are vulnerable and hurting. This emergent spirituality supports belief in these high ideals even in this cynical age. Tommy Douglas, one of the founders of the Co-operative Commonwealth Federation (CCF), now the New Democratic Party (NDP), said it well: "It is never too late to build a better world." In a too-cynical world that so often disempowers people, the social justice advocates are a sign that compassion and solidarity can lead to social change.

Fifth, while this spirituality is known by its compassion, those who practise it are tough, resilient and persistent. They know how to fight. Echoing the words of the prophets of Hebrew Scriptures, their struggle is passionate and righteous. It is long-suffering and patient. But it is also fierce in its passion.

It is appropriate to be passionate about our neighbourhoods and communities, to fight for housing and hunger issues, equity and the environment. This passion is evident in the numerous people who come before committees of City Council to present their stories, or to encourage City Hall to support an organization or an action. When an advocate articulately presents the facts on hunger issues, and demands that the city take action, we see a spark of the Divine at work. When demonstrators refuse to leave City Council chambers during the debate over dumping garbage in Kirkland Lake, we are witnessing a spirit of ecological justice. The spirit of social justice is a feisty spirit. It knows its voices and it knows how to struggle against principalities and powers. It can be as gentle as a lamb, and as wise as a serpent.

Sixth, this emergent spirituality employs the model of being the church in the world. It encourages people not to "spiritualize" their spirituality. A God in heaven is too far away. This movement is about the God that we find among us, together, working as community. The church is not fully church when it turns inward and exclusively devotes its best energies to its members, or focuses on its formal sacramental life. It is fully church when it gives witness to the God present in history, leading the community away from that which is not life-giving and toward that which gives greater life.

Many congregations, churches, synagogues, mosques and temples are well integrated into their neighbourhood and local community. They are alive; they bring the outside in and the inside out. They are not islands exclusively for their weekend visitors.

Seventh, the spirituality of those who love justice is rooted in the "preferential option for the poor." The phrase comes from Latin American liberation theology and is present in the Puebla documents of the Latin American Catholic bishops. It is an expression, however, that carries weight for Christians involved in northern countries and in urban environments. It speaks of bias in the doing of social justice work: analyzing social and political situations and determining whose voices are *not* being heard, identifying those who are the powerless, and determining how their voices and power can be restored. Theologically, this bias is understood as God's bias. As a mother loves all her children but tends to the one who is ill, so too God, in Her love for all, is especially present to those on the margins. The suffering other, the marginalized other, is never far away in this spirituality. Where there is suffering, there God is found and there the justice advocate searches with mind and heart.

Last, the spirituality of social justice calls on us to make a vocation of our jobs. Cities have become the great entities they are because they are centres for employment and creative activity. Not everyone concerned about social justice can work in an organization devoted to social change. Social action groups like the Ontario Coalition for Better Child Care or the Urban Alliance on Race Relations are important. But social justice work cannot be compartmentalized. Many lawyers, planners, architects, workers and business owners integrate justice work into their profession and career. Their professionalism is pragmatic and competent, and they know how to work the system. They take professional risks.

There are several people at City Hall who embody this spirit. For example, Joan Campbell, who worked as the director of Toronto's Housing Division, was passionately concerned about homelessness in Toronto. As the director of a division, she was able to put together progressive policies and programs to promote housing, create a hostel structure to meet a growing demand for emergency shelters, and help position homelessness politically as a national issue. Other examples include city accountants who find money for particular programs when funding seems impossible, and city planners who fight developments proposed by land speculators to the Ontario Municipal Board that would force seniors out of affordable housing.

No one is exempt from the call to develop a spirituality of social justice. We are all called in our chosen area of work to integrate our labour into a vision of the reign of God.

Christians involved in urban social justice have a tremendous contribution to make to the broader body politic. They work in community organizations, form deputations to City Council or appear at public events. They are articulate and knowledgeable about their community and city, radiate a vibrant compassion and solidarity, possess a gentle but fierce passion for their issue, and check their egos at the door. Their struggle for spiritual well-being and their journey toward interiority draw them not to individualism but to a social agenda. The only thing Toronto needs is more of them. As the majority religious group in Toronto, Christians have a special responsibility to participate in this movement of the spirit, in this movement to heal the urban environment. This is how Christians live out their urban spirituality, how they are mindful of their ultimate concerns, how they discover the spirit of Jesus in their personal lives and in social contexts.

Notes

1 Gregory Baum, "The Retrieval of Subjectivity," *Canadian Journal of Community Mental Health* 2 (1982): 94.
2 See Victor Kramer, *Thomas Merton: Monk and Artist* (Kalamazoo, MI: Twayne, 1987).
3 Gustavo Gutierrez, *We Drink from Our Own Wells* (New York: Orbis Books, 1983).
4 *Toronto Report Card on Homelessness 2001* (City of Toronto, February 2001). See also Anne Golden, *Taking Responsibility for Homelessness: Report of the Mayor's Homelessness Action Task Force* (January 1999).
5 Ibid. The annual *Report Card* is an excellent resource for documenting trends in homelessness and poverty in the Toronto area.
6 Michael Ornstein, *Ethno-Racial Inequality in the City of Toronto: An Analysis of the 1996 Census* (City of Toronto, May 2000), 122.

7 Medical Officer of Health, *The Path Ahead: A Report on the State of the City's Health – Toronto 2001* (City of Toronto, January 2001).
8 *Toronto's Air: Let's Make It Healthy* (Toronto Public Health, December 2000).
9 T.S. Eliot, "East Coker," III, *Four Quartets* (London: Faber and Faber, 1972), 27.

Selected Bibliography of

Roger Hutchinson

1975 “The Canadian Social Gospel in the Context of Christian Social Ethics.” In Richard Allen (ed.), *The Social Gospel in Canada*, 286-316. Papers of the Interdisciplinary Conference on the Social Gospel in Canada, 21-24 March 1973. Ottawa: National Museums of Man. Reprinted in Bruce Hodgins and Robert Page (eds.), *Canadian History Since Confederation: Essays and Interpretations*, 497-511. Nobleton, ON: Irwin-Dorsey, 1979.

1976 “Inflation Has Moral Implications.” *The Chelsea Journal* 2/3: 113-16.

1977 “Religion, Ethnicity and Public Policy.” In Harold Coward and Leslie Kawamura (eds.), *Religion and Ethnicity in Canada*, 135-50. Waterloo, ON: Wilfrid Laurier University Press.

1977 “Religion, Morality and Law in Modern Society.” In Peter Slater (ed.), *Religion and Culture in Canada*, 187-223. Waterloo, ON: Wilfrid Laurier University Press.

1979 “La Souveraineté-association vue par un protestant ontarien” (trans. Albert Jordan). In Louis Balthasar et al. (eds.), *Le referendum: un enjeu collectif,* 167-74. Montréal: Fides, Cahiers de Recherche Éthique.

1979 “No Easy Answers.” *Exchange* 3/3: 12-14.

1979 “To Empower People: The Church as a Mediating Structure” and “Self-Reliance and Social Planning: In Memory of J.W.A. Nicholson.” In *Personal Life and Impersonal Society,* 188-215. 11th Annual Atlantic Seminar in Theological Education, 3-8 June, Truro, NS.

1980 “Church, Nation and World Order: A Changing Context.” In Graham Scott (ed.), *More Than Survival: Viewpoints Toward a Theology of Nation*, 23-33. Don Mills, ON: Canec Publishing and Supply House.

1981 "Love, Justice and the Class Struggle." *Studies in Religion/Sciences religieuses* 10/4: 473-79.

1982 "Contextualization: No Passing Fad." *Consensus* 8 (July): 18-24.

1982 "Cyprus Consultation on Political Ethics." *The Ecumenist* (January-February): 27-28.

1982 "Ecumenical Witness in Canada: Social Action Coalitions." *International Review of Mission* LXXI: 344-53.

1982 "Summary Statement" and "Conclusion." In Benjamin G. Smillie (ed.), *Political Theology in the Canadian Context*, 245-54. Studies in Religion Supplements, 11. Waterloo, ON: Wilfrid Laurier University Press.

1983 "Reinhold Niebuhr and 'Contextual Connections.'" *This World* 6 (Fall): 102-09.

1983 "Towards a Method in Political Ethics" (with Gibson Winter). In Koson Srisong (ed.), *Perspectives on Political Ethics: An Ecumenical Inquiry*, 163-73. Geneva: World Council of Churches and Georgetown University Press.

1984 "Response to Gibson Winter's 'Hope for the Earth: A Hermeneutic of Nuclearism.'" *Religion and Intellectual Life* 1/3: 67-74.

1984 "Towards a 'Pedagogy for Allies of the Oppressed.'" *Studies in Religion/Sciences religieuses* 13/2: 145-50.

1985 "Comparative Ethics and the Mackenzie Valley Pipeline Debate." *Toronto Journal of Theology* 1/2: 242-60.

1985 "The Dene and Project North: Partners in Mission." In William Westfall et al. (eds.), *Religion/Culture: Comparative Canadian Studies,* VII, 391-410. Ottawa: Association for Canadian Studies.

1985 "Ecumenical Social Action." In James H. Marsh (ed.), *The Canadian Encyclopedia*, 538-39. Edmonton: Hurtig.

1985 "Mutuality: Procedural Norm and Foundational Symbol." In Charles Amjad-Ali and W. Alvin Pitcher (eds.), *Liberation and Ethics: Essays in Religious Social Ethics in Honor of Gibson Winter*, 97-110. Chicago: Center for the Scientific Study of Religion.

1985 "Social Action and Mission in the Eighties." In Terry Brown and Christopher Lind (eds.), *Justice as Mission: An Agenda for the Church,* 85-94. Burlington,ON: Trinity Press.

1986 "A New Mission to the Nation." *Bloor Street Leap* (Bloor Street United Church) 3/3: 1-2.

1986 "The Public Faith of a Democratic Socialist." *Journal of Canadian Studies* 21/2: 26-37.

1986 "Religious Commitments and Political Judgements: A Contextual Connection." In Walter Block and Irving Hexham (eds.), *Religion, Economics and Social Thought: Proceedings of an International Symposium*, 221-32. Vancouver: The Fraser Institute.

1986 "A Response to Kroeker." *Toronto Journal of Theology* 2/1: 21-22.

1986 "Whatever Furthers the New Jerusalem Should Be Fostered." *Prairie Messenger* 63/34: 10.

1987 "Gregory Baum as an Ecumenical Theologian." *Toronto Journal of Theology* 3/2: 185-88.

1988 "Breaking Connections and Clarifying Options." In Pratt and Hutchinson, *Christian Faith and Economic Justice,* 76-88.

1988 *Christian Faith and Economic Justice: Toward a Canadian Perspective.* Ed. by Cranford Pratt and Roger Hutchinson. Burlington, ON: Trinity Press.

1988 "Religious Commitments and Public Choices" (with Cranford Pratt). In Pratt and Hutchinson, *Christian Faith and Economic Justice,* 1-9.

1988 "Study and Action in Politically Diverse Churches." In Pratt and Hutchinson, *Christian Faith and Economic Justice,* 178-92.

1989 "The Fellowship for a Christian Social Order: 1934-1945." In Wells and Hutchinson, *A Long and Faithful March*, 17-29.

1989 "Introduction." In R.B.Y. Scott and Gregory Vlastos (eds.), *Towards the Christian Revolution*, vii-xxxii. Kingston, ON: Ronald P. Frye and Company. Original edition, Chicago: Willet, Clark & Company.

1989 *A Long and Faithful March: "Towards the Christian Revolution" 1930s/1980s*. Ed. by Harold Wells and Roger Hutchinson. Toronto: United Church Publishing House.

1989 "Witnessing Against War: Peacemaking in the Changing Canadian Context." In Wesley Cragg, Laurent Larouche and Gertrud Jaron Lewis (eds.), *Challenging the Conventional: Essays in Honour of Ed Newbery*, 168-82. Burlington,ON: Trinity Press.

1991 "The Just War Tradition: Human Rights and Public Moral Discourse." *McMaster Journal of Theology* (Spring): 30-42.

1991 "A Response" (with Cranford Pratt). *Toronto Journal of Theology* 7/1: 51-52.

1992 "God and the Mackenzie Valley Pipeline Debate." *The Literary Review of Canada* 1/9: 13-16.

1992 *Prophets, Pastors and Public Choices: Canadian Churches and the Mackenzie Valley Pipeline Debate.* Waterloo, ON: Wilfrid Laurier University Press.

1993 "Human Responsibility and the Environment: A Christian Perspective." *Hindu-Christian Studies Bulletin* 6: 13-17.

1993 "The Limits of Ethics in a Militarized World." In *Defense Beyond Borders: Canada's Overseas Military Responsibilities,* 26-30. Waterloo, ON: Project Ploughshares Working Paper.

1993 "Religion and Public Life." In Mel Watkins (ed.), *Handbooks to the Modern World: Canada,* 596-609. New York: Facts on File.

1994 "Environmental Stewardship: A Christian Theological Understanding," 18- 26 and "Global Warming and Stewardship of the Planet's Health,"

9-17. In Mary Ann Beavis (ed.), *Environmental Stewardship: History, Theory and Practice. Workshop Proceedings (March 11-12, 1994)*. Occasional Paper 32. Winnipeg: Institute of Urban Studies, University of Winnipeg.

1994 "Missiology." In Christopher Lind and Joseph Mihevc (eds.), *Coalitions for Justice: The Story of Canada's Interchurch Coalitions,* 320-31. Ottawa: Novalis.

1994 "Piety and Politics: A Protestant Perspective." *Westminster Affairs: A Publication of the Westminster Institute for Ethics and Human Values* 7/2: 9-12.

1994 "Responding to Realism, Assessing Anabaptist Alternatives: Response to Mark Neufeld." *The Conrad Grebel Review* 12/2: 226-29.

1994-95 "Beyond the First Phase: Studying Our Commitment to Multiculturalism." *VicReport* 23/3 (Winter): 10.

1995 "Foreword." In Shirley Farlinger, *A Million for Peace: The Story of the Peacemaking Fund of the United Church of Canada*, ix-xiii. Toronto: United Church Publishing House.

1995 "Introduction." In Peter Wyatt, *The Page That Fell Out of My Bible: A Selection of Sermons Preached at Trinity-St. Paul's United Church Between 1990 and 1995,* vii-viii. Toronto: Trinity-St. Paul's United Church.

1996 *Christianizing the Social Order: A Founding Vision of the United Church of Canada*. Ed. by Phyllis D. Airhart and Roger C. Hutchinson (Special issue of the *Toronto Journal of Theology* 12/2). Waterloo, ON: Wilfrid Laurier University Press.

1996 "Christianizing the Social Order: A Three-Dimensional Task." In Airhart and Hutchinson, *Christianizing the Social Order*, 227-36.

1996 "Embedded Beliefs." *PMC: The Practice of Ministry in Canada* 13/3: 7-11.

1997 *Action Training in Canada: Reflections on Church-Based Education for Social Transformation*. Ed. by Ted Reeve and Roger Hutchinson. Toronto: Centre for Research in Religion, Emmanuel College.

1997 "Foreword." In Renate Pratt, *In Good Faith: Canadian Churches against Apartheid*, ix-x. Waterloo, ON: Wilfrid Laurier University Press.

1997 "Social Ethics and Social Transformation." In Reeve and Hutchinson, *Action Training in Canada,* 115-28.

1998 "Beliefs About Jesus and the Reality of Faith." *Emmanuel College Newsletter* (Spring): 4.

1998 "Foreword" (with Phyllis D. Airhart). In Gwen R.P. Norman, *Grace Unfailing: The Radical Mind and the Beloved Community of Richard Roberts,* ix-x. Toronto: United Church Publishing House.

1998 "Social Ethics and Mission in a Post-Liberal Age." In Graham Brown (ed.), *Theological Education in Canada*, 29-48. Toronto: United Church Publishing House.

1999 "A Response to the Moderator's Letter on Faith and the Economy—Whose Faith? Which Economy?" In Ted Reeve (ed.), *The Church's Witness and Call for Action in Seeking a Moral Economy*, 6-9. Moderator's Consultation on Faith and the Economy. Toronto: United Church of Canada.

2000 "Ethical and Theological Reflections." In Nancy Palardy et al., (eds.) *Biotechnology and Genetic Engineering: Current Issues, Ethics, and Theological Reflections*, 83-94. Taskforce on the Churches and Corporate Responsibility. Toronto: United Church of Canada.

Contributors

Contributors

Phyllis D. Airhart is associate professor of the history of Christianity at Emmanuel College of Victoria University in the University of Toronto. Her publications in the area of religion in Canada include *Serving the Present Age: Revivalism, Progressivism, and the Methodist Tradition in Canada* (McGill-Queen's University Press) and a special issue of the *Toronto Journal of Theology* entitled *Christianizing the Social Order: A Founding Vision of the United Church of Canada,* which she co-edited with Roger Hutchinson.

Gregory Baum is professor emeritus at the Faculty of Religious Studies, McGill University, Montreal. He is editor of *The Ecumenist* and the author of several books, including *Compassion and Solidarity: The Church for* Others (CBC Massey Lectures), *Essays in Critical Theology* (Sheed and Ward), and *Nationalism, Religion and Ethics* (McGill-Queen's University Press).

David G. Hallman has served on the national staff of the United Church of Canada in a range of social justice portfolios for over twenty-five years, with a concentration on energy and environmental issues. Since 1994, he has also acted as the Climate Change Programme coordinator for the World Council of Churches. Hallman is the author and editor of numerous books on environmental issues, including *Ecotheology: Voice from South and North* (World Council of Churches) and *Spiritual Values for Earth Community* (World Council of Churches).

Cameron R. Harder is assistant professor of systematic theology at the Lutheran Theological Seminary in Saskatoon. His recently completed Ph.D. thesis, "The Shame of Farm Bankruptcy: A Theological and Sociological Investigation of Its Effects on Rural Communities," was directed by Roger Hutchinson. In addition to other writing in the field, he has been doing seminars and workshops across Canada on the church's role in rural revitalization.

C. Douglas Jay is former principal of and professor emeritus at Emmanuel College of Victoria University in the University of Toronto, and founding director of the Toronto School of Theology. He works in the areas of Christian ethics, theological education, ecumenism, interfaith dialogue and missiology, and is the author of, for example, *World Mission and World Civilization* (Board of World Mission, United Church of Canada), as well as a number of articles and reports.

Karen Krug is an associate professor in the environment program at Brock University in St. Catharines, Ontario. As principal investigator in a project funded by a Social Sciences and Humanities Research Council of Canada research grant, she is identifying strategies for building sustainable rural-urban agriculture in the Niagara region.

Marilyn J. Legge is associate professor of Christian ethics at Emmanuel College of Victoria University in the University of Toronto. She is the author of *The Grace of Difference: A Canadian Feminist Theological Ethic* (Scholars, Press), and the co-editor of *Liberation Theology: An Introduction* (Orbis Books). She contributes to various journals, networks and projects related to ecumenical and social justice ethics.

Christopher Lind serves as president of St. Andrew's College, Saskatoon and St. Stephen's College, Edmonton. He is the author of *Something's Wrong Somewhere: Globalization, Community and the Moral Economy of the Farm Crisis* (Fernwood), and the co-editor with Joe Mihevc of *Coalitions for Justice: The Story of Canada's Interchurch Coalitions* (Novalis). He is currently completing a manuscript with Maureen Muldoon entitled *Ethical Challenges in Ministry.*

Ian Manson is an ordained minister presently serving at Immanuel United Church in Winnipeg. He holds a Th.D. in the history of Christianity from Victoria University, and is completing a history of the social gospel in the United Church of Canada.

Joe Mihevc is an adjunct faculty member at the University of St. Michael's College, Faculty of Theology. His writing and teaching are in the area of social ethics and liberation theology. He is co-editor with Christopher Lind of *Coalitions for Justice: The Story of Canada's Interchurch Coalitions* (Novalis). He also serves as a city councillor in Toronto.

David Novak holds the J. Richard and Dorothy Shiff Chair of Jewish Studies at the University of Toronto and directs the Jewish Studies Program. His latest book, which has been awarded the American Academy of Religion's Award for Excellence in the Study of Religion in Constructive-Reflective Studies category for 2000, is entitled *Covenantal Rights: A Study in Jewish Political Theory* (Princeton University Press).

Cranford Pratt is an emeritus professor of political science at the University of Toronto. He co-edited, with Roger Hutchinson, *Christian Faith and Economic Justice: Toward a Canadian Perspective* and has published extensively on Canadian foreign policy, particularly in the Third World.

Gary L. Redcliffe is associate professor of pastoral theology at Emmanuel College of Victoria University in the University of Toronto. The investigation of communities of faith with a social mission is the focus of his academic work, while he maintains a keen interest in biomedical ethics, the subject of his doctoral thesis. He is currently researching a book exploring the dynamics of pastoral relationships in congregations.

Tracy J. Trothen is assistant professor of ethics and pastoral theology in the Faculty of Theology at the University of Winnipeg. She has written articles for various journals and books, and is involved in projects concerning social ethics and spirituality.

Harold Wells is professor of systematic theology at Emmanuel College of Victoria University in the University of Toronto. A former pastor in Ontario churches and a lecturer at the University of Lesotho, he is the author of *A Future for Socialism? Political Theology and the "Triumph of Capitalism"* (Trinity Press International).

Series Published by Wilfrid Laurier University Press for the Canadian Corporation for Studies in Religion / Corporation Canadienne des Sciences Religieuses

Editions SR

1. *La langue de Ya'udi : description et classement de l'ancien parler de Zencircli dans le cadre des langues sémitiques du nord-ouest*
   Paul-Eugène Dion, O.P. / 1974 / viii + 511 p. / OUT OF PRINT
2. *The Conception of Punishment in Early Indian Literature*
   Terence P. Day / 1982 / iv + 328 pp.
3. *Traditions in Contact and Change: Selected Proceedings of the XIVth Congress of the International Association for the History of Religions*
   Edited by Peter Slater and Donald Wiebe with Maurice Boutin and Harold Coward
   1983 / x + 758 pp. / OUT OF PRINT
4. *Le messianisme de Louis Riel*
   Gilles Martel / 1984 / xviii + 483 p.
5. *Mythologies and Philosophies of Salvation in the Theistic Traditions of India*
   Klaus K. Klostermaier / 1984 / xvi + 549 pp. / OUT OF PRINT
6. *Averroes' Doctrine of Immortality: A Matter of Controversy*
   Ovey N. Mohammed / 1984 / vi + 202 pp. / OUT OF PRINT
7. *L'étude des religions dans les écoles : l'expérience américaine, anglaise et canadienne*
   Fernand Ouellet / 1985 / xvi + 666 p.
8. *Of God and Maxim Guns: Presbyterianism in Nigeria, 1846-1966*
   Geoffrey Johnston / 1988 / iv + 322 pp.
9. *A Victorian Missionary and Canadian Indian Policy: Cultural Synthesis vs Cultural Replacement*
   David A. Nock / 1988 / x + 194 pp. / OUT OF PRINT
10. *Prometheus Rebound: The Irony of Atheism*
    Joseph C. McLelland / 1988 / xvi + 366 pp.
11. *Competition in Religious Life*
    Jay Newman / 1989 / viii + 237 pp.
12. *The Huguenots and French Opinion, 1685-1787: The Enlightenment Debate on Toleration*
    Geoffrey Adams / 1991 / xiv + 335 pp.
13. *Religion in History: The Word, the Idea, the Reality / La religion dans l'histoire : le mot, l'idée, la réalité*
    Edited by/Sous la direction de Michel Despland and/et Gérard Vallée 1992 / x + 252 pp.
14. *Sharing Without Reckoning: Imperfect Right and the Norms of Reciprocity*
    Millard Schumaker / 1992 / xiv + 112 pp.
15. *Love and the Soul: Psychological Interpretations of the Eros and Psyche Myth*
    James Gollnick / 1992 / viii + 174 pp.
16. *The Promise of Critical Theology: Essays in Honour of Charles Davis*
    Edited by Marc P. Lalonde / 1995 / xii + 146 pp.
17. *The Five Aggregates: Understanding Theravāda Psychology and Soteriology*
    Mathieu Boisvert / 1995 / xii + 166 pp.
18. *Mysticism and Vocation*
    James R. Horne / 1996 / vi + 110 pp.

19. *Memory and Hope: Strands of Canadian Baptist History*
Edited by David T. Priestley / 1996 / viii + 211 pp.
20. *The Concept of Equity in Calvin's Ethics**
Guenther H. Haas / 1997 / xii + 205 pp.
*** Available in the United Kingdom and Europe from Paternoster Press.**
21. *The Call of Conscience: French Protestant Responses to the Algerian War, 1954-1962*
Geoffrey Adams / 1998 / xxii + 270 pp.
22. *Clinical Pastoral Supervision and the Theology of Charles Gerkin*
Thomas St. James O'Connor / 1998 / x + 152 pp.
23. *Faith and Fiction: A Theological Critique of the Narrative Strategies of Hugh MacLennan and Morley Callaghan*
Barbara Pell / 1998 / v + 141 pp.
24. *God and the Chip: Religion and the Culture of Technology*
William A. Stahl / 1999 / vi + 186 pp.
25. *The Religious Dreamworld of Apuleius'* Metamorphoses: *Recovering a Forgotten Hermeneutic*
James Gollnick / 1999 / xiv + 178 pp.
26. *Edward Schillebeeckx and Hans Frei: A Conversation on Method and Christology*
Marguerite Abdul-Masih / 2001 / vi + 194 pp.
27. *Radical Difference: A Defence of Hendrik Kraemer's Theology of Religions*
Tim S. Perry / 2001 / x + 170 pp.

Comparative Ethics Series / Collection d'Éthique Comparée

1. *Muslim Ethics and Modernity: A Comparative Study of the Ethical Thought of Sayyid Ahmad Khan and Mawlana Mawdudi*
Sheila McDonough / 1984 / x + 130 pp. / OUT OF PRINT
2. *Methodist Education in Peru: Social Gospel, Politics, and American Ideological and Economic Penetration, 1888-1930*
Rosa del Carmen Bruno-Jofré / 1988 / xiv + 223 pp.
3. *Prophets, Pastors and Public Choices: Canadian Churches and the Mackenzie Valley Pipeline Debate*
Roger Hutchinson / 1992 / xiv + 142 pp. / OUT OF PRINT
4. *In Good Faith: Canadian Churches Against Apartheid*
Renate Pratt / 1997 / xii + 366 pp.
5. *Towards an Ethics of Community: Negotiations of Difference in a Pluralist Society*
James H. Olthuis, editor / 2000 / x + 230 pp.
6. *Doing Ethics in a Pluralistic World: Essays in Honour of Roger C. Hutchinson*
Phyllis J. Airhart, Marilyn J. Legge and Gary L. Redcliffe, editors / 2002 / viii + 264 pp.

Studies in Christianity and Judaism / Études sur le christianisme et le judaïsme

1. *A Study in Anti-Gnostic Polemics: Irenaeus, Hippolytus, and Epiphanius*
Gérard Vallée / 1981 / xii + 114 pp. / OUT OF PRINT
2. *Anti-Judaism in Early Christianity*
Vol. 1, *Paul and the Gospels*
Edited by Peter Richardson with David Granskou / 1986 / x + 232 pp.
Vol. 2, *Separation and Polemic*
Edited by Stephen G. Wilson / 1986 / xii + 185 pp.
3. *Society, the Sacred, and Scripture in Ancient Judaism: A Sociology of Knowledge*
Jack N. Lightstone / 1988 / xiv + 126 pp.
4. *Law in Religious Communities in the Roman Period: The Debate Over* **Torah** *and* **Nomos** *in Post-Biblical Judaism and Early Christianity*
Peter Richardson and Stephen Westerholm with A. I. Baumgarten, Michael Pettem and Cecilia Wassén / 1991 / x + 164 pp.